WHITMAN
EXPLORATIONS
IN FORM

WHITMAN
EXPLORATIONS IN FORM

Howard J. Waskow

THE UNIVERSITY OF CHICAGO PRESS

CHICAGO AND LONDON

LIBRARY OF CONGRESS CATALOG CARD NUMBER: 66–13892

THE UNIVERSITY OF CHICAGO PRESS, CHICAGO & LONDON
THE UNIVERSITY OF TORONTO PRESS, TORONTO 5, CANADA
© 1966 BY THE UNIVERSITY OF CHICAGO
ALL RIGHTS RESERVED. PUBLISHED 1966
PRINTED IN THE UNITED STATES OF AMERICA

TO BETSY

ACKNOWLEDGMENTS

I want first to thank my wife, who suffered gladly much of the otherwise thankless labor behind a book, and a good many self-righteous defenses of style. Then my parents, who typed, copyread, and sympathized. My friends, who endured in their own right—listening to my talk of Whitman and of form, or reading all or parts of the manuscript: Bell Gale Chevigny, John R. Cooper, Ann Congleton, William F. Davis, Jr., Robert K. Diebold, S. Hillhouse, and Phyllis Rackin. My teachers: Charles Feidelson, Jr., a generous and attentive overseer to the first version of this study, whose book, seminar, and conversation did much to gene-rate it, and whose open mind urged it along its way; Charles R. Anderson, Milton R. Stern, and R. W. B. Lewis, three other teachers of American literature who excited my interest in the field and who encouraged my progress; and the others who showed by ex-ample that reading, writing, and teaching are hard work and great joy—Mrs. Thea Hodes, Earl R. Wasserman, J. Hillis Miller, Don Cameron Allen, A. Dwight Culler, and Louis L. Martz. My stu-dents at the University of Pennsylvania and Reed College, who forced me to work out ways of explaining Whitman, and at times explained him to me. And, finally, the Whitman scholars, whose co-operative enterprise in editing, exhaustively and beautifully, *The Collected Writings of Walt Whitman*, crowns their labors of many years, which have supplied to students the necessary materials for an understanding of Whitman's poems. Permission to quote from

ACKNOWLEDGMENTS

Ezra Pound's "In a Station of the Metro," published in *Personae*, copyright 1926, 1954 by Ezra Pound, has been granted by the publishers, New Directions Publishing Corporation and Faber and Faber, Ltd., and Arthur V. Moore, Mr. Pound's literary agent. Permission to quote from "The Red Wheelbarrow," published in *The Collected Earlier Poems of William Carlos Williams*, copyright 1938, 1951 by William Carlos Williams, has been granted by the publishers, New Directions Publishing Corporation and MacGibbon and Kee, Ltd.

CONTENTS

INTRODUCTION

TOWARD THE END of his life, Walt Whitman sat half-paralyzed in Camden, New Jersey, dividing his acquaintances of the previous thirty years into "friends" and "enemies" of *Leaves of Grass* and fretting about the appraisal of the future. Although much of the time since then he has suffered at the violent hands of both enthusiasts and debunkers, Whitman would have delighted in the sheer amount of attention accorded him. His life has been investigated by several biographers in each of several generations; his philosophy and political creed have been appealed to by revolutionaries of various persuasions and nationalities; his editorials have been reprinted, his correspondence painstakingly transcribed, and his conversations lovingly recorded; and the *Leaves*, companion of his last forty years, has been scattered far and wide, in every sort of edition imaginable.

In the area of criticism, however, even with the quickening of interest provided by the 1955 centennial of the *Leaves*, there are serious gaps. When students of Whitman have turned to the poems themselves, they have concentrated on cultural influence and special attractions (thus we learn of Whitman's relationships to Hegel and Emerson and of his interest in science, opera, phrenology, and animal magnetism); on style, the unique rhythmical and metaphorical characteristics of Whitman's line; on the origin and growth of *Leaves of Grass*; and on the nature, as whole books, of various editions of that work. Important as these studies are, much remains to be done.

The process that has long been under way for Wordsworth,

1

Coleridge, and Keats, not to mention Donne and Eliot—a critical discussion about the matter and manner of single poems—is not very far along for Whitman. Aside from notes on particular passages, only these have addressed themselves to the subject: hardly more than a score of articles or sections of books, most of them on "Song of Myself" and "Out of the Cradle Endlessly Rocking"; the critical aids of Gay Wilson Allen and Charles T. Davis, interspersed with selections from the *Leaves*; and one full-length book, James E. Miller's *A Critical Guide to Leaves of Grass*.[1]

Helpful commentary on Whitman's literary modes or forms has been even more scarce, although the problem of Whitman's form has bothered readers for a long time. The easiest way out has been simply to declare the poetry "formless"; more satisfying, but still not very much so, have been various explanations by analogy—to the ocean or to music, for example.[2] Some critics, however, have sought to define the poems in their own terms. Sholom J. Kahn, finding in Whitman little of the "negative capability" that Keats praised in Shakespeare, sees him as no "story-teller or dramatist, . . . no Homer or Shakespeare," but as "a great lyric poet . . . who spoke out, passionately and eloquently, to the full range of his individual soul."[3] David Daiches attempts to identify the distinguishing characteristics of Whitman's poetry when he asks how Whitman's "lyrics" become "epics"; but he does not really know how to treat the poems when they shift suddenly, as many of Whitman's best poems do, instead of "develop [ing] cumulatively," which Daiches sees as Whitman's "true way."[4] Allen and Davis, who spend several pages on Whitman's "dramatic situations"; Miller, who displays Whitman's "dramatic structure" in a series of chapters; and Leslie Fiedler, in an illuminating paragraph on Whitman's "mode of reverie," all deal better than Daiches with those sudden shifts, revealing Whitman's mode to be "dramatic" in a way different from the one Kahn properly finds lacking: a way having to do not with negative capability but with the turns and modulations of the speaking voice.*[5] Yet, a truly useful definition

---

* Whitman himself, in a letter to William D. O'Connor (*The Correspondence*, edited by Edwin Haviland Miller [New York, 1964], III, 307), draws the distinction between the two kinds of drama: "The worry of Ruskin . . . with *Leaves of Grass* is that they are *too personal*, too emotional, launched from the fires of

of Whitman's mode still evades us, for Miller uses the term "dramatic structure" so loosely that very different sorts of poems—the Children of Adam and Calamus groups, "Out of the Cradle Endlessly Rocking," and "Song of Myself"—are all included under the rubric, and the other critics, who have set themselves to write brief introductions to Whitman, do not demonstrate in detail, in close study of specific works, just how Whitman's poems function. Only when we gather the work of several men—Walter Sutton's explications of some of Whitman's shorter poems; Paul Fussell, Jr.'s careful study of structure in "Cradle"; S. K. Coffman, Jr.'s close readings of "Crossing Brooklyn Ferry" and "Passage to India"; and the attempts of Thomas I. Rountree and John Lovell, Jr., dealing with "Song of Myself" and "Passage to India," respectively, to elucidate the strategy of "indirection"—do we begin to get a sense of both the extent and specificity of Whitman's forms.[6]

My purpose is to deepen that sense—to define Whitman's formal range by demonstrating how each of his forms works. The task turns out to involve an exploration of the relationship among the several forms. And here we enter a third area neglected by Whitman criticism, for there has been no real success in identifying Whitman's creative center, the unity that generates his different kinds of poems, as distinguished from the constructed unity of *Leaves of Grass*. There is no reason to assume that a given poet has such a center, but Whitman does, and although some steps have been taken toward defining it, as in Richard P. Adams' article on organicism in Whitman and A. H. Marks's on Whitman's "triadic imagery," [7] the job has not been fully done.

I have found it necessary to work simultaneously in all three of these neglected areas, for Whitman's essential unity, it seems to me, consists of a pattern of movement that informs his widely

myself, my spinal passions, joys, yearnings, doubts, appetites &c &c.—which is really what the book is mainly for, (as a type however for those passions, joys, workings &c *in all the race*, at least as shown under modern & especially American auspices). . . . R like a true Englishman evidently believes in the high poetic art of (only) making abstract works, poems, of some fine plot or subject, stirring, beautiful, very noble, completed within their own centre & radius, & nothing to do with the poet's special personality, nor exhibiting the least trace of it—like Shakspere's great unsurpassable dramas. But I have dashed at *the greater drama going on within myself & every human being—that is what I have been after—*"

3

various themes and forms as well as the relationship among his different kinds of poems. In the first part of this study, to provide a setting for the operation of that pattern in his poetry, I demonstrate the existence of the pattern in Whitman's extra-poetic materials, describing the way his mind plays over a given problem. After placing Whitman against a cultural background, I discuss his fundamental questions and the ideas and images with which he responds to the questions, and show how these questions and responses function in a theoretic context even more interesting to Whitman than to most poets—the problem of the relationship among external reality, the poet, the poem, and the reader.

In describing this imaginative design, Whitman's "habit of mind," I have drawn at will from the notebook jottings, editorials, letters, essays, and conversations of several decades. For the changes during the years in Whitman's sense of things are shifts in emphasis rather than new perceptions: the "Whitmans" who emerge after the "crisis" of 1859, after the Civil War, and after the paralytic stroke of 1873—all are implicit in the "early" Whitman, poet-publisher of the thin, remarkable volume of 1855. As the biographer Roger Asselineau has said, "Whitman's thought, like his technique, remained fundamentally the same. . . . Although it would be a very artificial game, one could almost deduce a posteriori the last poems from the very first." [8] Seen from a long view, the "contradictions" of which Whitman bragged are not contradictions at all, but consistent, sometimes predictable, variations upon several themes. They fall into a design that is reinforced by a "secret language" of metaphor and unusual vocabulary.

With this pattern and this language described, with the total setting for the poems in place, the way is opened for the second part of the study, in which I attempt to show in action the pattern delineated by the first part. Using the 1892 versions as a base and appealing to earlier ones where they are helpful, I present close readings of most of what I think are Whitman's major poems and arrange those poems according to their literary forms, in a pattern that imitates Whitman's characteristic design.

The 1892 edition of *Leaves of Grass* is convenient for presenting a way into the full range of Whitman's poetry because it more than any other is the record of attitudes explored throughout his poetic life, and although those attitudes may not have changed fundamentally, it is useful to have on hand as many representations of them as possible. Whether the "deathbed" edition is also Whitman's best poetry is a nice question. Claims have been made that, as a whole work, it is less successful than either the 1855 or 1860 edition;[9] and there is little doubt that, as in the excision of an impressive section in "The Sleepers," Whitman's editing was occasionally wrongheaded. The status as whole works of the various editions is, however, of little relevance to my particular concern. Moreover, it seems to me—and to others, though certainly not to all—that Whitman's editing was more often right than wrong; in any event, his excisions are retrievable, and I refer to them in my readings when they shed light on the poems that Whitman finally left us.

I do not mean to close this apologia, required of Whitman critics because of the poet's erratic taste and the existence of so many editions, simply in deference to Whitman's final choice. It is as much to the point that the only appropriate procedure other than following the 1892 edition would have been inconvenient editorially. Choosing the versions I prefer from among the various editions would have meant either reprinting those versions in this book, an obvious difficulty given Whitman's characteristic lengthiness and my desire to present extended readings, or leaving the reader, for whom the 1892 edition remains most familiar and most readily available, in ignorance of the poem being read.

To define individual poems by showing how they work, and to define Whitman's poetry by demonstrating the relationship among the various ways of working: these are the major purposes of this book. Approaching Whitman in this way is in one sense, of course, to limit him, for other possible approaches are necessarily deemphasized. I can only hope that my formulation of Whitman's poetry will reveal more than distort it. And one other hope: that, as I suggest in a speculative last chapter, the terms I develop here, which are responses to the demands of Whitman's poetry, will prove of some service in discussions of other literature.

PART ONE

WHITMAN'S HABIT OF MIND

I BACKGROUNDS: MECHANISM, ORGANICISM, AND WHITMAN

AT THE CENTER of Whitman criticism is a long debate between the idea of Whitman as dialectician and the idea of Whitman as organicist. Both ideas try to define Whitman's thought and the nature of his poetry, and although in some ways they overlap, at bottom they are contradictory. These contradictions of the critics result largely from a fundamental contradiction in the poet, a legacy of the profound cultural shift in which the philosophic and aesthetic mind moved from a conception of reality as mechanistic to a conception of reality as organic.

The case for Whitman as dialectician is stated early in this century by Thomas K. Smith, who prepares a lengthy list of the opposites toward which Whitman tends, and has since been pressed in various ways by Mody Boatright, Leon Howard, Floyd Stovall, A. H. Marks, David Daiches, and Richard Chase.[1] In this view, Whitman is conceived as accepting the terms of the Cartesian dualistic universe—as opposing matter to spirit, body to soul. The argument for Whitman as organicist begins, aside from the poet's own explanations of his work, with Whitman's disciple John

Burroughs and is developed by Edward Carpenter, Sculley Bradley, F. O. Matthiessen, Gay Wilson Allen, Charles Feidelson, Jr., and Richard P. Adams.[2] It sees Whitman as committed to a monistic world—a fluid world in which relationships among things, not the separate things themselves, are most important.

The essential difference between the two positions is revealed in a disagreement that Chase, making the argument for Whitman as dialectician, has with Feidelson. Feidelson considers Whitman to be a pure type of symbolist, who works inside a unified world of his own making.[3] To say that Whitman is a pure symbolist is actually to say that he is as much committed to organicism as a man can be; for, in Feidelson's terms, the symbolistic vision centers on language as the most indeterminate and creative element in an organic universe. Whitman, "militantly hostile to reason,"[4] abandons "the habit of mind which views the material world as separable from ideas and speech."[5] His symbolistic point of view focuses on the act of perception, the seeing, rather than the seer or the thing seen, thereby eliminating the distinction between subject and object, poet and reader. His poems enact a metaphysical journey, "a process in which the known world comes into being";[6] the self disappears into the seeing, and the aesthetic act is the real reality: ". . . attention is deflected from 'ideas' and 'objects' to a symbolic medium; . . . the perception of a meaningful symbol is opposed to another kind of perception, which Hawthorne calls 'analysis.' . . . Since Whitman regards meaning as an activity of words rather than an external significance attached to them, language, together with the self and the material world, turns out to be a process, the pouring of the flood."[7]

Chase's answer to this explanation of Whitman's poetry, although it agrees to the presence of a tendency toward symbolism, is essentially an assertion of the terms of dualism. The ability of the self to become identical with all other selves, which for Feidelson is representative of a new way of seeing, is for Chase "an artistic device, . . . heavily taxing our powers of provisional credence."[8] And:

Despite the "merging" and "identifying" tendencies of the poet, despite the timeless, flowing universe he speaks of, he preserves . . . his modes of distinction and "extrication." On the whole he operates on the ordinary assumptions of his time that a poem expresses the self of the poet and reports facts from the world of nature and is therefore more or less continuous with these orders of reality. (Indeed in some of his utterances Whitman took an unusually low view of poetry, stating in various ways that he thought it a poor substitute for reality.) It should also be noted that he tended to think of language as expressing a dualistic universe, as when he says that slang words, being more poetic than other words, unite the "natural" and the "spiritual." [9]

For Feidelson, making the extreme statement of Whitman as organicist, Whitman's world is monistic; for Chase, it is dualistic. For Feidelson, Whitman's mode of perception is the identification of himself with all the world; for Chase, Whitman preserves his analytic detachment. For Feidelson, the real reality for Whitman is the aesthetic act; for Chase, Whitman's "real reality" is reality itself, and the aesthetic act a mere substitute. Richard P. Adams in effect seeks to reduce the distance between these two positions by reminding us of the connection between the dialectic and organicism: ". . . Whitman succeeds considerably better than Emerson in getting away from the old dualities of Platonic idealism (which seems to have been merely turned upside down by the scientific materialists), the basic distinction between mind and matter, soul and body, idea and its wordly embodiment. Whitman's use of these opposites is genuinely dialectical; he succeeds in fusing them in terms of the organic metaphor." [10] The fact remains, however, that in his very conception of things as opposites Whitman is operating from dualist premises. If he is exploring the possibilities of the new metaphor of organicism, he is nevertheless still grounded in the old world–view. As Adams recognizes, he does not take the sudden, total leap.

It seems proper to say, indeed, that Whitman lives in both a mechanistic world and an organic world, and adopts, at either extreme of this double commitment, both the Cartesian and the symbolist points of view. We can represent Whitman's metaphysics with two intersecting circles. One circle would be the area of his belief in a dualistic, mechanistic universe, the typical construction of the metaphysical mind from Descartes until the late eighteenth century. In this static world, mind is coexistent with matter but

11

separated from it; and the imagination is an analytic, measuring and combining, non-creative activity, in which the mind "turns toward the body, and contemplates in it some object conformed to the idea which it either of itself conceived or apprehended by sense." [11] The other circle would be the area of Whitman's belief in a monistic organic world, the birth of which is prepared for by Kant's "Copernican revolution" and hastened by Fichte's radical concept of a subjective mind that makes things at its will, unrestricted by Kantian categories. Mind in this world is not separated from matter, for reality is the joining of the two, the activity of an imagination that is at once perceptive and creative.

Neither of these worlds provides all the answers for Whitman. The mimetic and pragmatic theories of poetry—to which the Cartesian imagination, with its analytic selection and ordering of material, is particularly attracted—and the organic theory of the Romantics all hold both promise and danger for the poet. Meyer H. Abrams' explanations of each theory provide terms for comparison:

. . . for the representative eighteenth-century critic, the perceiving mind was a reflector of the external world; the inventive process consisted in a reassembly of "ideas" which were literally images, or replicas of sensations; and the resulting art work was itself comparable to a mirror presenting a selected and ordered image of life.[12]

Looking upon a poem as a "making," a contrivance for affecting an audience, the typical pragmatic critic is engrossed with formulating the methods—the "skill, or Crafte of making" as Ben Jonson called it—for achieving the effects desired. These methods . . . are formulated as precepts and rules whose warrant consists either in their being derived from the qualities of works whose success and long survival have proved their adaptation to human nature, or else in their being grounded directly on the psychological laws governing the responses of men in general. The rules, therefore, are inherent in the qualities of each excellent work of art, and when excerpted and codified these rules serve equally to guide the artist in making and the critics in judging any future product.[13]

Through [the] . . . perspective [of the archetypal plant], Coleridge saw the mind as growing into its percepts, conceived of the activity of the poetic imagination as differing from this vital, self-determining, assimilative process in degree rather than kind, and thus was able to envision the product of artistic genius as exhibiting the mode of development and the internal relations of the organic whole.[14]

The best possibility for the mimetic poet is that he can be an ingenious rearranger of external reality; the worst the theory holds for him is that, as in the *Republic*, he can be considered foolish, a falsifier of truth, and thus disruptive of the health of the state. The poet in the pragmatic theory is at best a teacher of morality; the danger for him is that he is liable to reduction before critics who know the rules to which he tries to adhere. He comes to men, not men to him: "The aim of the artist and the character of the work [are ordered] to the nature, the needs, and the springs of pleasure in the audience." [15]

The great promise for the poet in the organic theory is, as Abrams suggests, that he is a real creator, something of a god, instead of an imitator tied to external reality or a pragmatic poet tied to his audience. Still, the organic theory too can threaten the artist. The first danger is that the poet can lose his individuality. If "the activity of the poetic imagination [differs] from [the] vital, self-determining, assimilative process [of the mind] in degree rather than kind," then the poet is not very different from other men: he is a poet rather than a reader only by accident. As Whitman puts it, "The greatest poet hardly knows pettiness or triviality. . . . He is a seer— . . . he is complete in himself—the others are as good as he, only he sees it, and they do not." [16] This can mean, when someone like Emerson or Whitman presses the organic theory to its extreme, that everyone is a poet, each man a god; but at the same time, it diminishes the significance of the individual artist. The second danger, expressed in a criticism of Coleridge by Walter Pater, is concerned immediately with the poet and his language; eventually, however, it also involves the poet and his readers and is therefore very closely related to the first danger. "What makes his view a one-sided one is, that in it the artist has become almost a mechanical agent: instead of the most luminous and self-possessed phase of consciousness, the associative act in art or poetry is made to look like some blindly organic process of assimilation." [17] This criticism implies some troubling questions. Where in its organic

13

world does the creative imagination stop? If everything flows into everything else and grows out of everything else, how can a poem be controlled? And, if it need not be controlled, is the man who utters the flowing language of any particular importance?

Given these various benefits and dangers, Whitman does not finally choose between the mechanistic world and the organic world: they overlap in his mind and press upon each other. To the degree that the organic world impinges upon mechanistic dualism, that dualism is qualified, and the restraints of the analytic mind are bent by the force of the creative imagination. To the degree that the mechanistic world impinges upon organic monism, that monism is qualified, and the flight of the creative imagination is restrained by the analytic mind. This is not to say that Whitman stands precisely between the mechanistic and organic worlds. Because one of his commitments is to extreme organicism, the symbolistic vision of reality as the ceaseless flowing of everything into everything else, Whitman leans, certainly, toward organicism. But it is even more true to say that he shifts back and forth among various attitudes toward the two worlds: among certainty, the acceptance of one or the other world; uncertainty, the movement from one to the other world; and transcendence of the problem, the creation of a new conception of reality out of the various components offered by mechanism and organicism.

Thus, for instance, Whitman is capable of statements that bring him to the borders of each world. At times he sounds committed to the beginning assumptions of dualism:

The most profound theme that can occupy the mind of man—the problem on whose solution, science, art, the bases and pursuits of nations, and everything else, including intelligent human happiness, . . . subtly and finally resting, . . . is doubtless involved in the query: What is the fusing explanation and tie—what the relations between the (radical, democratic) Me, the human identity of understanding, emotions, spirit, &c., on the one side, of and with the (conservative) Not-Me, the whole of the material objective universe and laws, with what is behind them in time and space, on the other side? [18]

And at other times, denying the original split, he seems like a convinced monist: "Strange and hard that paradox true I give,/Objects gross and the unseen soul are one." [19] Usually, however, as even these statements indicate, he occupies the hazy ground between the two worlds, the area where our two circles intersect. Even as he assumes the existence of "Me" and "Not-Me," he is concerned about "fusing" them; and even as he argues the oneness of "objects gross" and "the unseen soul," he is aware that his argument is paradoxical. When Whitman answers his question about fusing the Me and the Not-Me, therefore, he qualifies the rigorous Cartesian logic that lies behind the question:

Theology, Hegel translates into science. All apparent contradictions in the statement of the Deific nature by different ages, nations, churches, points of view, are but fractional and imperfect expression of one essential unity, from which they all proceed—crude endeavors or distorted parts, to be regarded both as distinct and united. In short, (to put it in our own form, or summing up,) that thinker or analyzer or overlooker who by an inscrutable combination of train'd wisdom and natural intuition most fully accepts in perfect faith the moral unity and sanity of the most creative scheme, in history, science, and all life and time, present and future, is both the truest cosmical devotee or religioso, and the profoundest philosopher.[20]

Hegel's logical philosopher, put in Whitman's "own form," becomes the essentially contradictory man, the man guided by both "train'd wisdom" and "natural intuition." Not only is Descartes's dualism absorbed into unity, but the atmosphere of philosophical thought, Hegel's as well as Descartes', is warmed by organic intuition, though far from dispelled ("thinker or analyzer or overlooker").*

The haziness of this overall position produces the confused vocabulary that has disconcerted, and misled, many of Whitman's critics. The confusion is best seen as it affects two of Whitman's fundamental words, *body* and *soul*, which reflect both the separation and the overlapping of Whitman's mechanistic and organic worlds.

The following notation will start us toward an understanding of

* See also "Carlyle," *Prose*, I, 260–61.: "While the contributions which German Kant and Fichte and Schelling and Hegel have bequeath'd to humanity . . . are indispensable to the erudition of America's future, I should say that in all of them, . . . when compared with the lightning flashes and flights of the old prophets and *exaltés*, the spiritual poets and poetry of all lands, . . . there seems to be . . . something lacking—something cold . . . —a want of living glow, fondness, warmth."

the poet's mechanistic world and also of the way in which one world is modified by the existence of the other: "There are in things two elements fused though antagonistic. One, is that bodily element, which has in itself the quality of corruption and decease; the other is that element, the Soul, which goes on, I think, in unknown ways, enduring forever and ever." [21] This suggests an important implication for Whitman of the dualistic structure: that body, limited and susceptible to change, distinguishes man from man, thing from thing, while at the same time all are identical in the "enduring Soul." The notion is stated explicitly in "Democratic Vistas": ". . . in respect to the absolute soul, there is in the possession of such by each single individual, something so transcendent, so incapable of gradations, (like life,) that, to that extent, it places all beings on a common level, utterly regardless of the distinctions of intellect, virtue, station, or any height or lowliness whatever." [22]

Whitman's specific definition of the relation of body to soul is in some respects a simple restatement of Cartesian dualism: body, to replace Whitman's words with Descartes', "is only an extended and unthinking thing," and soul (or mind) "is entirely and truly distinct from . . . body and may exist with it." [23] Yet, similar as they are, there is an important difference between Whitman's definition and the one at the core of Descartes' system. For Whitman, body and soul, while "antagonistic," are "fused"; for Descartes, they are at most "very closely conjoined," [24] and finally wholly separable even this side of "corruption and decease." That this difference is significant, not just a careless emphasis resulting from two hundred years' wear on Descartes' original definition, can be determined by comparing Whitman's notation to a journal entry by Emerson that clearly distinguishes between a concept like Whitman's and the outright Cartesian split: "If, as Hedge thinks, I overlook great facts in stating the absolute laws of the soul; if, as he seems to represent it, the world is not a dualism, is not a bipolar unity, but is *two*, is Me and It, then is there the alien, the unknown, and all we have believed and chanted out of our deep instinctive hope is a pretty dream." [25] Whitman's man or thing, composed of two elements "fused though antagonistic," is not a Cartesian duality but Emerson's special kind of duality, a "bipolar unity"—a new entity that results from the mutual pressure of the unified and dualistic worlds.

Further indications of this pressure can be found in Whitman's contradictory, yet complementary, explanations of how the "antagonistic" halves of the universe are joined. One explanation tends toward materialism, the other toward idealism. ". . . I guess the soul itself can never be anything but great and pure and immortal; but it makes itself visible only through matter—a perfect head, and bowels and bones to match is the easy gate through which it comes from its embowered garden, and pleasantly appears to the sight of the world." [26] The universe is divided—the soul has its home in an "embowered garden" and body in "the world"—but Whitman bridges the gap by having the soul exist in visible form in matter. The opposite conception of the same divided universe gives two homes to matter instead of the soul:

> Why what do you suppose is the Body?
> Do you suppose this that has always existed—
>   this meat, bread, fruit, that is eaten, is
>   the body?
> No, those are visible parts of the body , . . .
> ?But there is the real body too, not visible.[27]

The giving of two homes to both body and soul—seeing each as independent of the other (the soul of the embowered garden, the visible body) and each as *in* the other (the soul that makes itself visible in matter, the body that is "real" only as it is not visible)—is the expression of a man somewhere between two worlds, the old dualism and a new organic world in which all would be one.

Body and *soul* also exist in an organic world, which, like Whitman's mechanistic world, is compromised by his tendency in the opposite direction. When in "Song of Myself" Whitman declares his faith in the soul and calls for its "valvèd voice," he is really echoing a familiar epic convention, the summoning of the poetic muse.[28] Soul in this world is the poetic imagination, an agent of perception and creation:

The soul or spirit transmits itself into all matter—into rocks, and can live the life of a rock—into the sea, and can feel itself the sea—into the

17

oak, or other tree—into an animal, and feel itself a horse, a fish, or bird —into the earth—into the motions of the suns and stars.[29]

When I walked at night by the sea shore and looked up at the countless stars, I asked of my soul whether it would be filled and satisfied when it should become god enfolding all these, and open to the life and delight and knowledge of everything in them or of them; and the answer was plain to me at the breaking water on the sands at my feet: and the answer was, No, when I reach there, I shall want to go further still.[30]

This "organic soul"—transmitting itself into all matter and making a whole world by "enfolding" all—contrasts to the "mechanistic soul," which lives behind matter. Individual things are identical *in* the "mechanistic soul" that survives their corrupt particularities, but are *made* identical, experience and become each other, by the "organic soul." *

"Organic body" is the restrainer, the shaper, of the free poetic imagination. It is, for instance, the "I," the questioner of the soul in the passage quoted above. "Organic body" is, to use the terms of an evaluation by Whitman of himself and Blake, the "visible, objective life," the "directing principle" spurned by Blake's "uncontrolled" imagination ("subjective spirit"):

Of William Blake & Walt Whitman   Both are mystics, extatics but the difference between them is this—and a vast difference it is: Blake's visions grow to be the rule, displace the normal condition, fill the field, spurn this visible, objective life, & seat the subjective spirit on an absolute throne, wilful and uncontrolled. But Whitman, though he occasionally prances off, takes flight with an abandon & capriciousness of step or wing, and a rapidity and whirling power, which quite dizzy the reader in his first attempts to follow, always holds the mastery over himself, &, even in his most intoxicated lunges or pirouettes, never once loses control, or even equilibrium. To the pe[rfect] sense, it is evident that he goes off because he permits himself to do so, while ever the director, or direct'g principle sits cooly at hand, able to stop the wild teetotum & reduce it to order, at any moment. In Walt Whitman,

* An example of the confusion caused by Whitman's vocabulary can be seen in Stovall, "Main Drifts," p. 5. Stovall says of the early Whitman: "In theory he was the poet of the soul, but in fact he was as yet the poet of the body almost exclusively. The supernatural he held of no account." If *soul* means "imagination," Stovall can be right about Whitman's lack of interest in the supernatural but wrong that he was not "the poet of the soul."

escapades of this sort are the exceptions. The main character of his poetry is the normal, the universal, the simple, the eternal platform of the best manly & womanly qualities.[31]

The very existence of a distinction between body and soul in the organic world reveals the pressure upon Whitman's organic imagination of the dualist world that finds distinctions useful. The role of the body as restrainer of the soul is of course further evidence of Whitman's reluctance to commit himself wholly to the extreme organic view, which would theoretically delight in the disappearance of the seer behind the seeing, the man behind Emerson's "transparent eyeball."

Like Thoreau, who writes, "When the poet is most inspired, . . . his talent is all gone, and he is no longer a poet," and "The best poetry has never been written," [32] Whitman knows the danger of becoming too good an organicist. To a poet searching for human expression in which form is inseparable from content, silence can be compellingly attractive. The search for plastic form overwhelms language, and the poet, giving full sway to his genius, abandoning the ordering checks of his logical faculties, falls into mute harmony with Nature.

Whitman's course toward that envelopment is easily plotted. In *An American Primer,* he is closest to asserting that man's language is *the* reality: "A perfect user of words uses things—they exude in power and beauty from him . . . —lilacs, clouds, sunshine, woman, poured copiously." [33] But even there the enthusiasm becomes an excitement about voice; the delight that centers on meaning and sound shifts slightly, toward a delight in sound itself: "What beauty there is in words! What a lurking curious charm in the sound of some words! Then voices! Five or six times in a lifetime, . . . you have heard from men or women such voices, as they spoke the most common word!—What can it be that from those few men and women made so much out of the most common word!" [34] Like the later symbolists,[35] Whitman imitates music in his poems (as when he uses "aria" and "recitative" in "Out of the Cradle Endlessly Rocking"); but he also goes so far as to prefer music to the poems themselves: "Listen. Pure and vast, that voice now rises, as on clouds, to the heaven where it claims audience. Now, firm and unbroken, it spreads like an ocean around us. Ah,

19

welcome that I know not the mere language of the earthly words in which the melody is embodied; as all words are mean before the language of true music." [36]

This desire for expression more plastic than language, a tendency typical of the symbolists, is, however, only partly responsible for what Chase calls Whitman's "unusually low view" of poetry.[37] If on the one hand Whitman is "too good" an organicist, on the other he is not a good organicist at all. The same habit of mind that separates the Me from the Not-Me produces the idea that poetry is but a distorted reflection of nature:

Perhaps the untaught Republic is wiser than its teachers. The best literature is always a result of something far greater than itself—not the hero, but the portrait of the hero. Before there can be recorded history or poem there must be the transaction. Beyond the old masterpieces, the Iliad, the interminable Hindu epics, the Greek tragedies, even the Bible itself, range the immense facts of what must have preceded them, their *sine qua non*—the veritable poems and masterpieces, of which, grand as they are, the word-statements are but shreds and cartoons.[38]

This idea of poetry is foreign to the organic theory. Here "poem" is not differentiated from "history." The poet is not God in small, creating a new work, or even a vessel overflowing with God's language, but merely a copyist of God's creations, performing the relatively menial mimetic task assigned to him by most literary theorists from Plato until the Romantics.[39] Poetry for this Whitman is neither its own means nor its own end: "No one will get at my verses who insists upon viewing them as a literary performance, . . . or as aiming mainly toward art or aestheticism." [40] "I do not value literature as a profession . . . it is a means to an end, that is all there is to it; I never attribute any other significance to it." [41] It is copied from nature and used for the health of society. The "test of a poem," Whitman scribbles in an early notebook, is "how far it can elevate, enlarge, purify, deepen and make happy the attributes of the body and soul of a man." [42] "Literature," he is still saying as an old man, "is to be the medicine and lever, and (with Art) the chief influence in modern civilization." [43]

Thus Whitman, for whom body and soul have meaning in two

contexts, is attracted by the merging characteristics of the organic imagination, and is attracted also by the separateness provided in the mechanistic system. He must be detached as well as involved, static as well as voyaging, scornful of the poetic act and committed to it as the final reality. He celebrates both his private identity and his ability to "become," "train'd wisdom" and restraint along with organic spontaneity. To the overlapping of Whitman's two worlds and the differences between them can be attributed both the subject matter of the major poems, in which the poet moves from one alternative to another or tries in various ways to mediate between alternatives, and the range of his poetic forms—from imagistic poems to didactic poems, narrative to dramatic.

21

II "BIPOLAR UNITY" IN IDEA AND IMAGE

THE VERY FIRST "INSCRIPTION" to *Leaves of Grass* answers succinctly two questions that are at the heart of Whitman's thought and poetry, the questions of identity and government:

One's-Self I sing, a simple separate person,
Yet utter the word Democratic, the word En-Masse.
. . . .
Of Life immense in passion, pulse, and power,
Cheerful, for freest action form'd under the laws divine,
The Modern Man I sing.[1]

Whitman's answers here—that variety exists within unity and that government by the individual exists under a larger law—represent only one of the three attitudes he adopts toward these questions in his writings as a whole. He also sees variety alone and unity alone; he also conceives of government by the individual alone and of government by the larger law alone. This complicated response to the central problems of his experience is typical of Whitman's total habit of mind—the vision of what Emerson calls "bipolar unity." Emerson's term, like his description of the ideal American poet, could have been made especially for Whitman, who in his response to almost any problem is committed simultaneously to each polar position and to the polar positions unified.

Knowing Whitman's various responses to his central questions will help us to identify the attractions and fears he dramatizes in his poems and to comprehend his "secret language," the particular words, images, and gestures which embody those responses. Furthermore, by revealing his ideas of the relationships between individuals, Whitman's answers will help us to discuss his ideas of poet and reader, and therefore his poetic forms. Finally, by indicating the range of his attitudes, they will enable us to measure particular moments in the poems against the whole context of Whitman's mind, and to expect certain shifts in the statement and stance of the poet.

The central Whitman is to be found in the answers expressed in "One's-Self I Sing," the answers that unify polar positions. He is the Whitman of paradox, a unifier of contradictions, who sees the world in pairs—body and soul, Me and Not-Me, male and female, land and sea, old and new, real and ideal, object and subject, material and spiritual, individual and community—and whose favorite words are *balance* and *fusion*. In this, Whitman is very much like Coleridge, of whom Alice D. Snyder says:

. . . even as he was averse to ultimate negation and contradiction, so was he to any forms of division, signifying, as it must, mutual exclusion. Distinction he would allow, but never, as a fundamental philosophical fact, division. "O! the power of names to give interest," he exclaims. "This is Africa! That is Europe! There is *division*, sharp boundary, abrupt change! and what are they in nature? Two mountain banks, that make a noble river of the interfluent sea, not existing and acting with distinctness and manifoldness indeed, but at once and one—no division, no change, no antithesis." . . . Anything of ultimate value must for Coleridge consist of elements which, while they may be distinguished, are yet capable of real fusion.[2]

For Coleridge this truth of nature is revealed also in the power of the creative imagination, which "reveals itself in the balance or reconcilement of opposite or discordant qualities: of sameness, with difference; of the general with the concrete; the idea with the image; the individual with the representative; the sense of novelty and freshness with old and familiar objects; a more than usual state of emotion with more than usual order; judgment ever awake and steady self-possession with enthusiasm and feeling profound or vehement."[3] Whitman, as we shall see, goes beyond Coleridge in

23

two directions: he can conceive, as Miss Snyder says Coleridge cannot, of complete division, the absolute separateness of things; and he can conceive of a unity that admits no distinctions. Yet the central Whitman holds precisely the position expressed by Coleridge: driven by his inclination to reconcile opposites, he even retrieves judgment and restraint from the mechanistic world.

For this Whitman, as indicated by "One's-Self I Sing," truth resides in the separate points of view of individual men, but also in a transcendent law:

It remains to be inquired . . . whether after all allowance for Kant's tremendous and unquestionable point, namely that what we realize as truth in the objective and other Natural worlds is not the absolute but only the relative truth from our existing point of view, . . . whether there is not probably also something in the Soul, even as it exists under present circumstances, which being itself adjusted to the inherent and immutable laws of things . . . does not afford a clue to unchangeable standards and tests—whether in its abysmic depths, far from ken or analysis, it (the soul) does not somehow, even now, by whatever removes and indirections, by its own laws, repel the inconsistent, and gravitate forever toward the absolute, the supernatural, the eternal truth.[4]

His definitions insist upon two aspects of reality: the relative and the absolute, the particular and the transcendent, variety and unity.

The self encloses two halves—"my soul and I": [5] it is, as we have seen, mortal and immortal, corruptible and pure,[6] limited by "standards and measurements" and supremely free.[7] It is set against a dual universe—"the material objective universe. . . , with what is behind." [8] The great question is how to join the two, the Me and the Not-Me; and the answer is the use of that curious compound of poetic intuition and Hegelian logic that I have already discussed. The restraints placed upon the unifying organic vision by the dualistic mechanistic vision actually help to make fusion successful, for they allow the Me to remain as an individual within the Not-Me. The universal depends upon the particular, and freedom upon the limitation of the individual:

. . . the tendencies of our day, in the States, (and I entirely respect them,) are toward those vast and sweeping movements, influences, moral and physical, of humanity, now and always current over the planet, on the scale of the impulses of the elements. Then it is also good to reduce the whole matter to the consideration of a single self, a man, a woman, on permanent grounds. Even for the treatment of the universal, in politics, metaphysics, or anything, sooner or later we come down to one single, solitary soul.[9]

To be all, man must be most himself. In his solitude and particularity he is most removed from nature and most open to it, has most to offer and most to receive:

Now I stand here in the Universe, a personality perfect and sound; all things and all other beings as an audience at the play-house perpetually and perpetually calling me out from behind my curtain.[10]

There, in abstraction and stillness, (I had gone off by myself to absorb the scene, to have the spell unbroken,) the copiousness, the removedness, vitality, loose-clear-crowdedness, of that stellar concave spreading overhead, softly absorb'd into me, rising so free, interminably high, stretching east, west, north, south—and I, though but a point in the centre below, embodying all.[11]

The central Whitman's ideal man mediates between pride and love, the assertive and the sympathetic movements. Whitman lists his characteristics in both a note to himself and an elaborate public document like "Democratic Vistas":

Perfect Sanity. Divine Instinct. Breadth of Vision. Healthy rudeness of body. Withdrawnness. Gayety. Sun-tan and air sweetness.[12]

True, the full man wisely gathers, culls, absorbs; but if, engaged disproportionately in that, he slights or overlays the precious idiocracy and special nativity and intention that he is, the man's self, the main thing, is a failure, however wide his general cultivation.[13]

The hero is rude of body and filled with the divinity of soul, insistent on his own peculiarity and eager to cull and absorb, withdrawn into a private world and endowed with "Breadth of Vision." He is not the ecstatic mystic, a primitive smitten by an overwhelming vision (which commentary like Santayana's would lead us to expect),[14] but above all "a superb calm character." [15] He is Merlin, "strong & wise & beautiful at 100 years old"; [16] or "some unconscious Indianian," unworldly, disinterested, "on whose birth the calmness of heaven seems to have descended," who encloses both "animal purity and heroism" and "a strange spiritual sweetness"; [17] or Whitman's mother, "the most perfect and magnetic character, the nearest combination of practical, moral, and spiritual"; [18] or, in sum, a combination of the men Whitman himself played at being, the "rough" of the 1855 edition and "the good gray poet" of during and after the Civil War:

> Me imperturbe, standing at ease in Nature,
> Master of all or mistress of all, aplomb in the
> midst of irrational things, . . .[19]

Ideal identity encloses tendencies in all directions and scrupulously avoids the excessive cultivation of any one tendency. Thus Whitman scorns Bronson Alcott and the nation for opposite faults:

Alcott had a lot of queerities—freakishness: not vegetarianism—I do not count that—but transcendental mummeries—worst of all a most vociferous contempt for the body, which I, of course, opposed.[20]

. . . the current that bears us is one broadly and deeply materialistic and infidel. It is the very worst kind of infidelity because it suspects not itself but proceeds complacently onward and abounds in churches and all the days of its life solves never the simple riddle why it has not a good time.—For I do not believe the people of these days are happy. The public countenance lacks its bloom of love and its freshness of faith.—For want of these, it is cadaverous as a corpse.[21]

If ideal identity is a combination of individuality and the sense of community, practicality and spirituality, pride and love, "withdrawnness" and engagement, then ideal government is a combination of freedom and law:

Strange as it may seem, we only attain to freedom by a knowledge of, and implicit obedience to, Law. Great—unspeakably great—is the Will! the free Soul of man! At its greatest, understanding and obeying the laws, it can then, and then only, maintain true liberty. . . . The shallow . . . consider liberty a release from all law, from every constraint. The wise see in it . . . the potent Law of Laws, namely, the fusion and combination of the conscious will, or partial individual law, with those universal, eternal, unconscious ones, which run through all Time, pervade history, prove immortality, give moral purpose to the entire objective world, and the last dignity to human life.[22]

Democracy unites the rights of the individual and the rights of the community, each half equally important, emphasized at different times as necessary to the other:

Not that half only, individualism, which isolates. There is another half, which is adhesiveness or love, that fuses, ties and aggregates, making the races comrades, and fraternizing all.[23]

. . . to democracy, the leveler, the unyielding principle of the average, is surely join'd another principle, equally unyielding, closely tracking the first, indispensable to it, opposite, (as the sexes are opposite,) and whose existence, confronting and ever modifying the other, often clashing, paradoxical, yet neither of highest avail without the other, plainly supplies to these grand cosmic politics of ours, and to the launch'd forth mortal dangers of republicanism, today or any day, the counterpart and offset whereby Nature restrains the deadly original relentlessness of all her first-class laws. This second principle is individuality, the pride and centripetal isolation of a human being in himself—identity—personalism. . . . It forms, in a sort, or is to form, the compensating balance-wheel of the successful working machinery of aggregate America.[24]

As the individual is to the community, so is the particular state to the Union:

There are two distinct principles—aye, paradoxes—at the life-fountain and life-continuation of the States; one, the sacred principle of the Union, the right of ensemble, at whatever sacrifice—and yet another, an equally sacred principle, the right of each State, consider'd as a separate sovereign individual, in its own sphere. Some go zealously for one set of these rights, and some as zealously for the other set. We must have both; or rather, bred out of them, as out of mother and father, a third set, the perennial result and combination of both, and neither jeopardized. . . . The problem is, to harmoniously adjust the two, and the play of the two. [Observe the lesson of the divinity of Nature, ever checking the excess of one law, by an opposite, or seemingly opposite law—generally the other side of the same law.] [25]

The political world mirrors the natural world: ideally it plays extremes against each other, "checking . . . excess," moving toward balance or fusion. The citizen in his community, the state in the Union, the man in nature—all pursue their particular paths but must also subordinate themselves to external control. Thus the poet who claims in the 1855 Preface that "obedience does not

27

master [the great poet] . . . , he masters it," [26] a year later, in an appendix if anything more arrogant than the boasts of 1855, can brag of having received a high score for "caution" in a phrenological examination.[27] And the poet who in "Enfans d'Adam" so flouts public morality that the poems later cost him his job,[28] can write, in the same edition in which those poems first appear:

> He is wisest who has the most caution,
> He only wins who goes far enough.[29]

The touchstone of fusion, the blending of two extremes, is applied to almost every area about which Whitman records an opinion. East must be fused with West, and the old with the new.[30] From the philosophy of Greece, which taught "the beauty of life," and that of Christianity, which teaches "how to endure illness and death," should be formed a third philosophy, "doing full justice to both." [31] A third religion is to emerge from the traditional view of religion, which ascribes our ancestry to "divine beings of vaster beauty, size, and power than ours," and the modern view, which "curiously revers[es] the antique" in claiming that men have "originated, developt from monkeys, baboons." [32] And, combining the paradoxes of identity and government, language is "both the free and compacted composition of all [,] . . . a sort of universal absorber, combiner, and conqueror." [33]

Whitman's practical politics as well as his political theory tends toward the middle way. Even the brash young journalist, evidently fired from an editorship a few years later because he refuses to suppress his political disagreement with the owner,[34] advises restraint in an editorial against the extension of slavery: "That a man has these notions of liberty does not infer that he 'goes' for setting at defiance all discretion, the settled laws of the land, the guaranteed power of citizens. . . . We wish for the downfall of despotism in Russia and Austria—wish it with all our heart; yet who would be so wild as to violate the organized system of those empires, and our treaties with them, in any way?" [35] Two friends, C. Q. Eldridge and Edward Carpenter, think of Whitman as conservative,[36] as, in fact, does Whitman himself,[37] although the poet also says, "I claim to be altogether radical—that's my chief stock in trade: take the radicalism out of the Leaves—do you think anything worth while would be left?" [38] Ambiguous as the terms are, it is less to the point to label Whitman than to recognize that almost all of his political judgments are based on a belief in compromise between the existing situation and the ideal, and between the needs and responsibilities of each individual (or state) and those of the government. Progress is to be by "degrees": "The two ideas of unity and progress. The great idea of humanity is progress—onward! onward! backing and filling—every step contested—sometimes a long interregnum—sometimes a retrogression —but still, by degrees, a sure, resistless progress." [39]

In the writings of Hegel, whom he calls "Humanity's chiefest teacher and the choicest loved physician of my mind and soul," [40] and Darwin, "whose life was after all the most significant, the furthest-influencing, life of the age," [41] Whitman finds support for his own belief in gradual evolution, a belief strong enough that he can call evolution "not the rule in Nature, in Politics, and Inventions only, but in Verse," [42] and say of "Passage to India": "There's more of me, the essential ultimate me, in that than in any of the poems. There is no philosophy, consistent or inconsistent, in that poem . . . but the burden of it is evolution." [43]

This interest in progress "by degrees" suggests, what is not often associated with Whitman, a tendency toward the idea of stages and categories, an impulse that also has a place in his doctrine of prudence:

. . . all that a male or female does that is vigorous and benevolent and clean is so much more profit to him or her in the unshakable order of the universe, and through the whole scope of it forever. The prudence of the greatest poet answers at least the craving and glut of the soul, puts off nothing, permits no let-up for its own case or any case, has no particular sabbath or judgment day, divides not the living from the dead, or the righteous from the unrighteous, is satisfied with the present, matches every thought or act by its correlative, and knows no possible forgiveness or deputed atonement. [44]

Prudence includes everything ("puts off nothing") and gives everything its own place ("matches every . . . act by its correlative"). Or, as Daiches explains, "everyone and everything moves according to its own laws and both fulfills its own destiny and plays its proper part in the general movement." [45] Like Thoreau's

29

economy, prudence is a word played off deliberately against its everyday meaning. It is more than ordinary caution; to live prudently the individual must in effect understand the proportions and rhythm of all life, so as to find his own place and fill it. The particular role and the universe complement and fulfill each other in the manner of the individual and the community. Seen against this setting, Whitman's painstaking rearrangements of his book take on a special significance. Whitman insists to Traubel that his poems must be seen "in their place in the book" to be understood,[46] and says of the book as a whole: "Leaves of Grass may be only an indication—a forerunner—a crude offender against the usual canons—a barbaric road-breaker—but it still has a place, a season, I am convinced."[47] Each poem has a role in the book, the book as a whole fills a special place in the world.

This Whitman who mediates between the particular and the universal, and who insists on moderation and "place" even as he celebrates progress and the destruction of barriers, embodies his vision in two images—marriage, the union of opposites, and the procession, a measured journey.

The contact of opposites does not always produce a true union. Sometimes, as in "Song of Myself" and "The Sleepers," it results in a wild dance—the flight of the imagination, which, barely acknowledging the doubts of the bodily element, breaks through all distinctions. Or sometimes, as at the beginning of "As I Ebb'd," there is a terrible paralysis, caused by the individual's overwhelming recognition of his natural and aesthetic pettiness in comparison to the unlimited worlds of spirit and the imagination. Usually, however, there is a mediation between the attractions of individuality and limitation on the one hand and those of the universal and the free imagination on the other: the opposite tendencies are more cooperative and therefore more productive, their union a marriage rather than a rape by either partner. Body and soul, the marrying halves of the self, make for the life of the universe: ". . . the soul of the Universe is the Male and genital master and the impregnating and animating spirit—Physical matter is Female and Mother and waits barren and bloomless, the jets of life from the masculine vigor, the undermost first cause of all that is not what Death is."[48] Whitman is not consistent with his assignment of roles, for the soul in his poems is more often female than male,[49] but he does consistently conceive of his merging opposites as sexual partners. The sea and the land that merge in "As I Ebb'd" are "mother" and "father"; [50] and the real democracy is produced by a fusion of the principle of the States and that of the Union, must be "bred out of them, as out of mother and father." [51]

As in Hegel's dialectic and Darwin's explicitly biological system, marriage results in a further stage, the birth of a third form.

> Urge and urge and urge,
> Always the procreant urge of the world.

> Out of the dimness opposite equals advance, always
>   substance and increase, always sex,
> Always a knit of identity, always distinction,
>   always a breed of life.[52]

Opposite tendencies both restrain each other and satisfy each other: the form that results from the pressure of each on the other is one beyond each of the original forms yet enclosing part of each; and the process is "by degrees, a sure, resistless progress." [53] Thus we have the image of a procession, the "march of improvement." [54] The great lesson of life, Whitman has his "science-friend" explain, is that

> ". . . we all are onward, onward, speeding slowly, surely
>   bettering,
> "Life, life an endless march, an endless army, . . .
> "The world, the race, the soul—in space and time
>   the universes,
> "All bound as is befitting each—all surely going
>   somewhere." [55]

As the second line indicates, this conception of orderly progress is behind Whitman's fascination with army movements, as in "Cavalry Crossing a Ford," "An Army Corps on the March," and "A March in the Ranks Hard-Prest, and the Road Unknown." "A young man's life is a battle any how," Whitman writes to one of his ex-soldier friends. "Noble—thrice noble is he who steadily carries throughout the march, through defeat or whatever happens, a gay, unconquered spirit." [56] Life is not undifferentiated flux, but a measured journey: "The earth neither lags nor hastens"; [57] "Nature

31

marches in procession, in sections, like the corps of an army." [58] At no time does the image deny differences or contradictions. At its easiest, the journey does not eliminate distinctions but uses them ("Nature marches . . . in sections"); at its most difficult, it confronts contradictions and presses slowly on.

Although the procession is not necessarily committed to poetry, which is just one way of reaching the "somewhere" at the end of the journey, it is no surprise to find the poet presented as both the maker of the procession—"Duly take places in his flowing procession, and step to the sound of the jubilant music, the essences of American things" [59]—and, as in "Adieu to a Soldier," a participant in it, a poet-soldier:

> Your mission is fulfill'd—but I, more warlike,
> Myself and this contentious soul of mine,
> Still on our own campaigning bound,
> Through untried roads with ambushes opponents lined,
> Through many a sharp defeat and many a crisis, often
> baffled,
> Here marching, ever marching on, a war fight out—
> aye here,
> To fiercer, weightier battles give expression.
> [Pp. 325–26.] [60]

Progress seen whole is a journey "by degrees"—a warlike march that "speeds slowly," not an instantaneous flight—precisely because it depends upon the individual's fulfillment of his role and because it must contend with contradictions, the rough edges of the world, which are confronted and made into parts of a larger, proportionate good:

The first inspiration of real wisdom in our souls lets us know that the self will and wickedness and malignity we thought so unsightly in our race are by no means what we were told, but something far different, and not amiss except to spirits of the feeble and the shorn.—as the freckles and bristly beard of Jupiter to be removed by washes and razors, under the judgment of genteel squirts, but in the sight of the great master, proportionate and essential and sublime.[61]

The images of marriage and procession are admirably suited to the Whitman of paradox, who stands somewhere between the

Cartesian mathematical conception of the universe and the Coleridgean organic conception. Emerson, committed in "The Over-Soul" to the organic idea of reality, makes a sharp distinction between it and the mathematical idea: "After [the soul's] own law and not by arithmetic is the rate of its progress to be computed. The soul's advances are not made by gradation, such as can be represented by motion in a straight line, but rather by ascension of state, such as can be represented by metamorphosis—from the egg to the worm, from the worm to the fly. The growths of genius are of a certain *total* character." [62] The image of marriage, the wedding of "organic body" to "organic soul," expresses the new whole that Whitman tries to make from Descartes' analytic imagination and the creative imagination of organicism. The image of procession also is a blending of the two worlds. With its emphasis on degrees and "sections," it has some affinity with the "gradation" and "arithmetic" that Emerson would dismiss. Yet, its fluidity, the relationship of "procession" to "process," is more in keeping with organicism than with mathematics. Variety and unity, gradation and fluidity fuse to form images that express accurately the central Whitman, who is an "analyzer" with "intuition," who sees opposites but insists on a "proportionate" whole.

On either side of this central Whitman stands an extremist Whitman, the Whitman of variety on the one hand, the Whitman of unity on the other, each asserting his existence against the Whitman of paradox, who would fuse them.

The Whitman of variety sees individual differences not as part of a proportionate whole but as whole in themselves: "Believing that the man is always stronger than the circumstances which surround him—that his nature is bounded by a circle beyond which the forces of matter cannot thrust him—we cannot suppose that the relative strength of reason and imagination is at all modified by the chances and changes of what we choose to denominate civilization and refinement." [63] There is a significant difference in emphasis between the man who insists on variety within unity and the one who likes individuality and variety for their own sake. The Whitman to whom "self will and wickedness and malignity" are "not amiss" tends slightly more toward unity than the Whitman who grants the god of revolt equal status to the gods of justice and mercy, as he does by including Satan within his "square deific," [64] and much more than the Whitman who makes himself the Satan:

> I am a hell-name and a curse:
> Black Lucifer was not dead;
> Or if he was I am his sorrowful, terrible heir;
> I am the God of revolt—deathless, sorrowful,
>   vast; whoever oppresses me
> I will either destroy him or he shall release me.[65]

It is the spirit of this last Whitman that Carpenter, recalling a friend's impression of the poet's "magnificent No!," thinks of as Whitman's "cussedness," [66] and that we hear in these words to Emerson: "Always America will be agitated and turbulent. This day it is taking shape, not to be less so, but to be more so, stormily, capriciously, on native principles, with such vast proportions of parts! As for me, I love screaming, wrestling, boiling-hot days." [67] In the next breath Whitman adds, "Of course, we shall have a national character, an identity . . ."; but it remains clear that he is sometimes so attracted by variety and resistance as to forget about an encompassing, mediating unity.

According to the Whitman of variety, then, the reality is not the combination of state and individual, but the individual alone: "(— Where Rousseau is yet undeveloped is, in not realizing that the *individual* man or woman is the head and ideal, and the State, City, Government, or what not, is a servant, subordinate,—with noth'g sacred about it—noth'g in a Judge or Court either—But all sacredness is in the individual,—and the other, at most, is but a reflection of the individual's.) [68] This answer to the question of identity is accompanied by a complementary answer to the question of government: the individual must be his own boss. "The citizen must have room. He must learn to be so muscular and self-possessed; to rely more on the restrictions of himself than any restrictions of statute books, or city ordinances, or police. This is the feeling that will make live men and superior women. This will make a great, athletic, spirited city, of noble and marked character. . . ." [69]

From this conception of reality spring two images very different from those used by the central Whitman, who mediates between opposites: the images of struggle and the solitary, static man, as against those of marriage and the procession. Struggle is admired because distinct things have their own integrity and because they strengthen other distinct things with which they wrestle. Desiring "a great, athletic, spirited city," Whitman asks:

Have you learn'd lessons only of those who admired you, and were tender with you, and stood aside for you?
Have you not learn'd great lessons from those who reject you, and brace themselves against you? or who treat you with contempt, or dispute the passage with you? [70]

Thus Whitman, who loves "screaming, wrestling, boiling-hot days," and who indeed in his sixties wrestles with young Harry Stafford,[71] speaks approvingly of the Egyptian ruler Sesostris, who "conquered Asia and Europe, honoring those who resisted him most,"[72] and finds one of the great strengths of the English language to be that "it is the powerful language of resistance—it is the dialect of common sense."[73] Simple love of conflict even more than patriotic fervor is what produces his celebrations of war, the mood of which contrasts so curiously with the elegiac quality of the rest of the Drum-Taps group:

Proud and passionate city—mettlesome, mad,
    extravagant city!

Spring up O city—not for peace alone, but
    be indeed yourself, warlike!
Fear not—submit to no models but your own O city!
. . . .
I chant and celebrate all that is yours—yet peace
    no more,
In peace I chanted peace, but now the drum of war
    is mine,
War, red war is my song through your streets,
    O city! [74]

"Submit to no models but your own": one wrestles to discover, or to demonstrate, his own identity. There is an obvious relationship to the other image used by this Whitman of variety, that of the static individual man, in which the tendency toward separation is given its purest expression. The wide range of the image

35

demonstrates Whitman's conviction that the integrity of individualism resides as much in man's profound loneliness and perplexity as in his euphoric sense of completeness within himself. The individual can be the whole man, the "overlooker," out of the game, as in "When Lilacs Last in the Dooryard Bloom'd" (Section 12) and "I Sit and Look Out":

> I sit and look out upon all the sorrows of the
>   world, and upon all oppression and shame,
> I hear secret convulsive sobs from young men
>   at anguish with themselves, remorseful
>   after deeds done,
> . . . .
> All these—all the meanness and agony without
>   end I sitting look out upon,
> See, hear, and am silent.   [Pp. 272–73.]

Or he can be the man in the center of things, whole, stable, like the narrator of "Out of the Cradle Endlessly Rocking"—enclosing the things pressing in on him rather than pulled in various directions by them. Or he can be the individual so much in the game that he is driven into retreat: the bird who has lost his mate in "Cradle"; the poet who mourns in "Lilacs" (Section 2); the poet at the beginning of "As I Ebb'd with the Ocean of Life," "baffled, balk'd, bent to the very earth"; or the Whitman whom the old poet, in a rare moment of confession, describes to Traubel: "I don't know if you have ever realized it—ever realized what it meant to be a horror in the sight of the people . . . when the enemy—and nearly all were enemy then—wanted for nothing better or more than simply, without remorse, to crush me, to brush me, without compunction or mercy, out of sight, out of hearing: . . . to rid themselves of me." [75]

The other extremist, the Whitman of unity, has no delight in "screaming, wrestling, boiling-hot days"; rather, he says: "We want satisfiers, joiners, lovers. These heated, torn, distracted ages are to be compacted and made whole." [76] He is thrilled by the idea of union in the completion of the Atlantic telegraph cable, not by mere "material considerations": ". . . neither the scientific nor the utilitarian relations of this grand experiment . . . can account

for the exultation with which it has been greeted. . . . It is the
sentiment of *union* that makes the popular heart beat and quiver.
It is the union of the great Anglo-Saxon race, henceforth forever to
be a unit, that makes the States throb with tumultuous emotion
and thrills every breast with admiration and triumph." [77] Identity is
not in the individual but in the mass; government is established not
by one's own restrictions but by "the divine, vast, general law":

If I were ask'd *persona* to specify the one point of America's people on
which I mainly rely, I should say the final average or bulk quality of the
whole.[78]

The common ambition strains for elevations, to become some
privileged exclusive. The master sees greatness and health in being part
of the mass; nothing will do as well as common ground. Would you
have in yourself the divine, vast, general law? Then merge yourself in
it.[79]

This third Whitman, who sacrifices wrestling to joining, the
individual to the mass, separateness to merger, is very close to the
Emerson of "The Over-Soul," who says:

What we commonly call man, the eating, drinking, planting, counting
man, does not, as we know him, represent himself, but misrepresents
himself. Him we do not respect, but the soul, whose organ he is, would
he let it appear through his action, would make our knees bend. When
it breathes through his intellect, it is genius; when it breathes through
his will, it is virtue; when it flows through his affection, it is love. And
the blindness of the intellect begins when it would be something of
itself. The weakness of the will begins when the individual would be
something of himself.[80]

Perhaps because of this resemblance to Emerson, the Whitman of
unity has received more critical attention than he is due. D. H.
Lawrence, for instance, represents him as the whole Whitman, and
proceeds to bludgeon his straw man:

Oh, Walter, Walter, what have you done with it? What have you
done with yourself? With your own individual self? For it sounds as if it
had all leaked out of you, leaked into the universe.[81]

I, who happen to be asleep under the bushes in the dark, hoping a
snake won't crawl into my neck; I, seeing Walt go by in his great fierce
poetic machine, think to myself: What a funny world that fellow sees!

ONE DIRECTION! toots Walt in the car, whizzing along in it.

Whereas there are myriads of ways in the dark, not to mention trackless wildernesses. As anyone will know who cares to come off the road, even the Open Road. . . .

God save me, I feel like creeping down a rabbit-hole, to get away from all these automobiles rushing down the ONE IDENTITY track to the goal of ALLNESS.[82]

Actually, as we have seen, the Whitman of unity is not even the central Whitman, let alone the whole Whitman. The central Whitman does not relinquish his individuality; he knows the danger of merging and himself distrusts the route of "ONE DIRECTION."

Whitman's idea of unity has two aspects, a duality that can probably be traced back to Plato's dual conception of divinity, as self-sufficient and immutable (the idea of God that A. O. Lovejoy calls "otherworldly") and as constantly creating new forms of itself ("this worldly").[83] Lovejoy explains the original split:

. . . Plato, tacitly making the crucial assumption that the existence of many entities not eternal, not superhensible, and far from perfect, was inherently desirable, finds in his otherworldly Absolute, in the Idea of the Good itself, the reason why that Absolute cannot exist alone. The concept of Self-Sufficing Perfection, by a bold logical inversion, was—without losing any of its original implications—converted into the concept of a Self-Transcending Fecundity. . . . With this reversal there was introduced into European philosophy and theology the . . . conception of . . . Two-Gods-in-One, of a divine completion which was yet *not* complete in itself, since it could not be itself without the existence of beings other than itself and inherently incomplete; of an Immutability which required, and expressed itself in, change; of an Absolute which was nevertheless not truly absolute because it was related, at least by way of implication and causation, to entities whose nature was not *its* nature and whose existence and perpetual passage were antithetic to its immutable subsistence.[84]

The aspect of Whitman's unity that is static and permanent is the realm of the soul (what I have called the "mechanistic soul"), which lies behind each distinct body and joins all:

. . . in respect to the absolute soul, there is in the possession of such by each single individual, something so transcendent, so incapable of gradations, (like life,) that, to that extent, it places all beings on a common level . . .[85]

What is Life itself? but a Vestibule to something, in the future, we know not what—but something as certain as the Present is certain. Nay, who that has reach'd what may be called the full Vestibule but has had strong suspicions that what we call the Present, Reality, &c. with all its Corporeal shows, may be the Illusion for reasons, & that even to this Identity of yours or mine, the far more Permanent is yet unseen, yet to come—like a long train of noble corridors & infinite Halls & Superb endless chambers, yet awaiting us.[86]

It is within the realm of this "absolute soul" that men can achieve immortality. And it is toward this permanent One, as for Hegel's Absolute Being, that the universe is moving:

> I swear I think now that every thing without
> exception has an eternal soul!
> The trees have, rooted in the ground! the
> weeds of the sea have! the animals!
>
> I swear I think there is nothing but immortality!
> That the exquisite scheme is for it, and the
> nebulous float is for it, and the cohering
> is for it!
> And all preparation is for it—and identity is
> for it—and life and materials are altogether
> for it! [87]

Or, in Emerson's more sober tones:

This is the ultimate fact which we so quickly reach on this, as on every topic, the resolution of all into the ever-blessed ONE. Self-existence is the attribute of the Supreme Cause, and it constitutes the measure of good by the degree in which it enters into all lower forms. All things real are so by so much virtue as they contain. Commerce, husbandry, hunting, whaling, war, eloquence, personal weight, are somewhat, and engage my respect as examples of its presence and impure action.[88]

Despite Emerson's talk of "good" and "virtue," the moral characteristics and demands of the One are not precisely defined. Its nature is allowed to be vague (Whitman's processions are going "somewhere"; the world of the One is "the unknown region"),[89] except for the basic characteristics of permanence and unity (the "absolute soul" is "incapable of gradations").

The other aspect of Whitman's unity is the "this worldly" All, the everlasting flux: "The varieties, contradictions and paradoxes of the world and of life, and even good and evil, so baffling to the superficial observer, so often leading to despair, sullenness or infidelity, become a series of infinite radiations and waves of the one sea-like universe of divine action and progress, never stopping, never hasting." [90] The flux is not only "process"; it is also "progress"—it moves toward the One. Like the realm of the One, the flux allows for no gradations. The flux, however, goes beyond cosmic democracy; it insists not only upon equality but upon no distinctions at all. The difference between the Whitman who conceives of this flowing unity and the Whitman of variety is that, although both are concerned with the stuff of this world, the former sees varieties and contradictions disappear into the large merging movement of the universe, become indistinguishable in the All, whereas the latter delights in distinction, celebrates the each rather than the All, resistance rather than merging. And the Whitman of unity differs from the Whitman of paradox as the image of flux differs from the image of procession: although the flux also is an image of progress toward the "absolute soul," it wholly eliminates the distinctions that the procession keeps as part of itself. It is the "floating vast" [91] or the "measureless float," [92] rather than "a procession with measured and perfect motion." [93]

These two aspects of unity work both with each other and against each other. The conception of the One gives some authority to the shifting All, some implicit purpose, however vague, beyond its own movement and proliferation of new forms; and the conception of the All, arising from the idea of divinity as continuously creative, overflowing with love, allows an escape from the idea that God completed his work on the last day of Creation and is now detached from this world. Yet, as always for Whitman, the fluidity and permanence also tend to drive each other out. On the one hand, the flux is everlasting and seems to have its own final validity—"a series of infinite radiations . . . , never stopping, never hasting." On the other, the flux is merely preparation for the absolute truth—the permanent One, realm of immortality. Fluidity can become attractive in itself, as it is for the speaker in "Song of Myself," who says, ". . . as to you Corpse I think you are good manure, but that does not offend me"; [94] and rest, the permanence that comes from joining the One, can tempt one to desert the living flux, as it tempts the thrush in "Lilacs."

In the same way, the two images by which Whitman expresses the participation of the individual in these aspects of unity are both at variance with each other and complementary. One image, that of comradeship, carries the atmosphere of peace and permanence, while the other image, of a wild dance or instantaneous flight, is fluidity itself. The thinking behind the image of comradeship demonstrates how far the Whitman of unity is from the Whitman of variety, who demands freedom for the individual: "Comradeship—yes, that's the thing: getting one and one together to make two—getting the twos together everywhere to make all: that's the only bond we should accept and that's the only freedom we should desire: comradeship, comradeship." [95] And the image differs from the central Whitman's image of marriage in that it assumes identity between the two comrades, a soulful union, whereas the image of marriage expresses both unity and variety—"Always a knit of identity, always distinction." [96] Whitman's comradeship is a quiet, lingering love that provides for the living what immortality does for the dead—participation in the permanent spirit that lies behind the changing faces of things. It is an alternative to the flux, which at its most dangerous produces in the individual a "terrible doubt of appearances":

> I cannot answer the question of appearances
>   or that of identity beyond the grave,
> But I walk or sit indifferent, I am satisfied,
> He ahold of my hand has completely satisfied me.[97]

The image of flight or a wild dance most often represents the play of the imagination, the engagement of the "organic soul" in the flux of the universe. The speaker in "The Sleepers," wandering in his vision, cries, "I am a dance—play up there! the fit is whirling me fast!" (Section 1, p. 426). And in "Song of Myself":

> I hear the train'd soprano (what work with hers
>   is this?)
> The orchestra whirls me wider than Uranus flies,

41

> It wrenches such ardors from me I did not know
>   I possess'd them,
> It sails me, I dab with bare feet, they are
>   lick'd by the indolent waves , . . .
>   [Section 26, p. 56.]

This sort of journey is an instantaneous flight, not the march of an army corps. Yet, if the images of comradeship and flight contradict each other—if one expresses quiet and permanence and the other frenzy and violent motion, if one refers to metaphysical engagement with the One and the other to poetic engagement with the flux—they also work for each other, even as the two ideas of divinity, logically contradictory, support and enrich each other. In this passage from a notebook of 1847, the images no less than the rhythm are characteristic of the poetry to come:

. . . my left arm shall hook you round the waist, and my right shall point you to the endless and beginningless road along whose sides are crowded the rich cities of all living philosophy, and oval gates that pass you in to fields of clover and landscapes clumped with sassafras, and orchards of good apples, and every breath through your mouth shall be of a new perfumed and elastic air, which is love.—Not I—not God— can travel this road for you.—It is not far, it is within the stretch of your thumb; perhaps you shall find you are on it already and did not know.— Perhaps you shall find it every where over the ocean and over the land, when you once have the vision to behold it.[98]

The poet may tell his reader to travel his road alone, but the telling follows upon an embrace. In the 1855 Preface the gesture of comradeship is not simply an imparting of strength; the "elder" and "younger" travel together: "Now there shall be a man cohered out of tumult and chaos—the elder encourages the younger and shows him how—they two shall launch off fearlessly together till the new world fits an orbit for itself, and looks unabash'd on the lesser orbits of the stars, and sweeps through the ceaseless rings, and shall never be quiet again." [99] It is, in fact, unusual when the start of a journey is not accompanied, as it is in "Song of Myself" and "Song of the Open Road," by a call for a comrade. The arm round the waist, the touch of hands, the request for company—all these, seen one way, are gestures of encouragement, for the excitements of elasticity are meant to be shared. Seen another way, they are gestures of need; even as the poet promises his listener those excitements, he himself, about to be caught up in the wild dance of the imagination, needs the stability and permanence of comradeship.

This struggle in the Whitman of unity between a unity that is unchanging and one that is fluid, between a unity that is One and a unity that is All, is simply a small version of the struggle that dominates Whitman's imagination. The same conflict takes place within the Whitman of variety. On the one hand, he uses the image of wrestling, which suggests the resistance to each other of various individuals (connection in spite of itself), and on the other hand, he uses the image of the solitary individual. And of course the struggle is apparent in the central Whitman, the mediator between unity and variety: the desire for private identity plays against, and complements, the desire to be all. Each tendency supports the other, yet each is so attractive that Whitman presses it to its extreme, making the opposite tendency impossible of fulfillment; then, however, the peculiar danger of the resulting situation demands the calling-forth, for defensive purposes, of the neglected tendency.

The second struggle, between freedom and restraint, cuts across the struggle between variety and unity. Like the answers to the question of identity, each answer to the question of government can result in complications for the individual. The abstract answers —reality is unity, reality is variety, government is individual, government is transcendent—do not solve the problem of action for the individual. Each answer merely erects an intellectual structure inside which the individual must act: invariably he can move in at least two directions.

For the Whitman of variety, each individual governs himself, but he is not necessarily free. He may be so free—"perfect and sound," complete in himself—that, from behind his curtain, he can ignore "all things and all other beings." [100] But he may also be trapped by setting himself off from the rest of the universe, caught by the realization of his own pettiness, as in "As I Ebb'd with the Ocean of Life."

For the Whitman of unity, all beings live under "the divine, vast, general law" of equality: in both the All and the One, there are no "gradations." The individual who knows this law, like Whitman himself, is either radically free or radically limited, either a god among gods or nothing at all. He can either float joyously in equality—"My ties and ballasts leave me, my elbows rest in sea-gaps," [101]—or, again as in "Ebb'd," drown in it:

> As the ocean so mysterious rolls toward me closer
>   and closer,
> I too but signify at the utmost a little wash'd-up
>   drift, . . .

[P. 254.]

For the individual who must be initiated, however, government is a different matter, not dependent on the relationship between himself and the One or All, but on the relationship between himself and his teacher, Whitman, the voice of the law. He is at once Whitman's inferior and his equal: he must be subservient in order to be released. As Whitman says, in one of his unsigned, third-person explanations:

Especially in the "Leaves of Grass" are the facts of eternity and immortality largely treated. Happiness is no dream, and perfection is no dream. Amelioration is my lesson, he [the poet] says with calm voice, and progress is my lesson and the lesson of all things. Then his persuasion becomes a taunt, and his love bitter and compulsory. With strong and steady call he addresses men. Come, he seems to say, from the midst of all that you have been your whole life surrounding yourself with. Leave all the preaching and teaching of others, and mind these words of mine.[102]

The central Whitman mediates between the idea of government as the business of the individual and the idea of government as divine law. According to his conception of government—freedom under law—this Whitman too is both free and restrained. His freedom is but a local manifestation in the larger order of things: it, and he, will be surpassed:

Democracy too is law, and of the strictest, amplest kind. Many suppose, (and often in its own ranks the error,) that it means a throwing aside of law, and running riot. But briefly, it is the superior law, not alone that of physical force, the body, which, adding to, it supersedes with that of the spirit. Law is the unshakable order of the

44

universe forever; and the law over all, and law of laws, is the law of successions; that of the superior law, in time, gradually supplanting and overwhelming the inferior one.[103]

Life for Whitman at the particular moment within this general conception is again both free and restrained. He makes his own freedom and conforms to a law, less vague than the "divine law," of his own making. He rebels against restraints, the "formules" of "bat-eyed and materialistic priests," [104] yet feels it necessary to construct restraints to protect himself against a world of absolute equality.

The whole Whitman, the Whitman of bipolar unity, tries to maintain all three positions: even as he moves to a position between two alternatives, he continues to hold firmly to the alternatives themselves. In his article on Whitman's "triadic imagery," Marks says that Whitman's images of three figures are attempts to embody Hegel's dialectic, that "curious triplicate process." [105] The dialectic, however, is a process of two entities merging into a third, not of all three remaining in tension. The real force of the image is that, as Marks himself says elsewhere in the article, "the Poet-self which [Whitman] created . . . was designed both to contain the extremes and to unify them." [106] This— the reconciliation of extremes and an insistence upon the validity of each extreme—forms the pattern of Whitman's inconsistencies.

We should come away from a survey of Whitman's habit of mind and "secret language" with an intellectual and metaphorical structure for Whitman's work that will help us to ask relevant questions. The structure should enable us to discuss, for instance, as a prelude to the close readings of Whitman's major poems, topics with which the whole Whitman is concerned.

One such topic is Whitman's conception of time. Most critics of Whitman, when they talk of his idea of time at all, speak like Allen and Daiches, to whom Whitman is a "time-binder," who conceives of a "flowing time" and "live[s] emotionally and imaginatively in an eternal present," [107] or a "visionary poet [who] often deliberately mixes his tenses." [108] These observations are accurate enough, except that they tell only part of the story. If the central Whitman really thinks and talks in the way I have described, we might expect a conception of time that treats it not as an undifferentiated flux or "duration" (Georges Poulet's word), [109] expressed by a mixture or confusion of tenses, but as a procession—that is, an orderly succession of stages, expressed by the use of tense as we normally expect it to be used. This idea is, in fact, basic to "Democratic Vistas":

For the New World, . . . after two grand stages of preparation-strata, I perceive that now a third stage, being ready for, (and without which the other two were useless,) with unmistakable signs appears. The First stage was the planning and putting on record the political foundation rights of immense masses of people. . . . The Second stage relates to material prosperity. . . . The Third stage, rising out of the previous ones, . . . I, now, . . . promulge, announcing a native expression-spirit, . . . to be evidenced by original authors and poets to come, by . . . growths of language, songs, operas, orations, lectures, architecture . . . [110]

This conception of time does not see the present as "an extent that is filled with all times, an eternity formed of the union of the three elements of duration [—past, present, and future]," [111] but as an area separate from the past and future. The "New World," says Whitman, has been through the stage of political growth, is now in the stage of material growth, and is anticipating the stage of literary growth. And, if it be objected that "Democratic Vistas" is, after all, more or less straightforward prose, we can turn to the metaphor of "A Song of the Rolling Earth," where we find not the flux but a measured journey:

Embracing man, embracing all, proceed the three hundred and sixty-five resistlessly round the sun;
Embracing all, soothing, supporting, follow close three hundred and sixty-five offsets of the first, sure and necessary as they.

[Section 1, p. 222.]

Each day grows out of the previous one, but can be distinguished from it; the third stage of American democracy rises out of the two previous stages; and a third century, out of the preceding two— "The Nineteenth Century . . . ripening into fruit the seeds of the two preceding centuries . . ." [112]

Thus Whitman usually conceives of time as the central Whit-

46

man, the Whitman of paradox, conceives of reality. He is full of the
sense of organic unity, but also conscious of separations:

> I raise the present on the past,
> (As some perennial tree out of its roots,
> the present on the past,) . . .[113]

. . . what a nation likes, is part of that nation; . . . its politics and
religion, whatever they are, are inevitable result of the days and events
that have preceded the nation, just as much as the condition of the
geology of that part of the earth is the result of former conditions.[114]

The present grows out of the past or builds upon it, but still is
distinguishable from the past, just as the "sections" of a procession
are distinguishable from one another. Time for the central Whitman is not the "measureless float," but an orderly progression,
what it is for most of us who live by the clock and calendar. We
should, therefore, expect the poems often to use past tense to
describe an action in the past, present to describe an action in the
present. Proper readings of "Song of Myself," "As I Ebb'd with the
Ocean of Life," "Out of the Cradle Endlessly Rocking," "When
Lilacs Last in the Dooryard Bloom'd," and "Passage to India" are
all very much dependent on this understanding of Whitman's use
of tense. It is important that we know when Whitman is telling a
story of the past in these poems and when he is acting out a private
drama and is no longer really a narrator.

Nevertheless, it is necessary to repeat that Allen, Daiches, and
Poulet have their point: Whitman does occasionally conceive of
time as "duration," just as the Whitman of unity can conceive of
all existence as flux. Thus:

> I know that the past was great and the future
> will be great,
> And I know that both curiously conjoint in the
> present time,
>
> . . . .
> And that where I am or you are this present day,
> there is the centre of all days, all races, . . .[115]

Nobody can possess a fair idea of the earth without letting his or her
mind walk perfectly easy and loose over the past. A few definite points
mark deeds and national eras, lists of titles and battles and the like make

up very little of the movement of humanity and events at any time. The best and most important part of history cannot be told. It eludes being examined or printed. It is above even dates and reliable information. It is surer and more reliable, because by far the greatest part of the old statistics of history are only approaches to the truth and often discrepant and suspicious.[116]

All this comes from the man who makes a meticulous study of his genealogy,[117] writes a long series of articles about the history of Brooklyn, filled with dates and detail,[118] and is a careful and knowledgeable Egyptologist.[119] The poet who is precise about separating past from present action also uses tense dramatically, as if to demonstrate how easily his mind walks over the past:

> Swiftly arose and spread around me the peace and
>   knowledge that pass all the argument of the earth,
> And I know that the hand of God is the promise of
>   my own,
> And I know that the spirit of God is the brother
>   of my own,
> And that all the men ever born are also my brothers,
>   and the women my sisters and lovers,
> And that a kelson of the creation is love, . . .[120]

But by now we should be accustomed to Whitman's contradictions. If our way through his poems will not always be certain—if we will not always be sure what he means by shifting stance or statement or grammar—at least, placing the particular incident against the whole context of his writings, we should be able to guess with some confidence. And this survey should help us also to discuss Whitman's poetic forms. We will find, as we might expect, that his habitual answers to the questions of identity and government inform his notions of what poets, poems, and readers do; and that the pattern of his poetic forms is analogous to the pattern of his other questions and answers, the other demands he makes of life and gestures he makes toward it.

III "BIPOLAR UNITY" IN POETIC THEORY

WHITMAN'S ATTRACTION toward opposites is apparent in nearly every paragraph of his widely scattered critical writings. When we press his unordered remarks into distinct categories—the poet and reality, the poet and the poem, and the poet and the reader— we find dominant the activity of paradox, Whitman's fusing of those opposites. We find a different drama, however, when we approach in a different way. When we trace theories that cut across the categories, such as Whitman's conceptions of "indirection" and "direction," we can see him take his stand at one extreme of a dialectic and move steadily toward the other extreme. Approaching in both ways should provide a comprehensive view of his ideas on poets, poetry, and readers.

First the Whitman of paradox. Whitman's prefaces and conversations are full of statements that make the universe—Nature and the human personality—the measure of poetry:

. . . to speak in literature with the perfect rectitude and insouciance of the movements of animals, and the unimpeachableness of the sentiment of trees in the woods and grass by the roadside, is the flawless triumph of art. If you have look'd on him who has achiev'd it you have look'd on one of the masters of the artists of all nations and times. You shall not contemplate the flight of the gray gull over the bay, or the mettlesome action of the blood horse, . . . or the appearance of the sun journeying through heaven, . . . with any more satisfaction than you shall contemplate him.[1]

In many cases—more often in the early writings than the late, and especially in the exuberant Preface of 1855—such identifications of poetizing with natural process are closely connected to declarations of universal love and total satisfaction:

The known universe has one complete lover, and that is the greatest poet. He consumes an eternal passion, and is indifferent which chance happens, and which possible contingency of fortune or misfortune, and persuades daily and hourly his delicious pay. . . . Nothing can jar him —suffering and darkness cannot—death and fear cannot. To him complaint and jealousy and envy are corpses buried and rotten in the earth—he saw them buried.[2]

But the original analogy between Nature and poetry does not require an undiscriminating embrace, and Whitman knows it. Such simpleminded distortions of organicism and of life are, at least in part, his way of steadying himself. Those flights into extremism are in their special way basic to Whitman's life and poetic vision, but so too are the moments when he pushes aside his own "concealments" and reveals an understanding of complexity. He thinks "Drum-Taps" his best work, he writes to his friend William O'Connor, because "it delivers my ambition of the task that has haunted me, namely, to express in a poem . . . the pending action of this *Time and Land we swim in,* with all their large conflicting fluctuations of despair and hope. . . ."[3] An even more personal statement of the sentiment is reported by John Burroughs:

. . . the statement of the *personality* of the man himself . . . becomes of first importance. . . . upon due analysis, we discover every case of marked and resplendent individualism to be a composition, a paradox. Can there by strong lights without shades—mountain peaks without intervening chasms? Walt Whitman himself has warned me that my essay was seriously deficient in not containing this distinct admission applied to him. "My friends," he said, "are blind to the real devils that are in me. My enemies discover fancy ones. I perceive in clear moments that my work is not the accomplishment of perfections, but destined, I hope, always to arouse an unquenchable feeling and ardor for them. It is out of struggle and turmoil I have written."[4]

Life is complicated, full of light and darkness; and the darkness *does* jar. Nature, the poet, the making of the poem, the reading of the poem—all are paradoxical, all made of opposites or involved in the struggle to reconcile opposites.

"The poets," Whitman notes in the margin of a magazine article on modern poetry, "are the divine mediums—through them come spirits and materials to all the people, men and women." [5] Here is the poet as joiner, blender: within himself he fuses the opposite aspects of reality ("spirits and materials"), and through him reality and readers join one another. The idea is made image in a late poem:

> —Then the full-grown poet stood between the
> two [Nature and the soul of man], and took
> each by the hand;
> And to-day and ever so stands, as blender, uniter,
> tightly holding hands,
> Which he will never release until he reconciles
> the two,
> And wholly and joyously blends them.[6]

If the poet is to be a "medium" between Nature and Man, if he is to "translate" truth into a universal tongue,[7] it follows that he must somehow both lose self and assert self. Taking issue with Keats's statement that "a poet is the most unpoetical of anything in existence, because he has no identity; he is continually in for and filling some other body," Whitman writes: "The great poet absorbs the identity of others, the exp[erience] of others, and they are definite in him or from him; but he p[erceives] them all through the powerful press of himself . . ." [8] He even outlines as an exercise for the perception of reality, the cultivation of self and non-self, particularity and universality:

Abstract yourself from this book; realize where you are at present located, the point you stand that is now to you the centre of all. Look up overhead, think of space stretching out, think of all the unnumbered orbs wheeling safely there, invisible to us by day, some visible by night, ... Spend some minutes faithfully in this exercise. Then again realize yourself upon the earth, at the particular point you now occupy.[9]

Like perceiving, creating for Whitman is the function of both the assertion and the yielding of self, "pride" and "sympathy":

The soul has that measureless pride which consists in never acknowledging any lessons or deductions but its own. But it has sympathy as measureless as its pride, and the one balances the other, and neither can stretch too far while it stretches in company with the other. The inmost secrets of art sleep with the twain. The greatest poet has lain close betwixt both, and they are vital in his style and thoughts.[10]

The ideal poet's "style and thoughts" and his craftmanship, his making of the poem, all must adhere to this fundamental principle: the fusion of self and non-self, body and spirit, particularity and universality.

Subject matter must reproduce reality, which, we remember, is made of "spirits and materials":

All through [sic] writings preserve the equilibrium of the truth that the material world, and all its laws, are as grand and superb as the spiritual world and all its laws. Most writers have disclaimed the physical world and they have not over-estimated the other, or soul, but have under-estimated the corporeal.[11]

The criterion is stringent: near-successes are admired; out-right failures scorned:

Of all portraits of me made by artists I like Eakins' best: it is not perfect but it comes nearest being me. . . . We need a Millet in portraiture—a man who sees the spirit but does not make too much of it—one who sees the flesh but does not make a man all flesh—all of him body. Eakins almost achieves this balance—almost—not quite: Eakins errs just a little, just a little—a little—in the direction of the flesh.[12]

Tone of Spencer's poetry is inwardly abstracted, contemplative in the highest degree—loving high themes, princeliness, purity, white garments —rather averse to reality—his personages being only half real. He is haunted by a morbid refinement of beauty—beauty three times washed and strained.[13]

Whitman's beloved Shakespeare, found wanting at other times because he is wordy, or too much in the feudal tradition,[14] comes off better on this count—so well, in fact, that he deserves comparison to Whitman's hero of heroes:

Washington . . . was essentially a noble Englishman. . . . Lincoln, underneath his practicality, was far less European, was quite thoroughly Western, original, essentially non-conventional, and had a certain sort of out-door or prairie stamp. One of the best of the late commentators on Shakspere, (Professor Dowden,) makes the height and aggregate of his quality as a poet to be, that he thoroughly blended the ideal with the practical or realistic. If this be so, I should say that what Shakspere did in poetic expression, Abraham Lincoln essentially did in his personal and official life.[15]

The "practical or realistic" and the ideal, the two kinds of subject matter that ideally are to be one subject matter, have their counterparts in style:

Rules for Composition—A perfectly transparent, plate-glassy style, artless, with no ornaments, or attempts at ornaments, for their own sake— . . .

Clearness, simplicity, no twistified or foggy sentences, at all—the most translucid clearness without variation.

Common idioms and phrases—Yankeeisms and vulgarisms—cant expressions, when very pat only.[16]

. . . I have not been afraid of the charge of obscurity, . . . because human thought, poetry or melody, must leave dim escapes and outlets— must possess a certain fluid aerial character, akin to space itself, obscure to those of little or no imagination, but indispensable to the highest purposes. Poetic style, when address'd to the soul, is less definite form, outline, sculpture, and becomes vista, music, half-tints, and even less than half-tints. True, it may be architecture; but again it may be the forest wildwood, or the best effect thereof, at twilight, the waving oaks and cedars in the wind, and the impalpable odor.[17]

Reality is associated with simplicity and concreteness; the ideal world with dimness, fluidity. Here Whitman emphasizes separately each stylistic principle. Closer to his usual critical position is a commitment to both of them at once:

Ossian must not be despised—it means that kind of thought and character growing among a rude, combative, illiterate people, heroic, dreamy, poetical, on mountains, *not* on rich lowlands, *not* with placid Gods and temples, *not* with cultivated benevolence, conscientiousness, agreeableness, or constructiveness.

How misty, how windy, how full of diffused, only half-meaning words! How curious a study! (Don't fall into the Ossianic, *by any chance.*)

53

Can it be a descendant of the Biblical poetry? Is it not Isaiah, Job, the Psalms . . . transferred to the Scotch Highlands? [18]

This is the kind of dramatic statement characteristic of Whitman's major poems: moving back and forth from one position to its opposite, the author leaves us with the impression that he has fused the two attitudes into one complex attitude or is at least keeping them in a precarious balance. First, "Ossian must not be despised" —a grudging admission of his worth; then the attraction becomes clear—"heroic, dreamy, poetical," and the excitement of "How curious a study!"; then the admonition to himself to be "translucid," its force multiplied by parentheses and underlining, as if he knows his own attraction to "the Ossianic"; finally the return to admiration, the comparison to the Bible, as grand a literary compliment as Whitman can give.[19]

The stylistic problem of clarity and obscurity overlaps with that of simplicity and richness. The following quotations reveal the complexity of Whitman's position: each, like the criticism of Ossian, is a dramatic statement, working against itself; and each also works against the other, stressing different sides of Whitman's internal argument:

The points of the "Inferno" . . . are *hasting on*, great vigor, a lean and muscular ruggedness; no superfluous flesh. . . .
It is a short poem. Dante's whole works appear to lie in a very moderate compass. It seems strange that he should stand as the highest type of Italian imaginative art-execution in literature—so gaunt, so haggard and un-rich, un-joyous. But the real Italian art-execution flourishes of course in other fields—in music, for instance . . .
Mark the simplicity of Dante, like the Bible's—different from the tangled and florid Shakespeare. Some of his idioms must, in Italian, cut like a knife. He narrates like some short-worded, superb, illiterat—an old farmer or some New England blue-light minister or common person . . .
Mark, I say, his economy of words—perhaps no other writer ever equal to him. One simple trail of idea, epical, makes the poem—all else resolutely ignored. This alone shows the master. . . . A great study for diffuse moderns.[20]

Shakespeare shows undoubted defects: he often uses a hundred words where a dozen would do: it is true that there are many pithy terse

sentences everywhere: but there are countless prolixities: though as for
the overabundances of words more might be said: as, for instance, that
he was not ignorantly prolific: that he was like nature itself: nature,
with her trees, the oceans: nature, saying "there's *lot* of this, infinitudes
of it—therefore, why spare it? If you ask for ten I give you a hundred,
for a hundred I give you a thousand, for a thousand I give you ten
thousand." It may be that we should look at it in that way, not
complain of it: rather understand its amazing intimations.[21]

Dante's "economy" is alternately "un-rich, un-joyous" and "superb"; Shakespeare's "prolixities," alternately "tangled and florid"
and "prolific" like nature itself. And the works being criticized are
not alone in changing; so also do the standards against which the
works are measured. The Bible, once associated with the "diffuse-
ness" and "mistiness" of Ossian, now is praised for its "simplicity";
Nature itself, often looked to as a model of "precision and
balance," [22] is here appealed to in an explanation of Shakespeare's
"overabundances." For Whitman everything has two faces.

That includes, of course, the maker of the poem. If perception
involves the assertion of self and the loss of self; if the subject
matter of the poem concerns particularity and universality, matter
and spirit, practicality and idealism; if the style of the poem is at
once clear and "misty, . . . windy," spare and overabundant—
then in the making of a poem a man must both assert his identity
and release himself from it, must concentrate on his particularity,
his bodily role as maker or shaper, and at the same time soar
unencumbered into the regions of the soul. The poet must, that is,
strike a balance between individuality and universality, and between restraint and spontaneity. Whitman notes shortcomings in
either direction—even in the work of his "Master," though there
with proper hesitation:

Coming . . . to R. W. Emerson, is not his fault, finally, too great
prudence, too rigid a caution? . . . I have generally felt that Emerson
was altogether adjusted to himself, in every attribute, as he should be
(as a pine tree is a pine tree, not a quince or a rose bush). But upon the
whole, and notwithstanding the many unsurpassed beauties of his
poetry . . . , I am disposed to think (picking out spots against the
sun) that his constitutional distrust and doubt—almost finical in their
nicety—have been too much for him—have not perhaps stopped him

55

short of first-class genius, but have veiled it—have certainly clipped and pruned that free luxuriance of it which only satisfies the soul at last.[23]

[Hugo] runs off into the craziest, and sometimes (in his novels) most ridiculant, literary botches and excesses, and by almost entire want to prudence allows them to stand.[24]

The best poet is always in control—even of his own freeness:

Goethe is never carried away by his theme—he is always Master. He is the head person, saying to a pupil: Here, see how well this can be done.[25]

I call it one of the chief acts of art, and the greatest trick of literary genius (which is a higher sanity of insanity), to hold the reigns firmly, and to preserve the mastery in its wildest escapades. Not to deny the most ecstatic and even irregular moods, so called—rather indeed to favor them—at the same time never to be entirely carried away with them, and always feeling, by a fine caution, when and wherein to limit or prune them, and at such times relentlessly applying restraint and negation. Few even of the accepted great artists or writers hit the happy balance of this principle—this paradox.[26]

Here Whitman's principle of paradox escapes the boundaries of the organic vision: even organicism, which feeds the paradoxical sensibility, and feeds upon it, must be qualified by its opposite principle. The poem must have life, a certain irregularity; but at the same time its free growth must be limited, "pruned," by the "directing principle" of mechanism.

Whitman encourages in the ideal reader the same combination of freedom and restraint that he requires of the ideal poet. If on the one hand a style with "no twistified or foggy sentences" is meant to transmit the poet's vision directly and with no confusion to the reader, on the other hand a style that cultivates "half-tints" is meant to be "suggestive" or "indirect," to allow the reader movement of his own. Whitman thinks of the relationship between poet and reader as being very much like the relationship between government and individual:

I say the mission of government . . . is not repression alone, and not authority alone, not even of law, . . . but . . . to train communities through all their grades, beginning with individuals and ending there again, to rule themselves . . .

The purpose is not altogether direct; perhaps it is more indirect. . . . To be a voter with the rest is not so much; and this, like every institute, will have its imperfections. But to become an enfranchised man, and now, impediments removed, to stand and start without humiliation, and equal with the rest; to commence, or have the road clear'd to commence, the grand experiment of development . . . — that *is* something.[27]

"Indirection" is stressed a bit more here than its opposite, but both are necessary to this idea of government and the analogous idea of poetry. The government (the poet) is not an authority "alone," but it is an authority: it does set guidelines for the community or individual (the reader). If the individual makes his own journey of development, the government has cleared the road.

"Indirection" and "direction" represent two basically different conceptions of the relationships between reality and the poet, the poet and the poem, the poem and the reader. There are various reasons why Whitman moves away from an extreme statement of indirection—or why, distrusting it from the beginning, he holds the opposite theory in tension against it, and takes a whole range of positions moving toward that opposite theory. Some of the reasons are personal; some, inherent in the critical problem itself. We can, in fact, anticipate the possibilities for him by tracing a cultural pattern, the course taken away from extreme indirection by a number of English and American literary figures directly preceding and contemporary with Whitman.

Thomas De Quincey, in the essay on Pope that defines the literature of knowledge and the literature of power, states precisely the distinction between "direction" and "indirection":

The function of the first [literature of knowledge] is to *teach*; the function of the second is to *move*; the first is a rudder, the second an oar or a sail. The first speaks to the mere discursive understanding; the second speaks ultimately, it may happen, to the higher understanding or reason, but always through affections of pleasure and sympathy. . . . It is certain that, were it not for the literature of power, . . . ideals would often remain amongst us as mere arid notional forms; whereas, by the creative forces of man put forth in literature, they gain a vernal life of restoration, and germinate into vital activities. . . . hence the preeminency over all authors that merely *teach*, of the meanest that moves, or that teaches, if at all, indirectly by moving.[28]

Both De Quincey's language and his choice of poetic mode are typical of the organicist: the literature of knowledge, Pope's direct statement of "arid notional forms" and direct appeal to the reader, "merely" teaches; the literature of power, the Romantics' "creative" poetry, "moves," teaches indirectly.

De Quincey's insistence on indirect teaching expresses the prevalent Romantic idea, which results from the theory of the creative imagination and the image of the poem as organism, that poetry is autonomous, has a special validity that is superior to the mundane truths of society. The world must learn by going to the poet, overhearing his truth, rather than having the poet come directly to it. Thus Keats says, "I never wrote one single line of Poetry with the least Shadow of public thought"; [29] and Shelley can with consistency assert his abhorrence of didactic poetry [30] and claim that "poets are the unacknowledged legislators of the world." [31]

Just as the literature of power transforms ideals from "arid notional forms" into "vital activities," so does it seek to urge the reader into his own life and movement instead of considering him as a passive entity to be turned toward a predetermined course. De Quincey actually leans toward the position of the extreme organicist, for he is uncomfortable about the poet's having to teach at all. The organicist, as we shall see, can conceive of the poet as a hero with special knowledge to communicate; but the extreme organicist, after allowing for a temporary accidental difference between the poet and other men, expects communication to be automatic. The approach to the reader is so indirect that it is barely a gesture: once the poet has "moved" other men—the work of but an instant —all men will be poets, no man a teacher or follower. Emerson, in "The Over-Soul," argues himself into citizenship in that marvelous democracy:

The great poet makes us feel our own wealth, and then we think less of his compositions. His best communication to our mind is to teach us to despise all he has done. Shakespeare carries us to such a lofty strain of intelligent activity as to suggest a wealth which beggars his own; and we then feel that the splendid works which he has created, and which in other hours we extol as a sort of self-existent poetry, take no stronger hold of real nature than the shadow of a passing traveller on the rock. The inspiration which uttered itself in Hamlet and Lear could utter things as good from day to day for ever. Why then should I make account of Hamlet and Lear, as if we had not the soul from which they fell as syllables from the tongue? [32]

Walter Pater's protest that Coleridge's organic theory makes the poet "almost a mechanical agent" ignores the fact that Coleridge is not an extreme organicist; but it does make a telling point about pure organic theory. Carried to its logical extreme, as Emerson carries it in "The Over-Soul," the organic conception of language results in the disappearance of private responsibility and significance for the poet, who becomes merely a vessel for the language that flows of itself. For the extreme organicist, neither the poet nor the listener should have to approach the other party; for either party can be the poet, and absolute spontaneity of expression should be indistinguishable from absolute receptivity.

When things do not work out this way, the extreme organicist is hard put for an explanation:

. . . all men live by truth and stand in need of expression. In love, in art, in avarice, in politics, in labor, in games, we study to utter our painful secret. The man is only half himself, the other half is his expression.

Not withstanding this necessity to be published, adequate expression is rare. I know not how it is that we need an interpreter, but the great majority of men seem to be minors, who have not yet come into possession of their own, or mutes, who cannot report the conversation they have had with nature. . . . Every touch should thrill. Every man should be so much an artist that he could report in conversation what had befallen him. Yet, in our experience, the rays or apulses have sufficient force to arrive at the senses, but not enough to reach the quick and complete the reproduction of themselves in speech. The poet is the person in whom these powers are in balance, the man without impediment, who sees and handles that which others dream of, traverses the whole scale of experience, and is representative of man, in virtue of being the largest to receive and to impart.[33]

To admit, as Emerson here does in "The Poet," that in many men, even most men, "the rays or apulses have . . . not enough [force] . . . to . . . compel the reproduction of themselves in speech" is to admit that in most men the organic flow of language simply will not work, the plant will not flower. It is to admit the existence of a great gulf between the ideal and "our experience," the existence of evil in what seemed to be an organically harmonious world.

Like Melville's dreaming lookout, Emerson voyages too far in his pantheistic reverie and finds, when he "moves [his] foot or hand an inch," that he hovers over "Descartian vortices." [34] He saves himself from drowning by borrowing from Descartes' world of distinctions, modifying his extreme organicism. He retreats from Seeing to Man Seeing, from the Over-Soul to the Poet, from the conception of poet and reader as organically cooperative to the conception of the poet as a man apart, able to receive most from nature and impart most to men. The poet as teacher has returned: not as envisioned by extreme organic theory, a teacher for the instant it takes to transform other men, but as the teacher in an older tradition, the "representative" of men who cannot become poets.

The English organicists, less extreme, do not press the organic theory so hard as to endanger the poet. Against the double threat of pure organicism—that the poet can become indistinguishable from his readers and that the poet can be considered merely a vessel overflowing with language instead of a maker and controller of language—are poised two defenses. The first defense, which we have already seen at work in the writings of De Quincey and Shelley, is constructed within the organic world. It creates for the poet an exhilarating new role. He is neither of the poets congenial to the mechanistic world of analytic imagination—not the mimetic poet, copying the signs of nature or at most rearranging them ingeniously, nor the poet of pragmatic theory, a teacher attempting to "delight and instruct," dependent upon the approval of his audience even as he instructs it. He is, rather, in Carlyle's words, a "Force of Nature," [35] a hero who simply plays out his life, requiring that his audience come to him. Instead of brushing off as accidental the poet's difference from other men, this conception of the poet insists upon that difference. Carlyle describes both poet and audience: "On the whole, Genius has privileges of its own: it

selects an orbit for itself; and be this ever so eccentric, if it is indeed
a celestial orbit, we mere star-gazers must at last compose ourselves;
must cease to cavil at it, and begin to observe it, and calculate its
laws." [36] In contrast to the mimetic poet, the poet as hero has built
his own true world; whole, above the mere direct teaching practiced
by the poet of the pragmatic theory, he requires that men come to
him to learn his truth. Yet, he is also unlike the poet of extreme
organicism: his independent existence is important; it does mean
something to be Shakespeare.

The second defense against the dangers of extreme organicism is
made from the language of the mechanistic world. It is Coleridge's
defense, a deliberate corruption of his own system of organicism,
that Pater criticizes as if it were pure. Coleridge celebrates not only
the creative imagination but also the intellect and reason, does not
abandon the mechanistic theory of poetry but, as Abrams tells us,
incorporates it into his system:

. . . despite Coleridge's intoxication with the alchemical change
wrought in the universe by his discovery of the organic analogy, he did
not hesitate to save . . . the mechanical he so violently opposed.
Mechanism is false; not because it does not tell the truth, but because it
does not tell the whole truth. . . . Coleridge's fully developed critical
theory . . . is deliberately syncretic, and utilizes not one, but two
controlling analogues, one of a machine, the other of a plant; and these
divided the processes and products of art into two distinct kinds,
and . . . into two orders of excellence.[37]

The two kinds of artistic activity are called *talent* and *genius,* terms
we have seen Whitman approximate. Talent, which lies in the
"understanding," that "faculty of thinking and forming judgments
on the notices furnished by sense," is the art of the mechanistic
universe, Jonson's "crafte of making"; it produces works of a lower
order, like those of Pope. Genius, which consists in "the action of
reason and imagination," is the creative spirit of organicism, but is
recognizable in all works of a higher order, like those of Dante
and Milton.[38] And the greatest works display both talent and
genius: "great as was the genius of Shakespeare, his judgment was
at least equal." [39] Coleridge thus joins the poet as inspired hero,
teaching indirectly, to the poet as craftsman and pragmatic teacher.

The promises and threats of organicism, therefore, create these various positions: that of Emerson in "The Over-Soul," whose poet is an agent of the language which flows through him; that of Emerson, Carlyle, and Coleridge in their celebrations of the poet as hero; and that of Coleridge in his use of the mechanistic poet. We shall watch Whitman make a journey of the same sort, which by analogy to these other Romantics we may attribute to the nature of organicism. But we shall also see him go far beyond Coleridge's, and his own, position—the fusion of talent and genius, direction and indirection. Whitman's drive all the way to "direction" is finally due, probably, to personal reasons—his idea of himself as savior of the land, or perhaps, more fundamentally, his sensibility of paradox, his intense cultivation of opposites of all sorts.

"Indirection" depends always upon Whitman's belief in a spiritual world as well as a world of disparate materials; "direction," of which there are two kinds, sometimes involves a world of spirit and sometimes does not. What finally separates one conception from the other is method—the way of perceiving, creating, communicating.

Whitman's most extreme idea of indirection is that of the optimistic symbolist, the extreme organicist—the idea of Emerson in "The Over-Soul." It conceives of the poet as a "divine medium," an agent through whom reality, spirit and matter in one, passes to readers; language and reality shape themselves to each other, and a "perfect poem" becomes:

The poetic quality is not marshal'd in rhyme or uniformity, or abstract addresses of things, . . . but is the life of these and much else, and is in the soul. The profit of rhyme is that it drops seeds of a sweeter and more luxuriant rhyme, and of uniformity that it conveys itself into its own roots in the ground out of sight. The rhyme and uniformity of perfect poems show the free growth of metrical laws, and bud from them as unerringly and loosely as lilacs and roses on a bush, and take shapes as compact as the shapes of chestnuts and oranges, and melons and pears, and shed the perfume impalpable to form. . . . All beauty comes from beautiful blood and a beautiful brain. If the greatnesses are in conjunction in a man or woman, it is enough—the fact will prevail through the universe; but the gaggery and gilt of a million years will not prevail. Who troubles himself about his ornaments or fluency is lost.[40]

The poet's approach to reality, to the poem, and to the reader is so indirect that it is not really an approach at all. Reality, poet, poem, and the ideal reader all are one. The reader will be approached by "abstract addresses" no more than will the spiritual world, nor will he have to struggle for meaning; "the fact will prevail through the universe" because the reader will be like the poet, a man of "beautiful blood and a beautiful brain," a poet by nature.

A poem embodying this theory would represent the poet as careless of the reader, turned neither toward him nor away from him: the attitude of the speaker, the mask of the poet, would indicate the poet's confidence that the reader can come to the poem without assistance. And this poem would have as its focus a list of things: the poet would concentrate on the teeming life of the universe, his subject requiring no pointing to hidden meanings because meanings are in the things, and will be spontaneously sensed by the reader. Such a poem, that is, would be wholly made of one of Whitman's catalogues—a poem like "Spontaneous Me," whose title indicates that it is indeed the expression of an extreme organicist.

When the spiritual world is no longer in the material world—when the organicist has for some reason lost his optimism—the problems of perception and expression become much more difficult:

. . . I wish you to realize well that our boasted knowledge, precious and manifold as it is, sinks into niches and corners, before the infinite knowledge of the unknown. Of the real world of materials, what, after all, are these specks we call knowledge?—Of the spiritual world I announce to you this—much gibberish will always be offered and for a season obeyed . . . but to make a statement eludes us—By curious indirections only can there be any statement of the spiritual world—and they will all be foolish—Have you noticed the [worm] on a twig reaching out in the immense vacancy time and again, trying point after point? Not more helplessly does the tongue or the pen of man, essay out in the spiritual spheres, to state them. In the nature of things nothing less than the special world itself can know itself—[41]

Now the poet must strain to reach the world of soul, must seek for it in special ways and state it in special ways. It is with the new difficulties of perception, expression, and communication—the difficulties of a world that is no longer one—that Whitman's theory of indirection deals. The building of the method, in fact, is Whitman's first step away from his extreme indirection. Whereas extreme indirection is an instinctive process, the method implies conscious strategy. Perception, creation, communication—none is automatic: the poet must slant his vision to perceive the world of spirit, and creation and communication have their own special rules.

The subject matter of poems of indirection must concentrate upon those odd moments or scenes in which the "special world" seems to filter through to the world of materials—upon "the forest wild-wood, or the best effect thereof, at twilight, the waving oaks and cedars in the wind, and the impalpable odor." [42] Burroughs is more clear about this matter than the poet himself. Writing in a chapter called "Suggestiveness" (Whitman's alternative word for "indirection"), he says:

In the world of experience and observation the suggestiveness of things is enhanced by veils, concealments, half lights, flowing lines. The twilight is more suggestive than the glare of noonday, a rolling field than a lawn, a winding road than a straight one. In literature perspective, indirection, understatement, side glimpses, have equal value; a vocabulary that is warm from the experience of the writer, sentences that start a multitude of images . . .[43]

As Burroughs indicates, there is a special style that accompanies the special subject matter. If new perception of reality (or perception of a new reality) is possible only if the poet looks by "side glimpses," so the expression of this reality requires that the poet somehow twist his language: "Slang, or indirection," Whitman writes in his essay "Slang in America," is "an attempt of common humanity to escape from bald literalism, and express itself illimitably, which in highest walks produces poets and poems . . ." [44]

And the best poem should require the best reader to approach itself in the way that the poet approaches his reality:

At its best, poetic lore is like what may be heard of conversation in the dusk, from speakers far or hid, of which we get only a few broken murmurs. What is not gather'd is far more—perhaps the main thing.

Grandest poetic passages are only to be taken at free removes, as we sometimes look for stars at night, not by gazing directly toward them, but off one side.[45]

Sometimes, just as the poet's act of perception can be difficult, like a worm's "reaching out in the immense vacancy," the reader's "gazing . . . off one side" can become very much like work. "Books are to be call'd for, and supplied," Whitman preaches in "Democratic Vistas," "on the assumption that the process of reading is not a half-sleep, but, in highest sense, an exercise, a gymnast's struggle; that the reader is to do something for himself, must be on the alert, must himself or herself construct indeed the poem, argument, history, metaphysical essay—the text furnishing the hints, the clue, the start or frame-work." [46] What the reader does for himself, in his wrestling with the complex and ambiguous reality that is the poem, is to discover his identity. Whitman's warnings are also promises:

Dear friend! I put not in the following leaves melodious narratives, or pictures for you to con at leisure. With such the world is well enough supplied. But of Suggestiveness alone out of the things around us, with steady reference to the life to come, and to the miracles of every day this is the song—naught made by me for you, but only hinted, to be made by you yourself. Indeed I have not done the work, and cannot do it. But you must do the work to really make what is within the following song —which, if you do, I promise you return & satisfaction earned by you yourself far more than ever book has given you. For from this book Yourself, before unknown, shall now rise up & be revealed.[47]

A poem that is to suggest rather than state, that is to guide implicitly, indirectly, rather than directly, can rest neither on thing, a speck from the material world, nor on idea, an entity from the world beyond particular things. Instead, in its search to reach the unknown world from the perspective of the material world, the poem of indirection would focus upon action, motion, the development of things:

One of my cherished themes for a never-achieved poem has been the two impetuses of man and the universe—in the latter, creation's incessant unrest, exfoliation. . . . Indeed what is Nature but change, in all its visible, and still more its invisible processes? Or what is humanity, in its faith, love, heroism, poetry, even morals, but *emotion?* [48]

The mask of such a poem, the attitude in which the poet represents himself, would be inseparable from the action, for the interest of the poet would be wholly in the drama of development, the drama in which meaning reveals itself. A poem of indirection, therefore, would be essentially dramatic: a poem in which the speaker, at times turned toward the reader and at times away, is going through an action—a poem like "Song of Myself" or "As I Ebb'd with the Ocean of Life."

If building this theory of indirection removes Whitman from the pole of extreme indirection, his next position finds him exactly between "indirection" and "direction," and demonstrates his fundamental split between organicism and mechanism. It is expressed in his answer to his overwhelming question—"What is the fusing explanation and tie—what the relations between the . . . Me . . . and . . . the . . . Not-Me?"—for the answer comes in the voices of mechanism and organicism, of Descartes, Coleridge, and Carlyle. The hero who will merge the Me and the Not-Me is an "analyzer or overlooker" with "an inscrutable combination of train'd wisdom and natural intuition," who is "both the truest cosmical devotee or religioso, and the profoundest philosopher." [49] He is the "analyzer" and "train'd" craftsman of Descartes' universe; but at the same time he is the poet as hero, a "cosmical devotee," a "deathless Individual" who builds his own true world:

Amid the vast and complicated edifice of human beings . . . he builds, as it were, an impregnable and lofty tower, a part of all with the rest and overlooking all—the citadel of the primary volitions, the ever-reserved right of a deathless Individuality—and these he occupies and dwells, and thence makes observations and issues verdicts. [50]

If, like the indirect poet, he ignores other men, forcing them to come to his truth, he also "makes observations" and "issues verdicts"; if one of his techniques is suggestion, he is also a scientist and a prophet.

He is, simply, a man in the middle, squarely between suggestion and statement, indirection and direction. His kind of poem would be one step further toward direction than the poem of indirection, in which the mask does not offer guides into the action because it is experiencing the action. This kind of poem would focus on an action, which is suggestive in that it allows the reader latitude, but at the same time it would separate the mask from the action, making it something of a director. The poem of this man in the middle would, that is, be a narrative, a poem like "Out of the Cradle Endlessly Rocking," in which the mask describes an action but is at the same time turned toward the reader.

Push this poet toward one of his opposite tendencies and we push him into poetry of direction. He "makes observations" and "issues verdicts": we are back in the old poetry, back with the mimetic and the pragmatic, the descriptive and the moral. The theory of indirection, we have seen, is actually a rejection of two very different attitudes toward reality. Based on the anti-Cartesian premise that the ideal world is not finally separable from the material world, and committed to the equal importance of each world, it insists, in its extreme form, on seeing the ideal world and the material world as *in* each other; in its more moderate form, it sees the ideal world from the perspective of the material world. Thus the theory of indirection denies that the material world should finally claim man's attention and that the ideal world can be achieved in a direct leap or expressed in a direct statement. It is reasonable, then, for the impulses away from indirection to take two radically different forms—toward didacticism, the issuance of verdicts, and description, the making of observations.

Didactic poetry is made from a focus upon idea and the mask of an authoritarian. The man who, excited by the possibilities of indirection, praises Goethe's autobiography because "it . . . does not bear every now and then the inscription, 'See the moral of this!',"[51] can also commit himself to direct teaching. Perhaps motivated by the example of Emerson, he dreams of himself as a public lecturer, confiding his plans, in the summer of 1857, to an unidentified correspondent: "I have thought, for some time past, of beginning the use of myself as a public speaker, teacher, or lecturer. (This, after I get out the next issue of my 'Leaves') . . ."[52] The parenthesis hints that Whitman knows where his real talents lie, and most of the time he does have on the platform is spent not in didacticism, but in narrative, his annual description of the day of Lincoln's death. Still, the didactic impulse is there, to be seen in notebook jottings like "Spinal idea of a lesson" [53] and this urgent reminder to himself: *"Tell the American people their faults*—the departments of their character where they are most liable to break down—speak to them with unsparing tongue—carefully systematize beforehand *their faults*." [54] Didacticism and systemization go hand in hand: here Whitman shows us a face infrequently displayed. We are more familiar with his revolt against system, and with statements about evoking the "invisible processes" of life; but he is altogether capable, as in these remarks to Traubel, of adopting different priorities: "The first thing necessary is the thought—the rest may follow if it chooses—may play its part—but must not be too much sought after." [55] "The idea must always come first—is indispensable. Take my own method— if you can call it that. I have the idea clearly and fully realized before I attempt to express it." [56]

Yet even as he admits to method he denies it—perhaps because he has in fact several methods. Didacticism is direct, but the poetry of description has directness of a very different sort. In the margin of a magazine review dating from before the first edition of *Leaves of Grass*, Whitman applauds the critic's argument for use of concrete detail in poetry, writing, "Materialism as the foundation of poetry" and "Cramming Poetry with too many thoughts." [57] Instead of thinking of a poem as music, like the theoretician of indirection, or as the vehicle of an idea, like the didactic poet, he says that poems are "merely pictures." [58] And he tells Traubel, in complaint about his portraits: "I find I often like the photographs better than the oils—they are perhaps mechanical, but they are honest. The artists add and deduct: the artists fool with nature— reform it, revise it, to make it fit their preconceived notion of what it should be." [59] Both the suggestive "half-tints" of indirection and the "preconceived notion" (the "idea [which] must always come first") are rejected for straight scientific reporting.

Such a theory seems to separate the material world completely from the ideal world, and to celebrate it for its own sake. A poem to embody the theory would focus on a particular thing; and even though the mask would be turned away from the reader, the poem would be direct in the sense that the poet would be calling the reader's attention to a natural fact. Thus a poem like "A Paumanok Picture" seems to be simply a carefully made description of a scene in Nature. But, as we shall see, it is very difficult to focus attention on a thing without giving that thing some meaning external to its own physical nature. The directness of descriptive poetry is so different from the directness of didactic poetry because it is always capable of becoming indirect: meaning is not openly stated but is nevertheless always possible, if not always suggested. So if in one sense Whitman's "picture" poems are direct, they also are, or can be, very much like the poems of extreme indirection—poems which proceed on the premise that there is special, spiritual meaning in things and which do not guide the reader toward that meaning because the other part of their premise is that the reader knows the meaning, is himself a poet.

Whitman's bipolar unity, then—his split between mechanism and organicism, which reveals itself as simultaneous drives toward extremes and paradox—produces a wide range of poetic attitudes. These attitudes, expressed in Whitman's choices among various foci (action, thing, and idea) and among various masks (teacher, descriptive "overlooker," storyteller, and actor), are complex gestures to the reader. Because they imply degrees of direction or non-direction of the reader, and degrees of identification or non-identification between poet and reader, they can be thought of as answers to Whitman's fundamental questions about freedom and restraint, separateness and engagement. The interplay of mask and focus produces forms that, we shall see, require us as readers to play suitable roles, to make complementary gestures. The success of the poems will depend largely on what robes Whitman makes us wear and on how well we wear them.

PART TWO

WHITMAN
AT WORK

IV DIRECTION AND NON-DIRECTION: DIDACTICISM AND IMAGISM

THERE WAS A TIME when Whitman's Calamus poems were accepted as statements of a beautiful *cameraderie* * and when the Children of Adam poems were considered so sucessfully erotic that they were

---

* R. M. Bucke, for instance, in *Walt Whitman*, p. 166, says, ". . . Calamus presents to us . . . an exalted friendship, a love into which sex does not enter as an element"; and William S. Kennedy, like Bucke a not altogether undiscriminating admirer of Whitman, calls the Calamus group, in his *Reminiscences of Walt Whitman*, pp. 133–34, "Whitman's beautiful democratic poems of friendship," continuing, "a genuine lover speaks in the Calamus pieces: a great and generous heart there pours forth its secret. Set side by side with these glowing confessions other writings on friendship seem frigid and calculating." To these can be added the judgment of an anonymous Russian review of the second edition of Kornei Chukovsky's translation of Whitman, a review that appeared in *Biulleteni Literaturi i Zhizni*, No. 22 (July, 1914), pp. 1253–58, translated by Stephen Stepanchev, *Whitman Abroad*, edited by Allen, pp. 158–69: "The chivalrous adoration of woman, proper to the Middle Ages, the cult of the Beautiful Lady which ennobled sexual love and achieved social refinement, is now insufficient: the future of humanity needs a cult, too—the cult of the comrade, the cult of democratic union, for a new tenderness suffuses the hearts of men, a love of the fellow warrior, co-worker, fellow traveler, of him who journeys with us shoulder to shoulder and takes part in the general movement; it is this still weak feeling, this embryo or beginning of feeling, that the poet strengthened in his gigantic soul, brought to flame, to passion, to that all-encompassing, grand emotion with which, as he believed, he transfigured himself in a vision of the world triumph of democracy.

"He anticipated the future even in this. And if today his odes to comrades, to

73

banned in Boston and their author in the Department of the Interior.[1] More recently, however, the Calamus poems have been read as hints at homosexuality, and in that role, they have been both rejected and admired; and the Children of Adam poems have been dismissed as flat and unconvincing—their women, the argument runs, have no faces and their boastings are an attempt, perhaps unconscious, to camouflage with heterosexual vigor the true homosexual passion that lies behind the companion poems.*

those whom he called *camerado*, seem unreal, strange, and remind one of serenades to a lover—they are excessively pleading and flamingly affectionate—that is so because the days have not yet come when our hearts, too can flame with such magnificent passion. . . .

"Words have not yet been found for such a feeling. The formal word *comradeship* does not express it. This is a burning, stormy, almost alarming love of man for man, and without it, as the poet believed, democracy is only a shadow, an illusion." (Pp. 168–69.)

* John Addington Symonds, *Walt Whitman, A Study*, pp. 75–100, is the outstanding exception to this rough chronological categorization of critical response, for he both points up the absence of romantic feeling in the Children of Adam group and hints that homosexuality is the dominant passion of the Calamus poems. A letter from Eldridge to Burroughs, shortly after the publication of Symonds' book (quoted in Clara Barrus, *Whitman and Burroughs: Comrades*, p. 313), indicates, like the statements of Bucke and Kennedy, the more usual attitude of those contemporaries of Whitman who were interested in his poetry: "Have you seen Symonds's book on Walt? A part of it reaches the high water mark of criticism, but a part of it is abominable, and contains the very worst things ever said about Walt. It seems that 'Calamus' suggests sodomy to him, and, from some remarks, I judge that he was suspicious about Walt's relations with Peter Doyle. It appears that Walt made an indignant denial of any such construction of his poems, but, notwithstanding all, Symonds put it in. Truly, I think much learning, or too much study of Greek manners and customs, hath made this Englishman mad. Was ever such folly or madness shown before by a professed friend?"

The modern position, by and large, follows Symonds. Both Mark Van Doren and Clark Griffith, for example, assume that the Calamus poems are essentially homosexual, though they respond somewhat differently to what they see. Van Doren, in "Walt Whitman, Stranger," *The Private Reader*, p. 42, asks, "His democratic dogmas—of what validity are they when we consider that they base themselves upon the sentiment of 'manly love,' and that manly love is neither more nor less than an abnormal and deficient love?" Griffith, in "Sex and Death: The Significance of Whitman's Calamus Themes," *Philological Quarterly*, XXXIX (January, 1960), p. 18, while basing his argument on the deathlike, "negative" aspects of what he takes to be the Calamus passion, says that, ". . . *Calamus* . . . certainly contains the only authentic love poetry Whitman was ever to write."

Welcome exceptions to the present-day line are James E. Miller's interpretation ("Whitman's 'Calamus': The Leaf and the Root," *PMLA*, LII [March, 1957], 244–71; also printed in *Guide*, pp. 52–79), in which he emphasizes the "spiritual" aspects of the Calamus love, and that of Gilberto Freyre (abridged from *O Camarada Whitman* [Rio de Janeiro, 1948], translated by Benjamin M. Woodbridge, Jr., *Whitman Abroad*, pp. 223–34: "So fraternal was [Whitman] in his sense of life and of human relations and so capable of tenderness in those relations

The change in reception results, of course, from a change in the eye of the beholder. Readers of late, with some exceptions, have thought of both groups of poems as personal love lyrics: they have demanded from the "heterosexual" poems, therefore, a "sincerity" that Emerson and the official censors did not miss and from the "homosexual" poems a frank statement of love that Whitman did not find appropriate. Earlier readers must have sensed, or perhaps they simply read the explanations Whitman wrote, that the poems are about loving rather than love, addressed primarily to the general human situation, not to a particular man or woman. So Whitman suggests, in a note to himself about the Children of Adam group: "Theory of a Cluster of Poems the same *to the passion of Women-Love* as the 'Calamus-Leaves' are to adhesiveness, manly love." [2] More than that, as Whitman all but says in the 1876 Preface, the two groups of poems are about complementary ways of knowing, for which ways of loving are metaphors: the Children of Adam poems about "amativeness," pride, "a sense of the life . . . of flesh and blood, and physical urge, and animalism"; [3] the Calamus poems about "adhesiveness," the spiritual quality that matches the "brawn," the "appetite for sympathy" rather than pride, "this universal democratic comradeship." [*] The

---

—a tenderness which, generally speaking, in the civilizations where the sexes are most intensely differentiated, is accepted only in women—that some of his attitudes and some of his poems have been interpreted as affirmations or sublimations of narcissism and even of homosexuality, which has been confused with bisexualism. It is bisexualism of attitude, not of action, born of empathy, not of vice, that is found in Whitman. . . . He seems principally to have had the courage of great friendships with other men (sometimes, perhaps, with a remote homosexual basis) alongside enthusiasms for "perfect women"—a fact which emphasizes the bisexualism of his attitude. . . .

"That was what overflowed most abundantly from Whitman into his books: a personalistic and fraternalistic sense of life and of the community, a sense so vibrant as to seem at times homosexualism gone mad whereas it was probably only bisexualism sublimated into fraternalism. Whitman was not, as a poet, much less as a writer, impersonal, inhuman, esoteric, cut off from his condition as a man, a person, a citizen. Poet, citizen, and man formed in him a complex of inseparable activities and conditions." (Pp. 227–29.)

There is more agreement, in interpretation and attitude, about the Children of Adam group. Louis Untermeyer, in his introduction to *Whitman, Poetry and Prose*, pp. 47–48, and Paul Lauter, in "Walt Whitman: Lover and Comrade," *American Imago*, XVI (1959), 407–35, are representative of modern evaluation, Untermeyer complaining that the poems lack tenderness, and Lauter that they are "adolescent," a cover-up for the Calamus love that Whitman really felt.

[*] "Preface, 1876," *Prose*, II, 471, footnote. See also "Democratic Vistas," *Prose*, II, 381: "Not that half only, individualism, which isolates. There is another half,

relationship of the groups to each other (and to the whole of *Leaves of Grass*) is frankly schematic. "If there was any weakness in his position," Whitman tells Traubel about his dispute with Emerson over the Children of Adam poems,[4] "it was in his idea that the particular poems could be dropped and the Leaves remain the Leaves still: . . . he did not see that if I had cut sex out I might just as well have cut everything out—the full scheme would no longer exist—it would have been violated in its most sensitive spot." [5] But the schematism is their strength, not their weakness. For each group celebrates a principle: on the one hand, pride, spontaneity, assertion of self, all the characteristics of "body"; on the other hand, sympathy, calmness, yielding of self, the characteristics of "soul." Together they represent Whitman's idea of the perceptual abilities of "Yourself, your own Identity, body and soul." [6]

We will probably never know why Whitman deleted from the Calamus poems several specific references to homosexual love—why, for instance, he changed *man* to *woman* in the manuscript version of "Once I Pass'd Through a Populous City" [7] and printed the poem in the Children of Adam group, or why in 1867 he rejected a poem in which he promises, "I will go with him I love," to the one "who . . . is jealous of me, and withdraws me from all but love" (p. 596). There is some pretty convincing evidence that Whitman was homosexual by inclination if not by action,[8] and the deletions may have been attempts to hide the inclination, like his protest to the suspicious Symonds that his life had been "jolly bodily," so heterosexual that it had produced six children.[9] We know anyhow that he could think of "adhesiveness" as something

---

which is adhesiveness or love, that fuses, ties and aggregates, making the races comrades, and fraternizing all"; and, *Prose*, II, 414–15, footnote, "It is to the development, identification, and general prevalence of . . . fervid comradeship, (the adhesive love, at least rivaling the amative love hitherto possessing imaginative literature, if not going beyond it,) that I look for the counterbalance and offset of our materialistic and vulgar American democracy, and for the spiritualization thereof. Many will say it is a dream, and will not follow my inferences: but I confidently expect a time when there will be seen, running like a half-hid warp through all the myriad audible and visible worldly interests of America, threads of manly friendship, fond and loving, pure and sweet, strong and life-long, carried to degrees hitherto unknown—not only giving tone to individual character, and making it unprecedently emotional, muscular, heroic, and refined, but having the deepest relations to general politics."

more dangerous than spiritual love, and tried to suppress it, if not
to conceal it: "Depress the adhesive nature," he admonished
himself in a notebook; "It is in excess—making life a torment/ All
this diseased, feverish disproportionate *adhesiveness*." [10] Yet, if
"adhesiveness" could mean homosexual passion, if the Calamus
poems did in 1860 sound a personal note not heard in the poems
then called "Enfans d'Adam," and if it is possible that Whitman
made the excisions to protect himself against the charge of
homosexuality, it is also possible that the impulse to rewrite was
artistic rather than strictly personal. For he left in as many
homosexual references as he cut (in "When I Heard at the Close
of Day," p. 123, for instance: ". . . his arm lay lightly around my
breast—and that night I was happy"), and even the final version of
Leaves of Grass invites speculation like Symonds':

> Here the frailest leaves of me and yet my
>   strongest lasting,
> Here I shade and hide my thoughts, I myself
>   do not expose them,
> And yet they expose me more than all my other
>   poems.[11]

It may be that there is method in Whitman's seemingly
unreasonable editing. Perhaps we should read the Calamus poems
not as bowdlerized love lyrics, but as a group of poems with an
abstract theme that is given substance, symbolized, by several
deliberately personal references; and perhaps we should read the
Children of Adam poems as a "cluster" concerning a complementary abstract theme that requires deliberate impersonality.

"Native Moments" and "One Hour to Madness and Joy,"
typical Children of Adam poems, are about knowledge sharp and
quick: even the titles, which repeat parts of the first lines, celebrate
spontaneity. Both poems dramatize the condition of the "body
electric"—the leaping-out of the self, not in sympathy but in pride,
assertion. "Native Moments" begins the instant before the hot joy
of discovery overcomes the poet:

> Native moments—when you come upon me—ah you
>   are here now,
> Give me now libidinous joys only,

77

> Give me the drench of my passions, give me life
>   coarse and rank,
> To-day I go consort with Nature's darlings, . . .
>
>   [P. 109.]

The rest of the poem pretends to enact the journey the poet takes in his new world, but it is more notable for its description of that world than for a delineation of action. The world is rude and reckless, like the poet—a world of dancing, drink, and "midnight orgies," with persons "rude, illiterate," where the poet will come stripped of convention:

> I will play a part no longer, why should I exile
>   myself from my companions?
> O you shunn'd persons, I at least do not shun you,
> I come forthwith in your midst, I will be your
>   poet,
> I will be more to you than to any of the rest.
>
>   [P. 109.]

In "One Hour" the poet, anticipating the moment of final release, seems already seized by "madness and joy." The trance of love, which half makes the poet and is half made by his exultant exclamations, is hard to distinguish from the wild dance of the imagination:

> To be absolv'd from previous ties and conventions,
>   I from mine and you from yours!
> . . . .
> To drive free! to love free! to dash reckless
>   and dangerous!
> To court destruction with taunts, with invitations!
> To ascend, to leap to the heavens of the love
>   indicated to me!
> To rise thither with my inebriate soul!
> To be lost if it must be so!
>
>   [P. 106.]

Against this love—in which rude self-reliant man, "listen[ing] to no entreaties," [12] thrusts himself into the world—is poised the love of the "I" in "I Saw in Louisiana a Live-Oak Growing":

> I saw in Louisiana a live-oak growing,
> All alone stood it and the moss hung down from
>   the branches,
> Without any companion it grew there uttering
>   joyous leaves of dark green,
> And its look, rude, unbending, lusty, made me
>   think of myself,
> But I wonder'd how it could utter joyous leaves
>   standing alone there without its friend near,
>   for I knew I could not, . . .
>
> [Pp. 126–27.]

This Calamus lover and poet looks like the "live-oak," the "rude, unbending, lusty" Children of Adam lover and poet; but there are important differences of attitude. The Calamus lover avoids the pageants, spectacles, and feasts of the "city of orgies," seeking instead for the "swift flash of eyes offering . . . love." [13] Amid the "noises coming and going," he sits with a youth, the two "content, happy in being together, speaking little, perhaps not a word"; [14] or he is "yearning and thoughtful," [15] patiently waiting to meet with some lover. Whereas the Children of Adam lover glories in the uncontrolled dance, delights in change, daring even his own destruction, this lover retreats from "shifting tableaus," [16] the "coming and going," into the sure, permanent love of comradeship. [17] He and his comrade are "two boys together clinging," [18] saved from uncertainty, the terrible spin of things and the world, by the touch of their hands:

> Of the terrible doubt of appearances,
> Of the uncertainty after all, that we may
>   be deluded,
> That may-be reliance and hope are but spec-
>   ulations after all,
> That may-be identity beyond the grave is a
>   beautiful fable only,
> May-be the things I perceive, the animals, plants,
>   men, hills, shining and flowing waters,
> The skies of day and night, colors, densities,
>   forms, may-be these are (as doubtless they are)
>   only apparitions, and the real something has
>   yet to be known,
> . . . .

79

To me these and the like of these are curiously
    answer'd by my lovers, my dear friends,
When he whom I love travels with me or sits a
    long while holding me by the hand,
. . . .
I cannot answer the question of appearances or
    that of identity beyond the grave,
But I walk or sit indifferent, I am satisfied,
He ahold of my hand has completely satisfied me.[19]

The Calamus perception is not imaginative: it does not enfold other identities, does not "become," but rather finds an identical identity in the world of the spirit, a mirror-image of the self, which can be trusted.

The complementary groups of poems are not only about two kinds of perception. The "live-oak," a symbol of the "rude, . . . lusty" Children of Adam poet, "utter[s]" its leaves "without its friend near"; the Calamus poet, wondering at the live-oak, needs a listener. These different attitudes toward companionship, involving utterance as they do, finally are indicative of opposite theories of poetry.

The "children" of Adam, the unfallen Whitman, are products of his tongue as well as his loins. Singing and procreating are nearly indistinguishable:

> I, chanter of Adamic songs,
> Through the new garden the West, the great cities
>   calling,
> Deliriate, thus prelude what is generated, offering
>   these, offering myself,
> Bathing myself, bathing my songs in Sex,
> Offspring of my loins.[20]

Thus in "Spontaneous Me"—which, along with "I Sing the Body Electric" and "Aching Rivers," is thematically and stylistically central to the Children of Adam group—the subject matter is only superficially about "Love-thoughts, love-juice, love-odor, love-yielding, love-climbers, and the climbing sap" (p. 104). The poem goes beyond spontaneous love to the subject of spontaneity itself, the quality of anything (not just "Me") caught in its special moment

—and it is finally about spontaneous writing, expression that makes itself unique by catching the uniqueness of external things:

> The arm of my friend hanging idly over my shoulder,
> The hillside whiten'd with blossoms of the mountain
>   ash,
> The same late in autumn, the hues of red, yellow,
>   drab, purple, and light and dark green,
> The rich coverlet of the grass, animals and birds,
>   the private untrimm'd bank, the primitive
>   apples, the pebble-stones,
> Beautiful dripping fragments, the negligent list
>   of one after another as I happen to call them
>   to me or think of them,
> The real poems, (what we call poems being merely
>   pictures,) . . .
>   [P. 103.]

Since "the real poems" are things, "Beautiful dripping fragments," the best writing will simply describe them: the "joyous leaves of dark green" uttered by the live-oak are really, when we substitute "Children of Adam poet" for "live-oak," little imagistic poems, strung through the poem like leaves on a branch. And the whole poem is like a fruit that the tree drops "at random" from itself:

> The oath of procreation I have sworn, my Adamic and
>   fresh daughters,
> The greed that eats me day and night with hungry
>   gnaw, till I saturate what shall produce boys
>   to fill my place when I am through,
> The wholesome relief, repose, content,
> And this bunch pluck'd at random from myself,
> It has done its work—I toss it carelessly to
>   fall where it may.
>   [P. 105.]

The tree that drops its fruit, the lover who drops his "bunch" of sperm,[21] the poet who drops his poem [22]—all fulfill their "oath of procreation," satisfy their natures and can achieve "repose." We recall what Whitman says in the Preface of 1855, published only a year before "Spontaneous Me":

The rhyme and uniformity of perfect poems show the free growth of metrical laws . . . and take shapes as compact as the shapes of chestnuts and oranges, and melons and pears. . . . The fluency and ornaments of the finest poems or music or orations or recitations, are not independent but dependent. All beauty comes from beautiful blood and a beautiful brain. If the greatnesses are in conjunction in a man or woman, it is enough—the fact will prevail through the universe . . .[23]

The tree, the lover, and the poet can be careless because their only responsibility is the accomplishment of their act: Nature assures that the ground, the woman, the reader are proper recipients. So for the poet of "Spontaneous Me," reader is Reader, with "beautiful blood and a beautiful brain," and woman is Woman, who should have no face, only a body from which the instinctive lover can turn after his act is done.

The rivers in "From Pent-up Aching Rivers" are rivers of the poetic imagination as well as rivers of "the climbing sap." We find at the end of the poem that the poet has emerged from the night to celebrate the "act divine." The night, of course, is a night of love-making and the act an act of love; but the night is also the night of imagination that we find in "The Sleepers," and the act is the merging act of the imagination, the act of "the soul fitful at random" (p. 91). This ambivalence generates the ambiguity of the opening lines:

> From pent-up aching rivers,
> From that of myself without which I were nothing,
> From what I am determin'd to make illustrious,
>   even if I stand sole among men,
> From my own voice resonant, singing the phallus,
> Singing the song of procreation,
> Singing the need of superb children and therein
>   superb grown people,
> Singing the muscular urge and the blending,
> Singing the bedfellow's song . . .
>
> [P. 91.]

Is the "blending" sexual or perceptual? Or is it poetic, inseparable from "singing"? What is "that . . . without which I were nothing"—the phallus, the sexual urge, the imaginative leap, or "my

82

own voice resonant"? Is there any difference among love-making, imagining, and singing?

The drama of the whole poem simply puts these questions a different way: the voice acts out the ambiguity. Even as the poet, "Singing the true song of the soul fitful at random," spins out his "divine list"—a list like the one "pluck'd at random" in "Spontaneous Me," but more specifically sexual—he has other things on his mind. In five asides, set off by parentheses, he does what the poet in "Spontaneous Me" never does—turns away from his singing and addresses other characters, demonstrating thereby a failure of spontaneity. In the first three asides, the addressee can be either the reader or the lover who lies waiting in the night:

> . . . (O resistless yearning!
> O for any and each the body correlative attracting!
> O for you whoever you are your correlative body!
>   O it, more than all else, you delighting!)
>   [P. 91.]
>
> (Hark close and still what I now whisper to you,
> I love you, O you entirely possess me,
> O that you and I escape from the rest and go
>   utterly off, free and lawless,
> Two hawks in the air, two fishes swimming in the
>   sea not more lawless than we;)
> . . . .
> (O I willingly stake all for you,
> O let me be lost if it must be so!
> O you and I ! What is it to us what the rest do
>   or think?
> What is all else to us? only that we enjoy each
>   other and exhaust each other if it must be so;) . . .
>   [P. 92.]

It really does not matter whether the listener is reader or lover, for at this point the poet feels that his sexual, perceptual, and poetic passions are the same thing—"The furious storm through me careering" (p. 92). He has not yet realized that singing is one step removed from imagining—that although the self can lose itself in the night both of love-making and imagination, in order to sing the self must leave the night.

83

That realization comes in the next moment, and is signaled by the fourth aside, "(I have loiter'd too long as it is,)" (p. 92). Whereas the poet in "Spontaneous Me" never ceases to sound like the Whitman who thinks that great poetry comes naturally, the poet in "Rivers" has come to understand that poetizing demands consciousness, that the reader is not necessarily the lover in the dream. Thus the fourth aside reveals the poet's sense that he has been talking too long, instead of "being"—that he has stayed too long in the day. The aside may still be addressed to both reader and lover, but to one it is a warning and to the other an apology. This tendency of the poet to desert his own singing becomes even more apparent in the last aside, "(Yet a moment O tender waiter, and I return)" (p. 93). Now the listener is frankly the lover, and the apology has become a promise that the poet will soon keep by ending his poem.

Yet if by the end of the poem the poet has realized that love-making and poetizing, life and art, are two different things—the second necessarily less spontaneous than the first—he nevertheless has celebrated singing as well as love-making and imagining as an "act divine." For his action has shown us that singing will out. Despite himself he has lingered "Yet a moment" in the day: we readers, who along with Woman have been treated so carelessly in "Spontaneous Me," discover that we ourselves have become attractive even as Woman has blossomed into a "tender waiter."

"I Sing the Body Electric" seems to be written out of a mood as optimistic as that behind "Spontaneous Me," but finally it demonstrates a doubt more severe than that in "From Pent-up Aching Rivers." The poet celebrates the body "electric"—the life of the body, "the charge of the soul," the oneness of the world:

> And if the body does not do fully as much as the soul?
> And if the body were not the soul, what is the soul?
>
> [P. 94.]

Yet the action of the poet is less spontaneous in this poem than it is in "Spontaneous Me": if "Spontaneous Me" is finally a poem about singing, this is a poem about the making of a song. Both poets admit the insufficiency of their poems, admit that things are the "real poems" and that "body . . . balks account"; but the

84

poet of "Spontaneous Me" goes on to act as if that is not true, singing in careless confidence, whereas the speaker in "I Sing the Body Electric" is conscious of working himself up to song.

His trial flight is successful enough: most of Section 2 echoes the "divine list" of "Spontaneous Me":

> The female soothing a child, the farmer's daughter
>   in the garden or cow-yard,
> The young fellow hoeing corn, the sleigh-driver
>   driving his six horses through the crowd,
> The wrestle of wrestlers, two apprentice-boys,
>   quite grown, lusty, good-natured, native-born,
>   out on the vacant lot at sundown after work,
> The coats and caps thrown down, the embrace of
>   love and resistance,
> The upper-hold and under-hold, the hair rumpled
>   over and blinding the eyes; . . .
>   [Pp. 94–95.]

But he is not content to stop here. He seems to use this singing to release his imagination, to "loosen [him]self," and make way for the rest of the poem:

> The march of firemen in their own costumes, the play
>   of masculine muscle through clean-setting
>   trowsers and waist-straps,
> The slow return from the fire, the pause when
>   the bell strikes suddenly again, and the
>   listening on the alert,
> The natural, perfect, varied attitudes, the bent
>   head, the curv'd neck and the counting;
> Such-like I love—I loosen myself, pass freely,
>   am at the mother's breast with the little child,
> Swim with the swimmers, wrestle with wrestlers,
>   march in line with the firemen, and pause,
>   listen, count.
>   [P. 95.]

This speaker is more conscious than the speaker of "Spontaneous Me" because he wants to do more. Whereas "Spontaneous Me" stops with a catalogue of movements like the ones described above, this speaker wants to count more than the gongs of the bell. He

85

wants to "pass" on to a catalogue of things themselves: he begins by celebrating the electricity of the body, but he wants eventually to indicate the electricity by celebrating the body.

Thus the poem becomes steadily more concerned with bodily form. From the description of swimming, hoeing, and wrestling, the poet moves to a detailed account of an old man "of wonderful vigor, calmness, beauty of person" (Section 3), pauses for direct praise of "beautiful, curious, breathing, laughing flesh" (Section 4), and goes on to brief discussions of the "female form" and the male (Sections 5 and 6), discussing male and female passions as much as physical matters, but concluding, "The man's body is sacred and the woman's body is sacred." Sections 7 and 8, which close the original version of the poem (p. 92 n.), consider the "body at auction," first the man's, then the woman's. They contain the lines most specifically addressed, thus far in the poem, to the particular parts of the body:

> I help the auctioneer, the sloven does not half
>   know his business.
>
> Gentlemen look on this wonder,
> Whatever the bids of the bidders they cannot
>   be high enough for it,
> . . . .
>
> Examine these limbs, red, black, or white, they
>   are cunning in tendon and nerve,
> They shall be stript that you may see them.
>
> Exquisite senses, life-lit eyes, pluck, volition,
> Flakes of breast-muscle, pliant backbone and
>   neck, flesh not flabby, good-sized arms and legs,
> And wonders within there yet.
>
> [P. 98.]

This sales pitch is only rehearsal for the poet's major celebration of the parts of the body. The long list that makes up Section 9 is the most notorious of Whitman's catalogues; but when read dramatically, as the song the poet has been preparing himself for, it makes sense as the climax of the poem:

86

> O my body! I dare not desert the likes of you
>   in other men and women, nor the likes of the
>   parts of you,
> I believe the likes of you are to stand or fall
>   with the likes of the soul, (and that they are
>   the soul,)
> I believe the likes of you shall stand or fall
>   with my poems, and that they are my poems,
> Man's, woman's, child's, youth's, wife's, hus-
>   band's, mother's, father's, young man's,
>   young woman's poems,
> Head, neck, hair, ears, drop and tympan of the
>   ears,
> Eyes, eye-fringes, iris of the eye, eyebrows,
>   and the waking or sleeping of the lids, . . .
>   [P. 100.]

Section 9 does not appear until the 1856 edition, one year after the publication of the original version, but it fulfills the logic of the rest of the poem. If things are "the real poems," as the poet says in "Spontaneous Me," then even the describing of things, which the poet does in "Spontaneous Me" and at the start of "Body Electric," will not be the best the poet can do; naming things, simply noting their existence, will be more true to reality. The body may finally "balk account," but the poet has achieved as much as he can by working himself up to a true song, a list of names: "I believe the likes of you shall stand or fall with my poems, and that they are my poems" (p. 100).

The faithfulness of Section 9 to the inner logic of the poem may save this particular poem for us, but its faithfulness to the larger logic of Whitman's contradictions is a warning that the poetry of "Spontaneous Me" and "From Pent-up Aching Rivers" is on the wane. Working oneself up to sing a list of names is actually working oneself up to the admission that poetry is not particularly important. "Spontaneous Me" is successful because the speaker ignores his own assumption that words cannot make "real" poems; and "From Pent-up Aching Rivers," because we see the speaker struggling against that assumption. "I Sing the Body Electric" may work dramatically, but the last section deserves its notoriety: its existence is evidence of capitulation to the doubt, capitulation that

leads to a kind of poetry very different from the great dramatic
poetry of the 1855 and 1856 editions.

The opening poem of the Calamus group, "In Paths Untrodden," says explicitly that the poet is about to treat a new subject
matter, and implies that the new subject matter will be offered in a
new shape:

> In paths untrodden,
> In the growth by margins of pond-waters,
> Escaped from the life that exhibits itself,
> From all the standards hitherto publish'd,
>   from the pleasures, profits, conformities,
> Which too long I was offering to feed my soul,
> Clear to me now standards not yet publish'd,
>   clear to me that my soul,
> That the soul of the man I speak for rejoices
>   in comrades,
> Here by myself away from the clank of the world,
> Tallying and talk'd to here by tongues aromatic,
> No longer abash'd, (for in this secluded spot
>   I can respond as I would not dare elsewhere,)
> Strong upon me the life that does not exhibit
>   itself, yet contains all the rest,
> Resolv'd to sing no songs to-day but those of
>   manly attachment, . . .

> [P. 112.]

Whitman's play on *publish'd* suggests that he thinks of the
Calamus group as being a new kind of poetry, or at least a different
kind of poetry from that he has previously sung. His shift in
symbolism is a still stronger indication. The key term is stated in
the title of the group and referred to in "the growth by margins of
pond-waters" and "tongues aromatic." "Calamus" leaves, it seems,
are to be distinguished from another kind of "leaves of grass," the
"joyous leaves of dark green" uttered by the live-oak.* As Whitman explains to M. D. Conway,

* Whitman at one time considered using the "live oak leaves" as a symbol for
"adhesiveness." We find this note in *N & F*, p. 169: "A string of Poems, (short
etc.) embodying the amative love of woman—the same as *Live Oak Leaves* do the
passion of friendship for man"; and "Live Oak with Moss" is the heading of an
early version of some of the Calamus poems (Bowers, *Whitman's MSS*, p. lxvii).
Bowers concludes that "the live oak preceded the calamus and was later engulfed
by it" (p. lxx); but the rejection seems to have been more severe than that, for in
the Calamus group as it finally appears the leaves of the oak are actually contrasted
to calamus leaves.

"Calamus" is a common word here. It is the very large & aromatic grass, or rush, growing about water-ponds in the valleys—[spears about three feet high—often called "sweet flag—grows all over the Northern and Middle States—(see Webster's Large Dictionary—Calamus—definition 2).] The recherche or ethereal sense of the term, as used in my book, arises probably from the actual Calamus presenting the biggest & hardiest kind of spears of grass—and their fresh, acquatic, pungent bouquet.[24]

Whereas in the Children of Adam group he ascends "to the garden the world" [25] and counts off the leaves he finds there, now his furthest drive is toward a leaf found in a region beyond the world:

> These I singing in spring collect for lovers,
> (For who but I should understand lovers and all
>   their sorrow and joy?
> And who but I should be the poet of comrades?)
> Collecting I traverse the garden the world, but
>   soon I pass the gates,
> Now along the pond-side, now wading in a little,
>   fearing not the wet,
>
> . . . .
> Plucking something for tokens, tossing toward
>   whoever is near me,
> Here, lilac, with a branch of pine,
> Here, out of my pocket, some moss which I pull'd
>   off a live-oak in Florida as it hung trailing
>   down,
> Here, some pinks and laurel leaves, and a handful
>   of sage,
> And here what I now draw from the water, wading
>   in the pond-side,
> (O here I last saw him that tenderly loves me,
>   and returns again never to separate from me,
> And this, O this shall henceforth be the token
>   of comrades, this calamus-root shall,
> Interchange it youths with each other! let
>   none render it back!)
>
> . . . .
> . . . what I drew from the water by the pond-side,
>   that I reserve,
> I will give of it, but only to them that love as
>   I myself am capable of loving.[26]

89

To walk untrodden paths among the calamus leaves—to be talked to by "tongues aromatic," to "tally" those tongues, and to give a leaf as a token to a comrade-reader—is to write poetry about the "ethereal sense" in a form particularly suitable to that sense.

What is the new relationship between poet and reader? In the Children of Adam poems, we have seen, the poet is a lover of the universe, so spontaneous that he merely ticks off the glories of life, meanwhile ignoring the reader as an individual because he thinks of all readers as equally beautiful, and ignoring readers as a group because he is sure that all of them will see his truth. Only when that confidence has been shaken, as in "From Pent-up Aching Rivers," does the relationship shift: doubt in the spontaneous poetry of catalogues suddenly makes the poet conscious of the reader as an individual, a competitor for the poet's loyalty against a lover who has been transformed from indiscriminate Woman into a "tender waiter."

The Calamus poems are, in effect, the way the poet talks when, turning to this new lover, he discovers that lover and reader are one —both "tender waiters," both comrades. When the poet has been struck by "the terrible doubt of appearances," safety can come in the shape of a comrade and in the shape of poems about comradeship:

> That shadow my likeness that goes to and fro
>   seeking a livelihood, chattering, chaffering,
> How often I find myself standing and looking at
>   it where it flits,
> How often I question and doubt whether that is
>   really me;
> But among my lovers and caroling these songs,
> O I never doubt whether that is really me.[27]

So the Calamus poet is far from careless. Instead of dropping his "bunch" at random, he is cautious and deliberate—conscious of himself, his poetry, and his audience. Agonizingly conscious, in fact, for behind the new deliberateness is a stabbing sense of vulnerability. He is one who "knew too well the sick, sick dread lest the one he lov'd might secretly be indifferent to him";[28] he stains every song he sings with blood from his wounds;[29] he knows that he could not utter leaves "without a friend a lover near," [30] will give the calamus token "only to them that love as I myself am capable of loving." [31] And he insists that the reader duplicate the poet's awareness: the poet must be known too, not as a type (an "Adam") but as an individual:

> Among the men and women the multitude,
> I perceive one picking me out by secret and
>   divine signs,
> Acknowledging none else, not parent, wife,
>   husband, brother, child, any nearer than I am,
> Some are baffled, but that one is not—that one
>   knows me.[32]

The reader must know even that the comrade may not be what he seems, that the world beyond appearances may be corrupted or unreal:

> Are you the new person drawn toward me?
> To begin with take warning, I am surely far
>   different from what you suppose;
> Do you suppose you will find in me your ideal?
> . . . .
> Do you suppose yourself advancing on real ground
>   toward a real heroic man?
> Have you no thought O dreamer that it may be all
>   maya, illusion? [33]

The central poem of the Calamus group, "Scented Herbage of My Breast," is about the discovery of this new subject matter and this new way of talking. The first lines show us a poet who is writing instinctively, out of a vague new sense of himself:

> Scented herbage of my breast,
> Leaves from you I glean, I write, to be
>   perused best afterwards,
> Tomb-leaves, body-leaves growing up above
>   me above death, . . .
>
>   [P. 113.]

He does not know, here at the start, about the expression, communication, or meaning of these different leaves. He thinks that they will express themselves ("out from where you retired you shall emerge again"), but he is wrong; he is hesitant about their acceptance ("O I do not know whether many passing by will discover you or inhale your faint odor, but I believe a few will"); and he is uncertain about their significance ("O I do not know what you mean there underneath yourselves"). But his failure to understand leads to knowledge. Even as he thinks of these leaves as being self-expressive, like the Children of Adam leaves, his thinking begins to unfold their meaning:

> O slender leaves! O blossoms of my blood! I
>   permit you to tell in your own way of the
>   heart that is under you,
> O I do not know what you mean there under-
>   neath yourselves, you are not happiness,
> You are often more bitter than I can bear, you
>   burn and sting me,
> Yet you are beautiful to me you faint tinged
>   roots, you make me think of death,
> Death is beautiful from you, (what indeed is
>   finally beautiful except death and love?)
> O I think it is not for life I am chanting here
>   my chant of lovers, I think it must be for death,
> . . . .
> Indeed O death, I think now these leaves mean
>   precisely the same as you mean, . . .
>
> [P. 114.]

The leaves, the poet discovers, mean "death and love"; but we, and the poet, do not yet know what kind of death and love. Further meaning must wait upon further expression: the poet calls upon his song to sound itself:

> Grow up taller sweet leaves that I may see!
>   grow up out of my breast!
> Spring away from the conceal'd heart there!
> Do not fold yourself so in your pink-tinged
>   roots timid leaves!
> Do not remain down there so ashamed, herbage
>   of my breast!
>
> [P. 114.]

But these leaves, unlike the leaves of the live-oak, the spontaneous language of Adam, will not come of themselves. Expression in the Calamus poems requires conscious effort from the poet:

> Come I am determin'd to unbare this broad breast
>   of mine, I have long enough stifled and choked;
> Emblematic and capricious blades I leave you, now
>   you serve me not,
> I will say what I have to say by itself,
> I will sound myself and comrades only, I will
>   never again utter a call only their call,
> I will raise with it immortal reverberations
>   through the States,
> I will give an example to lovers to take perma-
>   nent shape and will through the States,
> Through me shall the words be said to make death
>   exhilarating,
> Give me your tone therefore O death, that I may
>   accord with it,
> Give me yourself, for I see that you belong to me
>   now above all, and are folded inseparably
>   together, you love and death are,
> Nor will I allow you to balk me any more with
>   what I was calling life,
> For now it is convey'd to me that you are the
>   purports essential,
> That you hide in these shifting forms of life,
>   for reasons, and that they are mainly for you,
> That you beyond them come forth to remain, the real
>   reality,
> That behind the mask of materials you patiently
>   wait, no matter how long,
> That you will one day perhaps take control of all,
> That you will perhaps dissipate this entire show
>   of appearance,
> That may-be you are what it is all for, but it
>   does not last so very long,
> But you will last very long.
>   [Pp. 114–15.]

Discovery of a new kind of expression—discovery that the poet must say these new, secret truths by himself, in a voice clear and

93

carefully controlled—is inseparable from the discovery of meaning, just what these secret truths are. He can define the love that moves him only after he decides to reject the "capricious blades" and say what he has to say; and he can reveal death, to us and himself, only when he speaks in the "tone" of death.

The truth that informs both this love and this death, the reason that the poet sees them as "folded inseparably together," is the truth of fixity, permanence, that which "will last very long." The love is the quiet love of comrades, not the love of "madness and joy" described in the Children of Adam poems; and the death is immortality, participation in the world of spirit that lies behind the "shifting forms of life." This "real reality," this truth representative of the "special world," is of course opposite to the spontaneity that the Children of Adam poet has been "calling life," the truth of the shifting world of actuality. The "real reality" will necessarily not express itself: it is available to the actual world only by means of the poet's conscious effort—either his strategy of indirection, which we shall see at work in Whitman's major poems, or a strategy of direction, to which the end of "Scented Herbage" refers. When Whitman proclaims that he "will give an example to lovers to take permanent shape and will through the States," he means not only that he will live a pattern of love to be glorified and imitated by future generations, but also that he will make a pattern of discourse, create a poetic form which will embody permanence and yield stability.

The form of permanence is didacticism: the Calamus perception —direct, non-imaginative—eventually leads away from the shyness of poems like "Here the Frailest Leaves of Me" ("Here I shade and hide my thoughts") and produces expression that is direct. The voice that will "sound . . . comrades" and "make death exhilarating" is the voice of the prophet, the man who takes his solid stand, saying what he has to say "by itself"; and the focus of the poem, the concern of the speaker, will be not action, the shifting of forms, nor things, the "mask of materials," but the idea of comradeship and immortality—idea, which has to do with the abstract permanence behind materials and shifting. By the end of "Scented Herbage," the poet, who begins in perplexity, has clarified his own vague impulse toward fixity, finding the special kind of love and the special kind of death that partake of permanence; and in the process he himself has approached fixity, relief from the struggle between contradictions. The statements of the last lines—"you will one day perhaps take control of all, . . . you will perhaps dissipate this entire show of appearance, . . . you will last very long"—are at once the poet's final revelations to himself and the beginnings of the prophet's work. The poet is not quite didactic, for he is still addressing the "real reality" instead of readers; but in the course of the poem, working his way toward the celebration of an idea, he has learned the prophet's manner. Unhappy from the start of the poem with Adam's careless nudity, he comes to try on a cloak of consciousness and responsibility. Wistful perplexity gives way to confident assertion. Although the speaker is not yet confronting readers, his conception of them has changed enormously: whereas once he hopes that a few passersby will discover his faint sense of the new truth, by the end of the poem he predicts that his call will reverberate throughout the States, that the new truth, revealed by the poet, will "take control of all."

So didacticism is just around the corner. In "When I Heard the Learn'd Astronomer," a poem of the Calamus subject matter but not of the group, Whitman celebrates the permanence of the spiritual world in terms that require him to reject not only the astronomer's mechanistic vocabulary—"the proofs, the figures, . . . the charts and diagrams"—but also the very stance and manner of lecturing:

> When I sitting heard the astronomer where he
>   lectured with much applause in the lecture-room,
> How soon unaccountable I became tired and sick,
> Till rising and gliding out I wander'd off by
>   myself,
> In the mystical moist night-air, and from
>   time to time,
> Look'd up in perfect silence at the stars.
>
> [P. 271.]

But the Calamus vision has room for another attitude: it is no accident that Whitman inserts in the group a poem not written until 1871, "The Base of All Metaphysics" (p. 121), in which he presents himself as an "old professor" addressing his "crowded

95

course." The birth of this didacticism is a complicated matter, the product of contradictory emotions that lie within the Calamus vision. A shy and lonely individual, seeking the roots of his being in the "ethereal sense," becomes a comrade when the search turns outward and becomes a search for the constant love of another individual. The teacher or prophet appears when the quest for permanence is pressed yet further. The individual newly conscious of the frivolousness and perils of spontaneity, suddenly aware that he must control his actions and his singing, moves forth more vigorously than in his search for a comrade, and imposes control upon readers. This man exists just beyond the last lines of "Scented Herbage"; we can think of him as a man supremely confident that he has found his truth in the doctrines of democratic comradeship and immortality, and also as a man who hides his perplexity by wearing the mask of confidence, settling on "idea" as a rock amidst shifting appearances. We hear him in the didactic poems that sound persistently throughout the Calamus group—"Whoever You Are Holding Me Now in Hand" (pp. 115–16), "For You O Democracy" (p. 117), "Recorders Ages Hence" (pp. 121–22), "Are You the New Person Drawn Toward Me?" (p. 123), "Roots and Leaves Themselves Alone" (p. 124), "Behold This Swarthy Face" (p. 126), "I Hear It was Charged against Me" (p. 128), "A Promise to California" (pp. 130–31), "No Labor-Saving Machine" (p. 131), "A Leaf for Hand in Hand" (p. 132), "What Think You I Take My Pen in Hand?" (p. 133), "To the East and to the West" (pp. 133–34), "To a Western Boy" (p. 134), and "Full of Life Now" (p. 136).

The new form has the strengths and weaknesses of its origin. It is the very embodiment of the permanence sought and celebrated by the poet: it represents the poet as a stable, certain individual; it focuses upon idea, implying thereby the existence of a world of stable forms; and it assigns the reader a fixed role as listener. But of course its strength is also its weakness: the great danger of Whitman's didacticism is that it can embody stability, fixity, all too well.

The danger manifests itself in one way as a problem in the relationship between form and subject matter. It is more or less true of all the didactic poems in the Calamus group, but most true of "A Promise to California," that we are confronted with a poet who praises comradeship and democracy but acts like a master:

> A promise to California,
> Or inland to the great pastoral Plains, and on to
>   Puget sound and Oregon;
> Sojourning east a while longer, soon I travel toward
>   you, to remain, to teach robust American love,
> For I know very well that I and robust love belong
>   among you, inland, and along the Western sea;
> For these States tend inland and toward the Western
>   sea, and I will also.
>
> [Pp. 130–31.]

When we realize from neighboring poems (such as "Behold This Swarthy Face" and "I Dream'd in a Dream") that "robust love" means comradeship, the love of the "new city of Friends" (p. 133), the tone of the speaker becomes comically inappropriate—"I know very well . . . ," for instance. Some flaw is unavoidable, for a poet must elevate himself to talk about equality or anything else. But instead of allowing us to suspend our disbelief, to accept the incongruity as a necessary convention, Whitman shoves the incongruity, and himself, down our throats. His "tending" toward "the Western sea," which he represents as a slow and graceful natural movement, seems actually to be the loud push of a braggart.

More is wrong here, however, than Whitman's failure of tone, his personal inability to harmonize subject matter and form. There is a difficulty inherent in the didactic form itself that must be specifically overcome if didactic poems are to work. For neither mask nor focus allows the reader any room for action. If at the end of "Scented Herbage" the poet's position is not yet fixed, neither is ours as readers. Instead of being under "control," receiving passively the exposition of an idea, we remain active by tracing the movement of the speaker, who, still turned away from us, is just reaching the climax of his personal drama. In "A Promise to California," however, and in most of the other didactic poems in the Calamus group, the mask is rigidly assertive, and refers to an idea, which has life only in the sense that it can produce, not invite, action. If the reader is "moved," to use De Quincey's word, it is to action only outside of the poem. He may dance for joy at the

97

prospect of Whitman's arrival, or even sponsor a model community based on "robust love," but read the "promise" again he will not. The form of the discourse actively discourages the reader's engagement in it, and no stylistic niceties or surprises modify the discouragement: the discourse may work as message, but it does not work as poem.

It is perhaps because Whitman senses the deficiency of the didactic form that he attempts occasionally to camouflage it. "I Dream'd in a Dream" (p. 133) puts the idea of a "city of Friends" into a narrative setting, which is operative only in that it identifies the idea as a dream. Almost no possibilities of the narrative form are explored. There is no significant separation between the man telling the story and the men told about (only the use of past tense suggests that the present speaker is perhaps not himself a dreamer); there is no attempt to describe an important action; even the identification of idea as dream could have been done in a different way, with no appreciable change in the meaning of the discourse.

The same device and the same failure are found in Whitman's best known didactic poem, "By Blue Ontario's Shore," a transposition of the 1855 Preface.[34] The poem seems at times to be unabashedly didactic—Section 11 begins, "For the great Idea,/That, O my brethren, that is the mission of poets"—but the "Idea" is presented in an unconvincing narrative setting:

> By blue Ontario's shore,
> As I mused of these warlike days and of peace
> return'd, and the dead that return no more,
> A Phantom gigantic superb, with stern visage
> accosted me,
> *Chant me the poem*, it said, *that comes from the*
> *soul of America, chant me the carol of victory,* . . .
> [Sec. 1, p. 340.]

> I listened to the Phantom by Ontario's shore,
> I heard the voice arising demanding bards,
> By them all native and grant, by them alone
> can these States be fused into the compact
> organism of a Nation.
> [Sec. 9, p. 346.]

98

> Thus by blue Ontario's shore,
> While the winds fann'd me and the waves came
>   trooping toward me,
> I thrill'd with the power's pulsations, and
>   the charm of my theme was upon me,
> Till the tissues that held me parted their
>   ties upon me.
>
> And I saw the free souls of poets,
> The loftiest bards of past ages strode before
>   me,
> Strange large men, long unwaked, undisclosed,
>   were disclosed to me.
>
> [Sec. 19, p. 355.]

Around and between these points of narrative is sung the song of "proportion," America, and, above all, individuality—the sacred power of "you and me" (Section 17). Finally even the speaker cannot believe that the narrative is as important as the didactic song:

> O my rapt verse, my call, mock me not!
> Not for the bards of the past, not to invoke
>   them have I launch'd you forth,
> Not to call even those lofty bards here by
>   Ontario's shores,
> Have I sung so capricious and loud my savage song.
>
> Bards for my own land only I invoke,
> . . . .
> Bards of the great Idea! bards of the peaceful
>   inventions! (for the war, the war is over!)
> Yet bards of latent armies, a million soldiers
>   waiting ever-ready,
> Bards with songs as from burning coals or the
>   lightning's fork'd stripes!
> Ample Ohio's, Kanada's bards—bards of Cali-
>   fornia! inland bards—bards of the war!
> You by my charm I invoke.
>
> [Sec. 20, p. 355.]

We could speculate that "By Blue Ontario's Shore" is actually neither narrative nor didactic, but rather a dramatic poem, the enactment of a struggle between a narrative voice and a didactic voice, finally decided when the didactic voice asserts itself in the last section. A struggle not unlike that does, after all, take place in "Scented Herbage" and, we shall see, "The Sleepers." But those good dramatic poems are dramatic at the roots, with carefully made plot and believable character development, whereas "By Blue Ontario's Shore" seems to be narrative by mere device and dramatic only as an afterthought. It is predominantly didactic, and neither mechanical narrative nor sporadic drama saves it from the essential fault of didacticism.

But Whitman can make good didactic poems. "To You," written in the same year as "By Blue Ontario's Shore," unlike that poem meets head-on both major difficulties of Whitman's didacticism, the problem posed by Whitman's special subject matter and the problem of the form itself. As in "A Promise to California," the speaker asserts himself as master and teacher even as he argues for freedom and equality, the sanctity of the individual:

> Whoever you are, now I place my hand upon
> you, that you be my poem,
> I whisper with my lips close to your ear,
> I have loved many women and men, but
> I love none better than you.
>
> O I have been dilatory and dumb,
> I should have made my way straight to you
> long ago,
> I should have blabb'd nothing but you, I
> should have chanted nothing but you.
>
> I will leave all and come and make the hymns
> of you,
> None has understood you, but I understand you,
> None has done justice to you, you have not done
> justice to yourself,
> None but has found you imperfect, I only find
> no imperfection in you,
> None but would subordinate you, I only am he
> who will never consent to subordinate you,
> I only am he who places over you no master,

> owner, better, God, beyond what waits
> intrinsically in yourself.
>
> [P. 233.]

But here the tone is right. Whitman goes a long way toward justifying the necessary distinction between himself and his reader by giving his sureness a personal reason for being. His manner, he suggests, is the fruit of his own self-discovery: only a moment ago, he was, like the reader, "walking the walks of dreams"; he should have been a teacher "long ago."

As in this treatment of subject matter, Whitman solves his problem of form not by running from it—not, for instance, by pretending to tell a story—but by making the most of it. "To You" is addressed directly and frankly to the reader, "Whoever you are"; but it demonstrates nevertheless that the uses of didacticism can be subtle. "Whoever you are" in one sense has a public sound, for we often hear Whitman say this to mean any one of his readers; [35] but when we emphasize the *are*, as this poem in particular encourages us to do, the words take on private meaning as well, for they concern the existence of the individual identity:

> Whoever you are! claim your own at any hazard!
> . . . .
>
> The hopples fall from your ankles, you find an
>   unfailing sufficiency,
> Old or young, male or female, rude, low, re-
>   jected by the rest, whatever you are pro-
>   mulges itself, . . .
>
> [P. 235.]

Since the idea of the poem is that any man, whoever he is, can release himself by being himself, the double meaning is important to the subject matter of the poem; but it is at least as important to Whitman's formal strategy. For the complicated use of the term, the play between "whoever you are" and "whatever you are," forces a reader to surrender his passivity. The reader, whom the didactic form ordinarily relegates to a fixed position, here must think of himself in two ways, as a member of a group and as an

101

individual; moreover, he is induced to return to the poem to explore its verbal complexity.

This small subtlety of the address is merely an indication of the truth demonstrated by the movement of the whole poem—that a teacher and the didactic form have latitude. "To You" is a lesson in teaching; and the pattern of the lesson, a model for didactic poetry. If the relationship between student and teacher suffers from built-in disadvantages to active learning, and if the teacher-poet's problem is all the more difficult because he must finally involve the reader not in external activity but in the poem, "To You" shows that after all there are ways around the disadvantages. Although Whitman's prophetic purpose requires that he moralize, it does not require that he do so from the start. The pattern of "To You" is a pattern of shifting attitudes of the teacher toward his student, culminating in the imperative moral statement.

At the start of the poem, the speaker takes his stance as a prophet, a man with a vision of the reader's "true body and soul." But he is a friendly prophet, not an angry and demanding one: his warning is mild ("I fear you are walking the walks of dreams") and balanced by encouragement. By the second section, in fact, this teacher is no longer a prophet at all, but a comrade, who whispers instead of preaching; and in the third section, he turns his scorn toward himself rather than "you." The prophet returns in the fourth section—not to scold, however, but to praise, to assure the reader that he is a kind of god. The praise is continued in the fifth section, with the important difference that it is generalized ("I paint myriads of heads, but paint no head without its nimbus of gold-color'd light"): withdrawing from direct praise of the individual "you," the speaker has given the addressee a chance to breathe.

Halfway through the poem, therefore, the speaker has declared a direct, though mildly put, unfavorable judgment and has reinforced the judgment in various ways not so direct—by intimate coaxing, self-condemnation, specific and general praise. The resting place of the fifth section is preparation for the renewed drive of the second half of the poem, in which the teacher makes his case more vigorously and more directly. The sixth section begins with an exclamation of direct individual praise, bridging the tonal break in the poem by reminding the reader of the fourth section; and it shifts quickly to a harsh restatement of the first section, in which the half-cautious, half-condescending "I fears" of that section disappear:

> You have not known what you are, you have slum-
>   ber'd upon yourself all your life,
> Your eyelids have been the same as closed most
>   of the time,
> What you have done returns already in mockeries,
> (Your thrift, knowledge, prayers, if they do not
>   return in mockeries, what is their return?)
>
> [P. 234.]

In contrast to the movement of the first half of the poem, this excitement is not quieted but is allowed to grow and spill over into the next section, where the speaker restates in more rugged language the humanitarian promises he has made in the fourth section, and includes also an accurate description of his own quickening pursuit of the reader:

> The mockeries are not you,
> Underneath them and within them I see you lurk,
> I pursue you where none else has pursued you,
>
> . . . .
> The pert apparel, the deform'd attitude, drunk-
>   enness, greed, premature death, all these I
>   part aside.
>
> [P. 234.]

Then a brief withdrawal to quiet, the last "resting place" of the poem: the eighth and ninth sections, six lines in all, in which the teacher first gently praises the reader, then explains his own role again, this time with no scornful reference to his own "blab."

Finally the stage is set for the ultimate didactic voice, the prophet's insistence on moral action:

> Whoever you are! claim your own at any hazard!
> These shows of the East and West are tame com-
>   pared to you,
> These immense meadows, these interminable rivers,
>   you are immense and interminable as they,

These furies, elements, storms, motions of Nature,
  throes of apparent dissolution, you are he or
  she who is master or mistress over them,
Master or mistress in your own right over Nature,
  elements, pain, passion, dissolution.

[P. 235.]

Only now, prepared by all the devices of the teacher—mild
mockery and loud praise, aggressiveness and gentleness, authority
and comradeship—can the reader receive the "strong and steady
call," the direct "lesson" that Whitman claims elsewhere to have
in mind all the time: "Especially in the 'Leaves of Grass' are the
facts of eternity and immortality largely treated. . . . his persuasion becomes a taunt, and his love bitter and compulsory. With
strong and steady call he addresses men. Come, he seems to say,
from the midst of all that you have been your whole life surrounding yourself with. Leave all the preaching and teaching of others,
and mind these words of mine." [36]

Thus "To You," although it is not included in the Calamus
group, is the fulfillment of the poet's search in "Scented Herbage,"
as true a fulfillment of the whole Calamus vision as any of the love
poems. Whitman demonstrates that he has found his new poetic
way by writing a successful didactic poem. He does so by playing all
the roles generated by the Calamus vision of the ethereal world:
the uncertain searcher, condemning his own failures; the whispering comrade; the demanding prophet. He denies the fixity of
didacticism by working in a pattern of shifting stances toward the
end of "idea," requiring readers to take the several complementary
stances and to involve themselves in the process of tracing the
pattern.

At the same time as "To You" fulfills the Calamus vision, it is
testimony to the richness of that vision and the variety of the
Calamus group itself. For the multiplicity of masks in "To You"
recalls to us that the Calamus group itself includes the full range of
poetic forms implied by the special kind of perception and
expression that it celebrates. In this sense the Calamus poems are
more successful as a group than their companion group, which
stops short of its own implications in that it is almost completely
restricted to dramatic poems, poems either lyric or "monodra-

matic," which catch the speaker in the moment of working out a position for himself.[37] Still, just as the Calamus vision implies the creation of a form so different from drama as didacticism, so the Children of Adam vision clears the way for imagism.

If the special logic of the Calamus group allows a perplexed comrade to become a demanding master, the complementary logic of the Children of Adam group allows a joyful and spontaneous lover, a singer of all the things of life, to reappear in related poems as an austere "analyzer and overlooker," who turns away from the reader and concentrates on one thing at a time. When Whitman says in "Spontaneous Me" that the "Beautiful dripping fragments" are the "real poems" and that "what we call poems" are "merely pictures," he is beginning a psychic and aesthetic journey that will end in his writing poems which attempt to be nothing but "pictures." Typical of such poems, which start to appear in 1860 and are increasingly present in the editions of 1865 and afterward, is "A Farm Picture" (1865):

> Through the ample open door of the peaceful
>   country barn,
> A sunlit pasture field with cattle and horses
>   feeding,
> And haze and vista, and the far horizon fading
>   away.
>
>   [P. 274.]

Actually the roots of this poetry can be found even before "Spontaneous Me" in a poem called "Pictures," written (and rejected) before 1855,[38] in which Whitman makes a gesture toward the kind of catalogue we see in "Spontaneous Me" and the beginning of "Body Electric." But the difference between roots and the final fruit is considerable. In poems like "A Farm Picture," there is no flow from picture to picture and no fluctuation in the speaker's voice, which, as quiet, unchanging, and economical as a voice in a poem can be, sets a frame around both itself and the one scene on which it focuses.

The writer of such a poem could himself have set down the following principles of poetry, which were in fact agreed to by six poets who called themselves Imagists some fifty years after Whitman practiced the art:

105

1. To use the language of common speech, but to employ always the *exact* word, not the nearly-exact, nor the merely decorative word.

2. To create new rhythms—as the expression of new moods—and not to copy old rhythms, which merely echo old moods. We do not insist upon "free-verse" as the only method of writing poetry. We fight for it as a principle of liberty. We believe that the individuality of a poet may often be better expressed in free-verse than in conventional forms. In poetry, a new cadence means a new idea.

3. To allow absolute freedom in the choice of subject . . .

4. To present an image (hence the name: "Imagist"). We are not a school of painters, but we believe that poetry should render particulars exactly and not deal in vague generalities, however magnificent and sonorous. It is for this reason that we oppose the cosmic poet, who seems to us to shirk the real difficulties of his art.

5. To produce poetry that is hard and clear, never blurred nor indefinite.

6. Finally, most of us believe that concentration is of the very essence of poetry.[39]

Indeed, if we pick and choose among Whitman's contradictory critical writings, he did in effect write this manifesto of imagism, the Preface to *Some Imagist Poets* (1915). The first three points read like an editor's revision of the 1855 Preface; the last three, like a lucid, if less imaginative, version of Whitman's own notebook "Rules of Composition," which, as we have seen, call for "A perfectly transparent, plate-glassy style, artless, with no ornaments. . . . Clearness, simplicity, no twistified or foggy sentences, at all . . ."[40] The critical bias of the whole takes the same slant as Whitman's judgment of his own work in a letter to O'Connor:

[Drum-Taps] is in my opinion superior to Leaves of Grass—certainly more perfect as a work of art, being adjusted in all its proportions and its passion having the indispensable merit that though to the ordinary reader let loose with wildest abandon, the true artist can see that it is yet under control. . . . I see I have said I consider Drum taps superior to Leaves of Grass. I probably mean as a piece of art and from the more simple and winning nature of the subject and also because I have in it only, succeeded to my satisfaction in removing all superfluity—verbal superfluity, I mean. I delight to make a poem where I feel clear that not a word but is indispensable part thereof and of my meaning.*

* *Correspondence*, I, 246–47. Yet the Imagists by and large rejected him. Although a line from Whitman, "To have great poets there must be great audiences

Whitman's imagism is linked directly to the Children of Adam vision. Like the Calamus transformation from comrade to prophet, the transformation from spontaneous Adam to "overlooker" makes good contradictory sense. Adopting the role of the "overlooker" seems to be Whitman's extreme statement of the careless confidence he exhibits toward the reader in "Spontaneous Me." The "overlooker" is not the kind of prophet we observe in the Calamus group; rather, he is like De Quincey's and Carlyle's hero, who teaches "if at all, indirectly by moving," who does not trouble to address the crowd but insists rather that the crowd come to him to learn Truth. But playing this role, adopting the mask of a describer of things, is actually an expression of doubt as much as of confidence. For the foot-loose, spontaneous ego is haunted by the fear of drowning, a fear that on the one hand lends the voyage some of its wild excitement but that also eventually curtails it. Focusing upon thing, like focusing upon idea, slows down the world for the poet.

The emotion that drives the poet to "sing" the closing catalogue of "Body Electric" is, when we view it from one perspective, an overweening confidence—confidence that the poet can invoke the electricity of the thing and elucidate his private excitement to readers simply by naming things themselves. Seen from a different perspective, however, it is a belief that the "real poetry" is things, not words, and it is therefore an expression of doubt in the poet's significance. Explored, pressed by the poet, this contradictory emotion takes the form of imagism: the confident poet, the

---

too," served as the slogan for Amy Lowell's magazine, *Poetry*, where the Imagists tried their wings, the scornful reference to "the cosmic poet" in the Preface to *Some Imagist Poets* sounds very much like a direct allusion to Whitman. And, although Pound admitted that Whitman was his "spiritual father," praised his rhythms, and even called attention to his "deliberate artistry," still he insisted that Whitman was "in the large" rather than "in details" (all quotations from "Walt Whitman," first published in *American Literature*, XXVII [1955], 59–61)—and details were very important to the man who said, "it is better to present one Image in a lifetime than to produce voluminous works" ("Imagism," *Poetry*, I [March, 1913], 199). Whitman's influence on the Imagists is probably restricted to his free verse. His indirect influence on French Symbolism (see P. M. Jones, "Whitman and the Symbolists," *The Background of Modern French Poetry*, pp. 69–88) may have somehow worked back to the Imagists; and Fletcher was influenced by Whitman before the French poets reinforced the lesson (S. K. Coffman, Jr., *Imagism*, p. 100). But these are after all not very large effects.

naming magician, concentrates further his already private vision and consequently makes even more demands upon his readers; the fearful poet further distrusts his own flow of perception and language, and finds that he cannot reel off a list of things, but must concentrate on the particular lonely thing.

The danger in the imagistic form itself simply inverts the formal danger in didacticism. If Whitman's didactic utterances can be too direct, if the reader knows all too well his role and has all too little chance to involve himself in the poem, the imagistic poem can suffer from a failure of direction—not "indirection," but "non-direction." For the mask of the poem, the overlooker, offers the reader no aid toward understanding the importance of the thing he celebrates. Simply by beginning to talk about the thing—the farm scene, for instance—he indicates that it is of private importance to him, but he does not suggest what kind of importance. Like William Carlos Williams in "Red Wheelbarrow," he says that "So much depends/upon" the thing, but not why:

> So much depends
> upon
> a red wheel
> barrow
> glazed with rain
> water
> beside the white
> chickens.

And the focus itself, the thing, is no more considerate a guide—unlike an action, whose moments of climax and descent give it importance of its own which is at least semipublic, or an idea, which is necessarily public in that it requires statement in intelligible terms.

The poetic image is, as C. Day Lewis has said, "the myth of the individual"; [41] and imagistic poems are by nature private. If the mask and focus of a didactic poem work too much in cooperation, the mask and focus of an imagistic poem work too much against each other: the focus is wholly direct, the pinpointing of a particular thing, but at the same time the mask is wholly indirect, turned completely away from the reader. In contrast to the didactic form, which makes the reader feel like a political and aesthetic inferior instead of a comrade and active participant in the poem, the imagistic form perplexes the reader by relinquishing all direction. It in effect assumes that the reader is the poet's equal, a poet himself—perhaps, in fact, identical to the creator of the poem, for the reader is expected to respond to the same private image that stirs the poet.

Thus the Children of Adam imaginative perception, in which man leaps out of himself to enfold other things, yields expression opposite to the didactic poetry that grows out of the Calamus non-imaginative perception—expression that demands, perhaps, too much. The didactic form falls short of being poetry when it is too purely direct—when it calls forth from the reader that staticity which one part of Whitman so much admires. The failure of the imagistic form, on the other hand, can come when the reader is required to make too swift a journey, the instantaneous flight that is Whitman's metaphor for the immediate knowledge of the imagination. At best, when the poem happens to work, the reader can experience, as Pound hoped, a "feeling of sudden light," [42] a "sense of sudden liberation." [43] Guided simply by the poet's concentration on a special thing or scene, he can see what he has never stopped to look at before, or he can see familiar things differently because they have been put in strange relation to each other. But there is always the danger in imagistic poetry—more than in narrative or dramatic poetry—that the poet and the reader will not "click": that the wheelbarrow in the rain or the sunlit pasture will remain images merely private or merely pictorial.

This difficulty of form is, of course, closely connected to the problem of relating subject matter to form. If the subject matter of Whitman's didactic poetry assures the reader that he is an equal and the form proceeds to treat him like an inferior, the subject matter of imagistic poetry, simply by concerning a particular thing, implies that individuality, the uniqueness of each thing, is important to the poet, whereas the form, expecting the reader to respond to the image that excites the poet, treats the reader not like an individual but like a man identical to the poet himself.

The response to this problem is not, as in didactic poetry, to modify the stance of the speaker, but rather to modify the quality of the subject matter—to make it somewhat less particular and individual, so that the reader need not be so much like the poet. Thus a great deal of the success of "An Army Corps on the March" (p. 301) results from Whitman's concentration on the advancing of the corps, an aspect of thing that has at least a vague public meaning, having to do with struggle, development, progress. He evokes the same public meaning and achieves the same kind of success in "The Runner" (p. 275) and "Cavalry Crossing a Ford" (p. 300). Likewise the importance of "The Dalliance of the Eagles" (pp. 273-74) rests not only upon metaphorical brilliance ("a sudden muffled sound"; "a living, fierce, gyrating wheel"; "tumbling turning clustering loops") but also upon the symbolic, public quality of the scene—loving conflict, poised tension, separation. These poems work as Whitman edges them toward the indefinite line between imagism and symbolism.*

The response to the problem of the form itself is somewhat more

* Amy Lowell's ambiguousness in regard to Imagism and Symbolism is an indication less of fuzziness on her part than of the fuzziness of the distinction between the two movements. Coffman describes her position: "Her distinction between the attitudes she describes as *internality* and *externality* and her disapproval of the former place her at odds with the broad philosophical element in the Symbolist aesthetic. *Externality*, the Imagist and modern attitude, cuts the poet away from introspection and focuses his attention upon the object as interesting for itself alone. While she does not directly attack the Symbolists' transcendental view of external reality, she unquestionably condemns it by inferences. The line of demarcation is clear: the poet could hold, with Hulme and the Imagists, that his art should be confined to the precise, external, physical world, or, with the early Symbolists, that it should be an attempt to penetrate the external to the vague and shadowy life beyond . . ." (*Imagism*, p. 89). But on the other hand, "she . . . stated that the dominant quality of the modern idiom (in which she included Imagism) was suggestion, 'the invoking of a place or a character rather than describing it, implying of something rather than the stating of it, implying it perhaps under a metaphor, perhaps in an even less obvious way.' By supporting this assertion with two examples from Fletcher's poetry, she brought her definition to what is approximately the position of the Symbolist. On one she commented: 'The picture as given is quite clear and vivid. But the picture we see is not the poem, the real poem lies beyond, is only suggested.' " (*Imagism*, p. 172, quoting Amy Lowell, "A Consideration of Modern Poetry," *The North American Review*, XXV [January, 1917], 103-4.)

How, after all, can we finally separate "externality" from "internality," our description of a thing from our attitude toward the thing? Our very selection of the thing to describe implies that it has for us some "vague and shadowy life" beyond its physical dimensions. Thus the difference between Imagism and Symbolism must be one of degree rather than kind: the making of an "Imagist" poem necessarily involves and implies "internality," and Miss Lowell's critical theory, like Whitman's imagistic poems, edges toward Symbolism as she touches on that "internality."

difficult to manage than the response to the problem of didacticism, for there are many ways to approach a reader directly with an idea, as we have seen in "To You," but fewer ways to turn away from a reader and describe a thing. Perhaps this fundamental difficulty in the imagistic form is behind the split in the Imagist group in which each side seizes one of the two choices offered by the form. On one side is Aldington, who emphasizes the pictorial quality of imagism: "We wanted," he reminds Amy Lowell in a letter, "to write hard, clear patterns of words, interpreting moods by 'images,' i.e., by pictures, *not* similes." [44] The other side is represented by Hulme, who talks not about faithful reproduction of a thing but about the play between images: "Say the poet is moved by a certain landscape, he selects from that certain images which, put into juxtaposition in separate lines, serve to suggest and evoke the state he feels. . . . Two visual images form what one may call a visual chord. They unite to suggest an image which is different to both." [45]

The best example of the imagism Aldington defines is Williams's "Red Wheelbarrow"; of Hulme's imagism, Pound's "In a Station of the Metro":

> The apparition of these faces in the crowd;
> Petals on a wet, black bough.

Whitman is capable of Hulme's and Pound's latter-day metaphysical wit—all through *Leaves of Grass* are lines like "the beautiful uncut hair of graves" from "Song of Myself" [46]—but when he comes to make whole little poems of his images he chooses the pictorial method. "An Army Corps on the March," "The Runner," "Cavalry Crossing a Ford," "The Dalliance of the Eagles," "The Ship Starting" (p. 9), "The Torch" (p. 395), "Bivouac on a Mountain Side" (p. 300), and "A Paumanok Picture" (p. 461) are all attempts by Whitman to "paint the thing" as he sees it.

Given this original rejection of Hulme's kind of imagism, Whitman has only two strictly formal ways "out" of the difficulty of the form. The first way is to mix two forms—to fuse imagism with the dramatic form, for instance, a technique similar to his placing a narrative frame around the didactic poem "By Blue Ontario's Shore," but more convincing. At the center of "Bivouac on a Mountain Side" is the description of an army, much like the descriptions in "Cavalry Crossing a Ford" and "An Army Corps on the March." But in "Bivouac" Whitman includes himself, the overlooker, in the scene ("I see before me now a traveling army halting"); and the most important moment of the poem is when he gasps at the relationship of sky to army:

> The numerous camp-fires scatter'd near and far,
>   some away up on the mountain,
> The shadowy forms of men and horses, looming,
>   large-sized, flickering,
> And over all the sky—the sky! far, far out of
>   reach, studded, breaking out, the eternal stars.
>
> [P. 300.]

As in Wordsworth's "Composed upon Westminster Bridge," the real focus of the poem is dramatic, the poet's own "feeling of sudden light," his own discovery or rediscovery of meaning in a scene as he describes it.

The second way is to work inside the form. In "An Army Corps on the March," the corps is saved from being Williams's wheelbarrow because of the speaker's verbal emphases. The overlooker stresses the symbolic quality of the scene by substituting *advance* and *press on* in the body of the poem for *march*, the less charged word of the title: he guides the reader ever so slightly to the understanding that the poem has to do with the "unknown road" [47] of development. The same sort of subtle direction is at work in "A Sight in Camp in the Daybreak Gray and Dim" (pp. 306–7). If we read no more than the first section of "A Sight in Camp," we have an imagistic poem:

> A sight in camp in the daybreak gray and dim,
> As from my tent I emerge so early sleepless,
> As slow I walk in the cool fresh air the path
>   near by the hospital tent,
> Three forms I see on stretchers lying, brought
>   out there untended lying,
> Over each the blanket spread, ample brownish
>   woolen blanket,
> Gray and heavy blanket, folding, covering all.

112

The rest of the poem concerns, in three brief scenes, the spiritual beauty of the dead soldiers, ending:

> Then to the third—a face nor child nor old,
>   very calm, as of beautiful yellow-white ivory;
> Young man I think I know you—I think this face
>   is the face of the Christ himself,
> Dead and divine and brother of all, and here again
>   he lies.

We can get a sense of those last lines even from the first section. The emphasis on the gray-brown dullness of the blankets; the alliance of that dullness with the day itself, "the daybreak gray and dim"; the variations on heaviness, *ample, heavy, folding, covering* —all these hint at the smothering of purity by the gray world of war. The description is "suggestive" rather than merely graphic: Whitman finds ways to direct the reader even in a form that is by nature non-directive. It is the triumph of his didacticism in reverse.

Thus Whitman can make good poems, if minor ones, in forms that are to either side of his great dramatic center. And they are new poems. Although one half of Whitman's poetic theory returns to the mechanistic conceptions of pragmatism and mimesis, the poems that would seem to embody the theory are not quite the old mechanistic poems. The play in Whitman between mechanism and organicism yields "mechanistic" poetry with a new soul. His didacticism at its best depends upon individual "Personality," the poet's and the reader's, in a way not typical of Pope's "Essay on Man" or Swift's "City Shower"; and his imagism hints at the hidden life of things as the eighteenth-century descriptive poetry of James Thomson or even of William Bowles does not.

Yet, if Whitman's responses are new, the problems of the forms are the same for the centuries. For they remain a matter of control and freedom, separateness and involvement, direction and non- direction: the working of the poet to involve the reader in his poem and to control his responses; the working of the reader to know where he is and to come alive.

V DIRECTION: NARRATIVE

I F IMAGISM AND DIDACTICISM can be said to represent the two poles in Whitman's "bipolar unity," his total design, then his other forms represent the unity, for they fuse the characteristics of imagism and didacticism. They direct the reader less than didacticism and more than imagism. Whereas didacticism evokes stasis and imagism requires from the reader an instantaneous flight to imaginative Truth, the narrative, the monodrama, and the "poem of reader engagement" all urge the reader into something between stasis and instantaneous flight—a long, hard journey in which meaning is gradually revealed. In this sense all three forms are more or less indirect; but of the three, narrative is of course most direct. The reader may be presented with an action in which he can involve himself; but all the while his journey of involvement is being guided by the stable man who, focusing on an action rather than an idea or a thing, has turned from teacher or overlooker into storyteller.

Whitman seems not to have been very comfortable in the narrative form. Often he uses the narrative as a device to get on to something else—as he does, for instance, in the basically didactic "By Blue Ontario's Shores" and "Over the Carnage Rose Prophetic a Voice" (pp. 315–16), and the basically lyric "Year That Trembled and Reel'd Beneath Me" (p. 308). Even when he concentrates on the problem that is at the heart of the narrative form—the relationship between the manner and values of the present

114

teller of the story and the manner and values implied by the action he describes—Whitman slants away from using the form itself. Thus in "The Artilleryman's Vision" (pp. 317–18), where the peaceful hush of a soldier's home is contrasted to the remembered chaos of battle, Whitman makes the battle scene not a story but a "vision," a waking nightmare; so that the center of attention is upon a struggle in the present between actuality and imagined reality, instead of a relationship between past and present.

Yet, "Out of the Cradle Endlessly Rocking" is a narrative: at its center is the distinction between present telling and past experience.* The speaker in "Cradle" holds his position throughout. Even though Whitman's tendency toward present dramatic enactment results in a speaker who is man-boy ("A man, yet by these tears a little boy again"), less removed from the action he describes than, say, the mature Pip in *Great Expectations*, the fact remains

* The form of "Cradle" has been more closely examined than that of any other Whitman poem. In the process it has been convincingly demonstrated, if demonstration be necessary, that the problem of form or genre can be approached with reward from various directions. The poem I call "narrative," Faner, *Whitman & Opera*, calls an Italian opera in miniature; Northrup Frye, *Anatomy of Criticism*, calls a development of the genre of the riddle; and Richard Chase, " 'Out of the Cradle' as a Romance," *The Presence of Whitman*, pp. 52–71, calls, obviously, a romance. Of special interest are the definitions of Fussell, "Warble," *Presence*, and Leo Spitzer, "Explication de Texte Applied to Walt Whitman's Poem 'Out of the Cradle Endlessly Rocking,' " *ELH*, XVI (September, 1949), 229–49. Fussell suggests a genre he names "The American Shore Ode," whose characteristics are that "it is a lyric of some length and philosophic density spoken (usually at a specific place) on an American beach; its theme tends to encompass the relationship of the wholeness and flux of the sea to the discreteness and fixity of land objects" (p. 31); and he also remarks that "the structure attempts to fuse . . . the traditional orderliness of narration, or epic, with the traditional impulsiveness of apostrophe, or lyric" (p. 38). For Spitzer, too, estimating the place of "Cradle" in world literature, the poem is an ode, "if the ode may be defined as a solemn, leagthy, lyric-epic poem that celebrates an event significant for the community . . . Whitman has acclimated the ode on American soil and democratized it. The lyric-epic texture, the solemn basic tone and the stylistic variation, the whimsical word-coinages and the chaotic fragmentariness are preserved. The latter feature has even found a modern justification in the complexity of the modern world. For the rhymeless Greek verse, Whitman by a bold intuition found an equivalent to the Bible verset, but he used this meter in order to express a creed diametrically opposed to that of the Bible. . . . He replaces the pagan Pantheon by the deified eternal forces of nature to which any American of today may feel close. . . . As for the solemn event significant for the community which the ode must by its nature celebrate— this we have in the consecration of Walt Whitman as a poet, the glorification, not of a Greek aristocratic athlete born of Gods, but of a nameless American boy, . . . who, having met with nature and with his own heart, becomes the American national poet . . ." (pp. 247–49).

that the speaker is always somewhere within a strange middle area between the present and the past of which he tells.

We come to know this narrator by noticing first when he talks, then what he says and how he says it. He separates himself from the action by means of two structural devices. First, he defines himself in an envelope that surrounds the description (one side of the envelope ends with "A reminiscence sing," and the other begins with "Which I do not forget"); second, in the description itself he inserts reminders of his presence outside the action, stage-directions, as in the line "Demon or bird! (said the boy's soul)." These structural devices are especially necessary because the narrator is at times pulled back toward the action as he describes it. He occasionally addresses the bird instead of the reader, usually briefly; but once, in the passage beginning "O you singer solitary," he blends his voice with the child's for some eight lines. The line ". . . (said the boy's soul)" is especially clumsy if we do not understand that this speaker must finally remove himself from the story he tells, must keep us from forgetting that the voice uttering the whole poem is not the voice of the bird, or the boy, or the sea.

That controlling voice, we discover, is actually the voice of Whitman in all his complexity: "I, chanter of pains and joys, uniter of here and hereafter, /Taking all hints to use them, but swiftly leaping beyond them." He is the man who knows the joys and sorrows of both merging and separateness; who is thoroughly involved in the procession of time, both caught by the past and free of the past; who makes his song out of the things around him and out of himself. He is related to the boy, yet more than the boy; his voice partakes of the voices of boy, bird, and sea, yet is more than any one of them, and, since it includes his own continuing voice, more than the fusion of them:

> . . . [I] fuse the song of my dusky demon and brother,
> That he sang to me in the moonlight on Paumanok's
> gray beach,
> With the thousand responsive songs at random,
> My own songs awaked from that hour,
> And with them the key, the word up from the
> waves, . . .

[P. 253.]

116

The manner of his telling, his habit of style and structure, supports these more direct self-revelations. The whole voice is made of two styles: the "organic" style, which emphasizes the flowing-together of things, and the "mechanistic" style, which emphasizes orderliness, the distinction between things. Together they express the one poet who controls "Cradle": a man who feels at one with all things but also keeps his distance. The first style is most readily available in the envelope, where Whitman meditates upon his own organic inclusiveness; the second, at spots in the descriptive core, where Whitman almost always holds himself apart from things that have happened to him. More often than not, the first style intrudes upon the second, for the poet is conscious of the flowing-together of the things he recalls and of their intimate connection to himself even as he describes the distinctions among them and expresses the barrier between them and himself. But a look at the styles in their purity will help us to determine the significance of their fusion.

In the envelope, a swirl of adverbial, prepositional, and participial phrases plays through and depends upon the central "I." The swirl and the "I" thus become of equal importance: the poet is an organic being, both absorptive and creative:

> Out of the cradle endlessly rocking,
> Out of the mocking-bird's throat, the musical shuttle,
> Out of the Ninth-month midnight,
> Over the sterile sands and the fields beyond, where
>   the child leaving his bed wander'd alone, bare-
>   headed, barefoot,
> Down from the shower'd halo,
> Up from the mystic play of shadows twining and twisting
>   as if they were alive,
> Out from the patches of briers and blackberries,
> From the memories of the bird that chanted to me,
> From your memories sad brother, from the fitful
>   risings and fallings I heard,
> From under that yellow half-moon late-risen and
>   swollen as if with tears,
> From those beginning notes of yearning and love
>   there in the mist,

117

From the thousand responses of my heart never to cease,
From the myriad thence-arous'd words,
From the word stronger and more delicious than any,
From such as now they start the scene revisiting,
As a flock, twittering, rising, or overhead passing,
Borne hither, ere all eludes me, hurriedly,
A man, yet by these tears a little boy again,
Throwing myself on the sand, confronting the waves,
I, chanter of pains and joys, uniter of here and
    hereafter,
Taking all hints to use them, but swiftly leaping
    beyond them,
A reminiscence sing.

[Pp. 246–47.]

The descriptive style is much more straightforward—the lines shorter, the diction simple, the syntax more regular. The poet is a dispassionate observer and reporter:

Till of a sudden,
May-be kill'd, unknown to her mate,
One forenoon the she-bird crouch'd not on the nest,
Nor return'd that afternoon, nor the next,
Nor ever appear'd again.

[P. 248.]

Or:

He call'd on his mate,
He pour'd forth the meanings which I of all men know.

[P. 249.]

In the poem as a whole, the style of the envelope is dominant, for the straightforward style does not appear in the envelope, whereas the swirling style does run over into the core:

The aria sinking,
All else continuing, the stars shining,
The winds blowing, the notes of the bird
    continuous echoing,
With angry moans the fierce old mother
    incessantly moaning,

. . . .

118

To the boy's soul's questions sullenly timing,
    some drown'd secret hissing,
To the outsetting bard.

[P. 251.]

Yet, if the style of the whole voice emphasizes the organic quality of the poet, his recognition that he is at one with everything that has happened to him, the rigid structure which encloses the play of that voice (the existence of the envelope outside the core of the poem) is a reminder of the mechanistic quality of the poet, his insistence that he is separate from the action he describes.

When we take the next step in reading a narrative—when we measure the values of the action described against the values of the teller—we find that the narrator is indeed both the same as and different from the heroes of his reminiscence. The story centers upon a boy's triple discovery—of love, of death, and of poetry, a new kind of life. Yet in a larger sense the story is about Whitman's familiar problems—for the greatest significance of love, death, and poetry in "Cradle" is that they all concern separateness and involvement, freedom and restraint. If "death" is "the word stronger and more delicious than any," the "key" to this poet's songs, it is because the confrontation of death restates the confrontation of life, and in giving a name to the problem, the sea allows the poet yet a further statement of it, his confrontation of poetry.

There are three main characters in the story—the bird, the boy, and the sea. The first two are agents of perception, explorers of reality; the sea, more a steady representative of a truth about reality. In one sense, the several attitudes toward love, death, and poetry expressed by these characters are all creations of the boy: he "translates" both the bird's song and the sea's, and can do so only when he has achieved certain states of awareness. But the bird and the sea are also allowed their own integrity. Both their existence and their melodies, if not their words, have reality external to the boy's reality: we see the bird learn, and we see the boy, discovering as well as creating, learn from the bird and then from the sea. Truths are revealed in a strange "colloquy," a chorus of assertion and response, creation, and discovery, in which the bird sings to itself, the boy sings to himself, to the bird, and to the sea, and the sea simply sings. The various attitudes toward death and life we

119

will finally be able to place against the attitudes toward death and life of the man who has learned from all these characters, the man who sings the story. And the voices of the story, the tones and styles that, filtered through the boy's imagination, express the various attitudes, we will finally be able to place against the voice that talks to us in the present time of the poem.

The setting of the action is Paumanok in spring, an American Eden in which the "he-bird" and the "she-bird" live in blissful harmony, hovering brightly over new life. Outside this scene, observing it but not involved in it, "absorbing" it but not moved to action in it, is the boy—

> . . . I, a curious boy, never too close, never
> disturbing them,
> Cautiously peering, absorbing, translating.
> [P. 248.]

The song translated by the boy sounds very much like Whitman's exuberant song in the last movement of "Song of Myself." Its ecstatic exclamations, its brash ordering of the sun, its carelessness of place, of day and night, of even the seasons—all recall the Whitman who sings his own enormous sufficiency:

> *Shine! shine! shine!*
> *Pour down your warmth, great sun!*
> *While we bask, we two together.*
>
> *Two together!*
> *Winds blow south, or winds blow north,*
> *Day come white, or night come black,*
> *Home, or rivers and mountains from home,*
> *Singing all time, minding no time,*
> *While we two keep together.*
> [P. 248.]

The great difference, of course, is that Whitman sings "myself," whereas the bird sings "two together." The bird is not really self-reliant, and he does not understand how vulnerable he is made by his attachment.

When the blow does come—when the she-bird disappears, "May-be kill'd, unknown to her mate"—the bird's exclamatory

song is not quite so assured. Although he still is confident enough
to order the winds to their work ("Blow! blow! blow!"), his cry
expresses need, of course, for the help of those winds. When the
command is not obeyed, assurance yields completely to uncertainty. The bird's intense consciousness of the love in the universe
—his awareness of the waves "embracing and lapping" one another;
of the moon hanging low, "heavy with love"; of the mad embrace
of the sea with the land—is but the other face of his new sense of
loss and private perplexity. The disappearance of the she-bird is a
bolt from the blue: not only is she lost to the he-bird, but her
disappearance is the work of the unknown, carried out in unknown
ways. The resultant private uncertainty produces the pathetic turn
outwards in which the he-bird convinces himself that there is love
for everything but him. Soon the sense of love "out there" gives
way to the "terrible doubt of appearances" that lies behind it:

> Land! land! O land!
> Whichever way I turn, O I think you could give
>   me my mate back again if you only would,
> For I am almost sure I see her dimly whichever
>   way I look.
>
> . . . .
> . . . somewhere I believe I heard my mate
>   responding to me,
> So faint, I must be still, be still to listen,
> But not altogether still, for then she might
>   not come immediately to me.
>
> [P. 250.]

Finally uncertainty ("I am almost sure I see her dimly . . .")
becomes outright desperation. The bird is sure once more, but sure
now that he is alone, that death is final, that love is past, that the
past is all:

> O darkness! O in vain!
> O I am very sick and sorrowful.
>
> O brown halo in the sky near the moon, drooping
>   upon the sea!
> O troubled reflection in the sea!
> O throat! O throbbing heart!
> And I singing uselessly, uselessly all the night.

121

O past! O happy life! O songs of joy!
In the air, in the woods, over fields,
Loved! loved! loved! loved! loved!
But my mate no more, no more with me!
We two together no more.

[P. 251.]

If the bird has learned about loss, its mourning has its own kind of innocence. In feeling alone, the bird achieves a true perception of reality that the easily confident bird never approaches; but that perception too is limited, for it fails to see the whole context of experience, in which the finality of loss is nevertheless but part of the continuous process of death and life. The bird, who at the start is something of a fool, is now at once pathetic and comic—pathetic in that he has truly lost, is alone, comic in that he is after all not finally alone, just thinks he is alone. For his song is not "useless": there is someone to hear it—the "boy ecstatic," whom the bird's song makes "the outsetting bard." The boy, an observer and "absorber" at the start, now is involved and a creator—started toward the man's work of poetry:

Demon or bird! (said the boy's soul,)
Is it indeed toward your mate you sing? or
     is it really to me?
For I, that was a child, my tongue's use
     sleeping, now I have heard you,
Now in a moment I know what I am for, I awake,
And already a thousand singers, a thousand songs,
     clearer, louder and more sorrowful than yours,
A thousand warbling echoes have started to life
     within me, never to die.

[Pp. 251–52.]

The boy has learned about loss and love from the bird, a lesson that the narrator, in his least detached moment of the poem, both recalls and relives:

O you singer solitary, singing by yourself,
     projecting me,
O solitary me listening, never more shall I
     cease perpetuating you,

122

Never more shall I escape, never more the
    reverberations,
Never more the cries of unsatisfied love be
    absent from me,
Never again leave me to be the peaceful child
    I was before what there in the night,
By the sea under the yellow and sagging moon,
The messenger there arous'd, the fire, the
    sweet hell within,
The unknown want, the destiny of me.

                    [P. 252.]

The two discoveries are inseparable: the boy loves the bird because the bird has lost his love. In coming to love the bird, the boy himself knows both the joy of connection and the pain of separation: he knows the "sweet hell within." The "love in the heart long pent" is now loosed, but at the same time the boy experiences the bird's loneliness, and even, if we take the narrator's preoccupation with solitude to be a true re-creation of the boy's emotion, has a vague sense of his own loneliness, his separation from the bird. But the boy—perhaps because of his perspective outside the bird's drama, his knowledge that the bird's song is heard—unlike the bird does not retreat into despair. This is not to say that the boy is full of joy: rather that, most important, he is no longer the "peaceful child." The simultaneous discovery of separation and involvement, of loneliness and love, has branded in his heart the truth of contradictions.

Out of that new sense of contradiction comes utterance—but utterance showing us that although the boy has learned some things from the bird, he has not learned everything. For although the boy feels that he is now creator instead of mere observer, his cry is a cry of confusion—a cry that, the original version of the poem makes clear, is both ecstatic and fearful, frenzied in two directions at once:

O give me some clue!
O if I am to have so much, let me have more!
O a word! O what is my destination?
O I fear it is henceforth chaos!

O how joys, dreads, convolutions, human shapes,
    and all shapes, spring as from graves around me!
O phantoms! You cover all the land and all the sea!
O I cannot see in the dimness whether you smile or
    frown upon me!
O vapor, a look, a word! O well-belov'd!
O you dear women's and men's phantoms! [1]

The boy's distress here is not so much a sense of chaos as an overwhelming uncertainty, expressed in a violent alternation from ecstasy to fear. The uncertainty is the new poet's perplexity about what to do with his sudden vision; and thus it is a perplexity about love, death, and poetry all at once. The phantoms, whom we shall meet again in "The Sleepers," are creatures of the poetic imagination: in the unaccustomed dimness of his poetic night, the boy has both "joys" and "dreads," wonders whether the things of his creation are smiling or frowning, both thinks of them as specters from the grave and addresses them lovingly.*

But more important even than this uncertainty is the boy's response to the uncertainty: his cry for certainty, which is what Whitman preserves in the final version of the poem:

O give me the clew! (it lurks in the night here
    somewhere,)
O if I am to have so much, let me have more!

* On this point it is necessary to give particular notice to Stephen Whicher, "Whitman's Awakening to Death," *Presence of Whitman*, pp. 1–27, for his reading of these lines is bound up with an emphasis widespread among critics of "Cradle," on Whitman's "homosexual crisis." Whicher argues that in these lines "the boy is not just distressed, he is desperate with the desperation of the man of 1859" for "instead of the triumphant vision of Life which Whitman himself had known, when the whole world smiled on its conquering lover, nothing rises now before the outsetting bard but a dim phantasmagoria of death-shapes, . . . strengthless ghosts, like the power of vision from which their life had come." Such a reading overlooks, I think, the boy's hope that the phantoms are smiling, the fact that "joys" as well as "dreads" appear in the sudden vision, and the fact that for Whitman the image of springing from the grave can suggest awakening of new life as well as death-walking (Section 38, "Song of Myself," *Reader's Edition*, p. 720). The boy's uncertainty is not the uncertainty of a failing poetic vision (though I do think that the poem as a whole moves toward "As I Ebb'd with the Ocean of Life") but the uncertainty of whatever poetic vision, and especially that of an "outsetting bard." The vision in "The Sleepers"—published in 1855, well before the "homosexual crisis" on which so much criticism of "Cradle" centers—is as crowded with fear and death as the boy's vision.

A word then, (for I will conquer it,)
The word final, superior to all,
Subtle, sent up—what is it?—I listen;
Are you whispering it, and have been all
    the time, you sea-waves?
Is that it from your liquid rims and wet sands?
                        [P. 252.]

The boy's very poetic awareness rests upon a sense of contradiction, but the boy too has a special innocence. Recklessly he pushes forward to "conquer it"—to discover ultimate answers about love, death, and, as is stressed by his call for "A word," the "word final," about poetry as well.

The answer he gets is the word from the sea, which has been there "all the time," an "undertone" to the songs of the bird and boy. It is, in effect, the answer that love and death are one: the conception of death not as final, and painful to the living, but as "delicious," part of the everlasting love of the universe. The sea, "Delaying not, hurrying not," embodies the endless process of reality. Its answer is in its "liquid rims and wet sands"—"that suggesting, dividing line, contact junction, the solid marrying the liquid— . . . blending the real and the ideal, and each made portion of the other." [2] The word the sea whispers is, in this sense, not only *death* but *life*: the sea bathes the boy in a loving ceremony of renewal ("Creeping thence steadily up to my ears and laving me softly all over"); it is "the cradle endlessly rocking." The sea sings, then, "neither like the bird nor like my arous'd child's heart." Its lulling song contrasts to the bird's song, first joyful, then desperate, and the boy's song, at once ecstatic and pained, just as its truth of endless process contrasts to the bird's notion of love and discovery of loss and the boy's understanding of loss and love.

Yet, even though the boy learns from the bird and in learning comes to know more than the bird, and then learns still more from the sea, there is a truth that goes beyond even the sea's. If the bird does not push beyond the conception of death as final, the boy, whom we leave still listening to the sea's hypnotic song, does not seem to push beyond the sea's promise that death is lovely, part of

125

the endless love of merging. The last voice in the poem is not the sea's, whispering, "Death, death, death, death, death," but the narrator's, incorporating all the truths—the bird's, the boy's, the sea's. If the sea's word is a revelation to the boy of the soft beauty of blending, to the narrator it is a "key" in a different way—a restatement of the old problems. For the narrator, removed from the boy just as the boy is removed from the bird, knows something about the sea that the boy does not know: that the sea's voice, while melodious, is also a hiss; that the sea is a mother, but a "savage old mother"; that it is "swathed in sweet garments," but is nevertheless an "old crone"; that its "white arms . . . tirelessly tossing" are beautiful, but also grotesque, perhaps the arms of a siren; that it bathes, but perhaps, like the ocean in "As I Ebb'd with the Ocean of Life," will also drown. The narrator knows, in other words, that there is danger as well as deliciousness in the conception of existence as a "measureless float," a sea of things endlessly involving themselves with each other. Were we to yield wholly to the truth of the "float," we would lose the sense of things as separate: we would lose the bird's truth that death is final and life lonely and the boy's truth of a "sweet hell within." The sea may have been there "all the time," but its word is no truer than the word of the particular, lonely moment.

Thus the narrator's exploration of attitudes toward death and love brings us back to the voice and attitudes of the narrator himself. The mature voice of the narrator—combining style and structure to represent itself as both organic and mechanistic—plays against the voices of the characters in the story. Their separate styles are less true than the narrator's to the poet's reality, in the sense of being less comprehensive, just as their attitudes toward love and death are less true. Thus to the bird's proudly innocent song of self-gratulation ("Two together!") is juxtaposed Whitman's understated narrative—his revelation to us, itself appearing "of a sudden," that Eden was invaded by the unknown. The half-certain exclamations that follow ("Blow! blow! blow!") are answered by the poet's voice, first conversational ("Yes, when the stars glisten'd"), then increasingly caught up by the action it describes, until it moves from addressing the reader ("He call'd on his mate") to addressing the bird:

126

He call'd on his mate,
He pour'd forth the meanings which I of all
   men know.

Yes my brother I know,
The rest might not, but I have treasur'd every
   note,
For more than once dimly down to the beach gliding,
Silent, avoiding the moonbeams, blending myself
   with the shadows,
Recalling now the obscure shapes, the echoes, the
   sounds and sights after their sorts,
The white arms out in the breakers tirelessly
   tossing,
I, with bare feet, a child, the wind wafting
   my hair,
Listen'd long and long.

[P. 249.]

But the narrator, pulled into the past as he is, does not lose his identity for us, for we have been prepared by the envelope to expect this much latitude in his movement. There too he turns from us to the bird:

> From the memories of the bird that chanted to me,
> From your memories sad brother, from the fitful
>   risings and fallings I heard , . . .

[P. 247.]

Although the narrator may move from distant narrator, commenting on the action in the careful and regular tones of the observing reporter, to involved narrator, developing a swirling syntax and addressing the characters themselves, he never becomes wholly captivated by the bird's reality. He holds his own style—only very occasionally imitating the painful cry of the bird, which is dramatically valid but too full of "O's" and exclamation points to be the controlling voice of this poem. Nor does the narrator identify wholly with the style and tone of the boy's voice, which he carefully places as the product of "my arous'd child's heart." Even when the boy is talking on his own, not "translating" the bird's song, his style has certain of the idiosyncrasies of the bird's:

127

> O give me the clew! (it lurks in the night
> here somewhere,)
> O if I am to have so much, let me have more!
>
> [P. 252.]

Again, the voice of the awakening poet is not the voice of the mature poet, the voice with which Whitman controls the poem. If the bird is first too proud and then too pained, in that first it does not admit the possibility of loss and then cannot push beyond its discovery, the boy is at once too ecstatic and too fearful, too full of the importance of his discoveries and too eager to push beyond them to certainty. The sea's lulling voice, wearing away at the extravagances of both joy and fear, counters the songs of bird and boy; but it too cannot control the poem, for it only suffers these extravagances their statement, rather than believing in them as really important.

The only voice that encloses the largest truth of the poem is the voice of the narrator. Carefully he separates himself from any one of the characters in his story, joins himself to all of them and separates himself even from all of them together. The lulling cadences of his voice restate the voice of the sea, and its passionate breaking-away from those cadences, as in its addresses to the bird, restate the voices of the bird and boy—the narrator's voice reproduces the "colloquy" sung by bird, boy, and sea. And it does still more, for the largest truth of the poem is more even than the fusion of the attitude and voices of the three characters in the story: the narrator's occasional matter-of-factness ("Once Paumanok"; "Till of a sudden"; "He call'd on his mate"; "Which I do not forget") introduces an attitude of detachment not expressed in the songs of bird, boy, or sea.

Standing at a position between removal from the past and involvement in it, between a stance as observer and a stance as "experiencer," the narrator defines his identity in a series of paradoxes. He is above all a blender of things. The elements which have formed him, which have brought him to this place and moment, all seem to fuse contradictory characteristics. The "Ninth-month midnight" suggests both birth (the midnight of the womb) and death (the running out of the year); the "mystic play" of the shadows, "twining and twisting as if they were alive," seems horrible as well as mysteriously enticing; the bird's song has "fitful

128

risings and fallings"; the word of the sea is both "stronger" and "more delicious" than any. And the self-contradictory elements also contradict each other: the narrator has been "borne hither" out of contrary songs (the sea's rocking and the shuttling of the bird's throat), out of sterility and fertility (the "sterile sands" and "the patches of briers and blackberries"), out of darkness and light (the play of the shadows and "that yellow half-moon late-risen and swollen as if with tears"), out of advance and response (the call of "yearning and love" and the "responses" of his own heart). Finally —and this is the largest paradox of the narrator's situation— whereas on the one hand he has been "borne hither" (a pun on *borne* suggests itself) by all the things that have made his life, on the other hand he is free of them:

> Borne hither, ere all eludes me, hurriedly,
> A man, yet by these tears a little boy again,
> Throwing myself on the sand, confronting the waves,
> I, chanter of pains and joys, uniter of here and
>   hereafter,
> Taking all hints to use them, but swiftly leaping
>   beyond them,
> A reminiscence sing.

[P. 247.]

He is helpless, brought to this position by his memories, a man who passively embodies his past and a poet who is impelled to sing, a vessel of language; yet, at the same time he chooses his moment to sing ("ere all eludes me, hurriedly"), he is a free man leaping into the future and a poet who, "Taking all hints to use them," forms his work like a Jonsonian "craftesman."

This same combination of freedom and bondage he allows his readers—giving them their head, but not so much as the imagistic poet, and, less than the didactic poet, guiding their movement. If we are given the latitude of an action in which to roam, it is also true that we must return from time to time to measure our responses against the values embodied by the narrative voice.

Flexible as is the control in "Cradle" upon the narrative voice and upon the reader, "There Was a Child Went Forth" allows more freedom yet. The difference marks the difference between a narrative, which "Cradle" remains despite the narrator's occasional addresses to the bird, and something between a narrative poem, which focuses on an action outside the speaking voice, and a dramatic poem, which focuses on the action through which the speaking voice itself is going.

The title of "Child" sounds like the title of a narrative: this would seem to be a poem in which the mask is a narrator ("There Was a Child") and the focus an action (". . . a Child Went Forth"). And so it is, at the start:

> There was a child went forth every day,
> And the first object he look'd upon, that
>   object he became,
> And that object became part of him for the
>   day or a certain part of the day,
> Or for many years or stretching cycles of years.
>
> [P. 364.]

The mask stands outside the action, telling about it and providing the reader with guides into the action: the formed man, his voice descriptive rather than dramatic, separates himself from the boy who is ever in the process of change. Yet the 1860 title of this poem —"Poem of the Child that Went Forth, and Always Goes Forth, Forever and Forever"—is finally more apt than the title Whitman settled upon in 1871. Its clumsiness aside, the earlier title captures the fundamental truth of the poem, that it mixes the past and the present, is an amalgam of a descriptive narration and a dramatic enactment.

The action described by the poem is, as hinted by the phrase "stretching cycles of years," symbolic of the organic vision. From the start our attention is turned toward the "becomingness" of life: in the spring of the year, a time of awakening, the child and the things around him fuse identities.

The first things that become part of the child, and that he becomes, are the country things of Whitman's boyhood home, the center of the child's being:

> The early lilacs became part of this child,
> And grass and white and red morning-glories,
>   and white and red clover, and the song of
>   the phœbe-bird,

130

> And the Third-month lambs and the sow's pink-faint
>   litter, and the mare's foal and the cow's calf,
> And the noisy brood of the barnyard or by the mire
>   of the pond-side,
> And the fish suspending themselves so curiously
>   below there, and the beautiful curious liquid,
> And the water-plants with their graceful flat
>   heads, all became part of him.
>
>   [P. 364.]

Mixing images of fresh life with more ordinary scenes of Natural activity, Whitman is able to suggest that the child's journey of perception is a discovery, or a making, of new life. When seen by a clear, childlike eye, when experienced by a being ready to be transformed, each piece of life, even the mire, is new, "curious." Accepting each thing in its idiosyncrasy, the particular quality that makes its existence "miraculous," as Whitman says in the poem "Miracles" (pp. 388–89), the child moves out temporally—we now have "field-sprouts of Fourth-month and Fifth-month" instead of "the Third-month lambs"—and spatially, past the barnyard and the pond, through the fields and the weeds by the road to the people on the road itself: the drunkard, the schoolmistress, boys friendly and quarrelsome, children "fresh-cheek'd" and Negro. As the child "becomes" more and more, accommodating even the characteristics of the drunkard and the quarrelsome boys, which from a different perspective would be seen as unpleasant, so does the poem grow. The third section is eight lines long, double the length of the first section and two lines longer than the second.

The steady expansion is interrupted by the next section, only three lines long, in which we are reminded that the child has a past as well as a future, a local, particular existence as well as the potentiality for all-inclusiveness.

> His own parents, he that had father'd him and she
>   that had conceiv'd him in her womb and birth'd him,
> They gave this child more of themselves than that,
> They gave him afterward every day, they became part of him.
>
>   [P. 365.]

The child is returned by the poem to his parents, particularly to his birth-time, and to the numerous "births" that ensue, the results of

131

their "giving him" every day. The result for us of this return is that the child is reborn in the poem, in the sense that we see another dimension of him: the self does not just enclose other things but offers its own newness to the world.

Having established the particularity of the child, the poem, imitating his now rapidly expanding life, surges into its last section, which, twice the length of any previous section, moves the child swiftly toward merger with the busy things of the city, then the things of the seashore, the water itself, and finally "The horizon's edge, the flying sea-crow, the fragrance of salt marsh and shore mud." The journey of perception leads to the farthest reaches of the physical world.

So the story of the child is about merging and particularity, but wholly within the context of organicism, for the child's particularity is stressed only so that "crossing" between him and external life can be properly dramatized. Yet there is a tug against organicism, the particularity and withdrawal of the mechanistic impulse, which we find in the speaking voice itself. For the voice goes through an action just as surely as the child: it moves subtly between the tones and rhythms of the removed observer and guide and those of the man caught up in the action he describes. The stylistic and structural changes that imitate the child's movement also serve as guides to the action of the voice.

Thus the poem begins with quiet and orderly lines, in the style that emphasizes orderliness and separation, but, as it enumerates the experiences of the child's organically whole life, slides into a style much less "mechanistic," in which subjects and objects, speaker and action spoken of, swirl into each other, blend until they are sometimes indistinguishable.

The change is very gradual. The second and third sections of the poem, catalogues of the "changes" of country if not of city, take on some of the fullness and activity of their subject matter: individual lines as well as the sections are longer than at the start of the poem. Yet the syntax is orderly (there is just a touch of the "present participle" style that signals the full flight of the organic poet), and each section is framed by statements whose deliberateness and careful use of the past tense make the narrator a stable man who knows that he and the action he describes are separate. In the fourth section the mask reemphasizes this basic orderliness of its voice. The pattern of growth is interrupted: the withdrawal of this section to three lines indicates the narrator's presence at "home" as well as the child's—the narrator's insistence, that is, upon an attitude of calm removal. The syntax is still orderly—subject, predicate; the past tense, again obvious:

> They gave this child more of themselves than that,
> They gave him afterward every day, they became
>   part of him.

[P. 365.]

In the fifth section, however, the voice breaks loose from the constraints of ordered time, place, and grammar. The section starts quietly, its descriptions careful and subdued like those in sections two and three: style and subject matter (the mother "quietly placing the dishes on the supper-table") reinforce each other. But within this ordered style are hints of the other style to come: present participles replace the regular finite verbs of the earlier sections ("the mother . . . placing the dishes . . . , a wholesome odor falling off her person"), and the syntax is disturbed ("the mother with mild words, clean her cap and gown"). In the next lines those hints are fulfilled. The description of the unpredictable father ("manly, mean, anger'd, unjust") introduces a style that defies grammatical categories:

> The father, strong, self-sufficient, manly, mean,
>   anger'd, unjust,
> The blow, the quick loud word, the tight bargain,
>   the crafty lure,
> The family usages, the language, the company, the
>   furniture, the yearning and swelling heart,
> Affection that will not be gainsay'd, the sense
>   of what is real, the thought if after all it
>   should prove unreal,
> The doubts of day-time and the doubts of night-
>   time, the curious whether and how,
> Whether that which appears so is so, or is it
>   all flashes and specks?
> Men and women crowding fast in the streets, if
>   they are not flashes and specks what are they?

[P. 365.]

Suddenly, as the narrator meditates upon the experiences of the boy, the boy's "becomingness," his merging with other identities, is not so sure and pleasant: we remember the child's uncertainty in "Cradle." Perhaps there is no reality "out there." And, indeed, what is reality for us as readers? Is this the narrator's "terrible doubt of appearances" or the boy's? Is the narrator just now experiencing the doubt as he tells about the boy's discoveries, or is he remembering the doubt that assailed the boy's "yearning and swelling heart"? Here is the special moment of vertigo that is so often the mark of Whitman's dramatic poems, and that we have seen threaten to erupt in "Cradle." Tense shifts rapidly, experience suggests experience, nouns follow quickly upon one another and turn into relative clauses, and the controlling verb never comes. We cannot separate the speaker from his subject matter, nor know precisely where we stand. The moment represents a tangle of two different kinds of form, the narrative and the dramatic, and two different ways of experiencing reality: it is the poet's deliberate expression of a perception that is at once confusion and vision, an expression that itself is both perplexing and enlightening.

The climax passes quickly. This high point, where the poet is being pulled from the precise and orderly world of the mechanistic vision into the indeterminate float of the organic vision, with all its excitements and unsurenesses, yields to a quieter enumeration of the boy's experiences, a return toward the descriptive technique of the earlier sections. The words of motion still are participles rather than finite verbs, and the section extends in one long sentence through eighteen lines, broken only by the parenthetical question about men and women as "flashes and specks"; yet the flow of the section is toward an orderly closing sentence, reminiscent of the direct statements that surround the second and third sections:

> The horizon's edge, the flying sea-crow, the
> fragrance of salt marsh and shore mud,
> These became part of that child who went forth
> every day, and who now goes, and will always
> go forth every day.
>
> [P. 366.]

By the end, the mask has established a position somewhat less distant from the action than it is at the start of the poem, yet not immersed in the action, as it is in the middle of the last section. The speaker is now a man-boy ("That child . . . who now goes, and will always go forth every day"); the mask, a narrator-experiencer. The two actions of the poem, that of the child in his journey and that of the man in his struggle between withdrawal from the child's adventure and involvement in it, play against each other. That play, the largest action of the poem, makes impossible the kind of mold that keeps "Cradle" in the narrative form: Whitman is well along toward monodrama, and we are about to become more adventurous voyagers than we have been before.

VI INDIRECTION: MONODRAMA

T HE SLEEPERS" impels a modern mind toward James Joyce, Virginia Woolf, and William Faulkner. More than half a century before those revolutionaries, Whitman achieves a goal that Hawthorne, a dweller in the half-real world of "romances," sets for himself but never manages: "To write a dream which shall resemble the real course of a dream, with all its inconsistency, its strange transformations, which are all taken as a matter of course; its eccentricities and aimlessness,— with nevertheless a leading idea running through the whole. Up to this old age of the world, no such thing has ever been written." [1] We know from the first words of Whitman's poem that we are to be introduced to the world Hawthorne sketches, and before we are through a dozen lines we have had played out for us some of the "transformations, . . . eccentricities and aimlessness" of that world:

> I wander all night in my vision,
> Stepping with light feet, swiftly and noiselessly
>   stepping and stopping,
> Bending with open eyes over the shut eyes of
>   sleepers,
> Wandering and confused, lost to myself, ill-
>   assorted, contradictory,
> Pausing, gazing, bending, and stopping.

136

How solemn they look there, stretch'd and still,
How quiet they breathe, the little children in
    their cradles.

The wretched features of ennuyés, the white
    features of corpses, the livid faces of
    drunkards, the sick-gray faces of onanists,
The gash'd bodies on battle-fields, the insane
    in their strong-door'd rooms, the sacred
    idiots, the new-born emerging from gates,
    and the dying emerging from gates,
The night pervades them and infolds them.

[P. 424.]

Whitman thus makes art out of an awareness that Poe, writing early in his career, describes but complains he cannot "adapt language" to:

There is . . . a class of fancies, of exquisite delicacy, which are *not* thoughts, and to which, *as yet*, I have found it absolutely impossible to adapt language. I use the word "fancies" at random, and merely because I must use some word; but the idea commonly attached to the term is not even remotely applicable to the shadow of shadows in question. They seem to me rather psychal than intellectual. They arise in the soul (alas, how rarely!) only at its epochs of most intense tranquillity, . . . and at those mere points of time where the confines of the waking world blend with those of the world of dreams. I am aware of these "fancies" only when I am upon the very brink of sleep, with the consciousness that I am so.[2]

Putting aside the important questions raised by the common interest in this dream world of Poe, Hawthorne, Whitman, and the recent practitioners of "interior monologue," we are led to ask: Why this particular poetic world for Whitman? Is "The Sleepers" an oddity in Whitman's own work, or is it in some sense typical of a major tendency, the logical outcome of a special idea of form? *

To begin an answer to these questions, I go back to Hawthorne's

---

* "The Sleepers" was for a long time a rather neglected poem, considering its worth; but that fact has now been so frequently noted, that a fair-sized body of criticism on the poem exists. Fullest readings are Miller, *Guide*, pp. 130–41, and Chase, *Whitman*, pp. 54–57.

note, which is at once a description of the dream reality and a prescription for the poem to be written about the dream. It stresses two opposing principles: "all the inconsistency" and the "leading idea running through the whole," or, in the terms I have used in discussing Whitman's habit of mind, variety and unity. Hawthorne's concern is Whitman's. First, fascination with a subject that is both various and unified: thus the dream—miscellaneous images joined internally by a logic of metaphor, joined externally by the framework of the dream itself, which has a beginning, turning, and end. Second, a desire, in the presentation of such subject matter, to give the reader a sense of both variety and unity: to bring him into a world of profusion and new perspectives, to excite his interest in discovery, and yet to assure him that the separate experiences will somehow hang together, will be meaningful in a way larger than themselves. The problem that Hawthorne poses for the dream poet is how to juxtapose the images so that the internal logic has relevance not only for the recorder of the dream, the separate person in his private imagination, but also for readers, the observers of the dream statement. "The Sleepers" is a successful response to the problem. A way to give public meaning to the private dream image, a way to inform "eccentricities and aimlessness" with "a leading idea," is to focus the poem not upon the images themselves but upon the action of the experiencing hero, the perceiving of the images.

To say only this, however, would be to minimize the importance both of Hawthorne's charge to poets and of Whitman's poem, the response to the charge. For Hawthorne's problem is not just the problem of the dream poem, but of the new poetry in general, the poetry of "Personality" (to use Whitman's word), the intensely private poetry that is a great part of the Romantic revolution. In such a poetry, which explores strange worlds and tries to make new ones, all images are more or less private: the dream situation Hawthorne describes simply emphasizes the strangeness and privacy of the images. Similarly, "The Sleepers" is not merely a dream poem: its being a dream poem is symptomatic of its being the kind of poem I shall call the "monodrama," a poetic form that includes much of Whitman's best work—among others, "From Pent-up Aching Rivers," "Passage to India," "Song of the Broad-Axe," and,

138

as we shall see, "Song of Myself," "Song of the Open Road," and "As I Ebb'd with the Ocean of Life."

"Monodrama," a term suggested by Allen and Davis,* seems a convenient rubric for poems in which the focus is an action and the mask that of an "actor," a speaker involved at the present time in an action, not describing an action and giving us guides into it, like a narrator, but actually *going through* the action. The difference between a lyric poem and a monodrama would be that the mask of a lyric poem, the "experiencer," is always turned away from the reader, going through his drama while addressing himself or some imagined object or particular person, whereas the actor puts on at least two of the masks—the experiencer's, the overlooker's, the narrator's, or the teacher's. In these terms, "Scented Herbage" would be a lyric poem and "From Pent-up Aching Rivers" a monodrama.

It is important to distinguish the monodrama from the dramatic monologue. The former is uttered by a speaker who, if we cannot say he is at one with the superior intelligence that is the poet, seems to have his complete sympathy, whereas the speaker in the dramatic monologue is more clearly a "character," more clearly at some distance from the poet. The test is whether we feel easy about interchanging the poet's name and the term "the speaker," as I do in discussing Whitman's monodramas—and all his forms except dramatic monologues like "Vigil Strange I Kept on the Field One Night," where the speaker is a soldier who stands vigil for his dead son, and "Prayer of Columbus," where the explorer, seen as a "batter'd, wreck'd old man," states his faith and is rewarded with a sudden vision. That even these speakers represent familiar aspects of Whitman—the soldier, seen in mourning rather than in battle, thinks of the dead boy as a comrade, and Columbus seems very much a figure for the sick and disappointed poet—is a measure of

---

* *Critical Aids*, p. 27: ". . . in the best of Whitman's longer poems a conflict in his emotions, that is, the emotions of the 'I' in the poem, provides the dramatic situation, or tension, on which the structure rests. These poems might, therefore, be called monodramas: the speaker is racked by a mental or spiritual conflict, which he debates in a soliloquy or dramatizes in a symbolical dialogue. They are not dramatic monologues because they are obviously subjective instead of objective, though the exact degree to which the 'I' represents Walt Whitman, the man in actual life, need not concern us here because the artistic value of the poem does not rest upon this identification."

the relative unimportance of the dramatic monologue for Whitman, whose most significant works enact the turns and maneuvering of a speaker represented as very close to the poet's private self.

Although the dream poem is set in a private world especially strange and spontaneous, the experiences of its hero, and indeed of the hero of monodramas in general, are not merely miscellaneous, nor his images merely private. There is "plot" to the movement of the speaker in a monodrama: action among experiences, which is necessarily more public than the separate experiences themselves. The actor begins at a definable place, and the changes he undergoes are clearly related to the place where he ends. Thus, for instance, we saw the hero in "From Pent-up Aching Rivers" begin by addressing the reader and then steadily withdraw until he has entered the private world of himself and his lover. Actor and experiences inform each other: the reader travels with the hero through the particular moments, defining the experiences by observing their effect upon the moods and actions of the hero, and defining the hero by being alert to the implied connections among the things experienced.

The monodrama does things for the reader, and demands things of him, that Whitman's other kinds of poems do not. The imagistic and didactic poems avoid the problem Hawthorne sets— the imagistic poem emphasizing individual images rather than the interaction between them, the didactic poems having a "leading idea," but only that. Narrative poems, like "Out of the Cradle Endlessly Rocking," present the interaction between things from a point outside the action: a narrator, who is not in the process of change, provides guides to the reader. For that reason—the element of stability in the narrative and of certainty on the part of the reader—a narrative poem lacks some of the strangeness and excitement of a monodrama. We cannot say, as we have for a monodrama, that a narrative is simply a less strange "dream poem": slim as the role of the narrator might be (in "Cradle" it is considerable), the reader is deprived of, or is shielded from, the adventure of seeing the drama unfold as it happens, of having no perspective on it but his own. We have seen in "Cradle" how the narrative voice holds itself more or less steady and separate in its structural envelope, and, in contrast, we have seen in "There Was a

140

Child Went Forth" how the narrative voice shakes loose from its role and becomes involved in the action it describes. Just as the narrative voice "shakes loose" to become a dramatic voice, so does the reader of a monodrama escape from his predetermined, relatively passive role as a reader of narratives. He is suddenly vulnerable to perplexity as the reader of a narrative never is, but he is also open to new challenges and discoveries.

We can get a rough idea of the action in "The Sleepers" by noting what the speaker says about his own movement. At our first meeting we hear him, or overhear him, say that he is engaged in a dream of his own, a dream in which he observes other sleepers (Section 1—"I wander all night in my vision, / . . . Bending with open eyes over the shut eyes of sleepers"). Next the hero announces the abandonment of his position outside the other sleepers (Section 1—"Now I pierce the darkness, new beings appear, / . . . I dream in my dream all the dreams of the other dreamers, / And I become the other dreamers"); and then, after recording various dream images and scenes (Sections 2 and 3), his modification of that new position (Section 4—"I turn but do not extricate myself, / Confused, a past-reading, another, but with darkness yet"). Later, after more description of scenes and, a new element, some telling of stories (Sections 4, 5, and 6), the speaker predicts his withdrawal from his night vision (Section 7—"I am jealous and overwhelm'd with friendliness, / And will go gallivant with the light and air itself"); and finally he says that he is passing from the situation in which we first met him (Section 8—"I too pass from the night").

At the beginning of this action, the speaker describes himself as "Wandering and confused, lost to myself, ill-assorted, contradictory"; at the end he says to the night:

> I stay a while away O night, but I return to you
>   again and love you.
>
> Why should I be afraid to trust myself to you?
> I am not afraid, I have been well brought for-
>   ward by you, . . .
>
>   [P. 433.]

141

But are we convinced? Are the miscellaneous experiences really one grand experience? What after all has happened to make a whole man out of an "ill-assorted" man?

We will not be convinced—the poem will not work—if we listen only to the overt statements that the hero makes about his own action; for he tells us only what he is doing, not why. If we are to believe in the action, if the transformation of the speaker is to be important to us, not merely to the poet, we must search for the special logic that controls both the various experiences and the various moods and statements of the actor. When we read either a lyric or a monodrama, when we meet a speaker who describes an action happening in himself at the present time, as we listen to him, then we must *see* the action happen, not merely be told about it. Beneath the action described overtly by the speaker—the hesitation outside of the other sleepers, the piercing of the darkness, the passing from the night and assertion of confidence— must lie a more profound action, which includes the making of these statements. The actor's overt statements about his movement must be taken not as total guides to the action, as we would take a non-dramatic narrator's statements, but as parts of a different kind of statement—the change in the speaker's manner, his *actual* shifting from one position to another.

As the poem begins, the speaker is almost completely concerned with the problem of his own vision. He bothers about defining his actions; and the erratic quality of those actions—"Pausing, gazing, bending, and stopping"—reveals the "ill-assorted, contradictory" nature of the speaker. Then the speaker does in fact what he says earlier he is doing: his gaze turns toward the sleepers. The external movement reflects, or triggers, a change in attitude. The first particular description of the sleepers does not emphasize their variety, but comes to rest on "little children in their cradles." In two lines filled with images of peace, the actor records the first movement of stillness in his internal discontent:

> How solemn they look there, stretch'd and still,
> How quiet they breathe, the little children in
>   their cradles.

> [P. 424.]

Then he begins to list—corpses, drunkards, onanists, the "sacred idiots." The lines grow as variety is introduced; but the multiplicity is given form by repetition (contrast the deliberately chaotic nature of the lines in "There Was a Child Went Forth" when the speaker is being pulled back into the past), and the paragraph is rounded with a short and balanced line—"The night pervades them and unfolds them." The speaker seems already to be under the peaceful spell of the night.

The description continues to emphasize calmness and quiet love ("The married couple sleep calmly in their bed, / . . . The sisters sleep lovingly side by side in their bed") and is itself calm and quiet until the point where passive description unexpectedly becomes a pair of questions:

> The murderer that is to be hung next day,
>   how does he sleep?
> And the murder'd person, how does he sleep?
>   [P. 425.]

But that interruption is brief, and again the speaker is calm, his words lulling—"The enraged and treacherous dispositions, all, all sleep." So peaceful, in fact, is this speaker who began as "confused," that he can soothe the restless:

> I stand in the dark with drooping eyes by the
>   worst-suffering and the most restless,
> I pass my hands soothingly to and fro a few
>   inches from them,
> The restless sink in their beds, they fit-
>   fully sleep.
>   [P. 425.]

At this point the actor seems already to be Whitman's ideal figure of contentment—the "wound-dresser," if you will, calm, gentle, at peace with himself and eager to bring the world to peace. But the inner balance has yet to be tested. Like the boy in "Cradle," who watches the birds from a distance, "cautiously peering," the speaker in "The Sleepers" is at this point not really experienced, not really a man, for he has not yet really involved himself in things outside himself. Now, no longer unsure, he takes the plunge:

143

> Now I pierce the darkness, new beings appear,
> The earth recedes from me into the night,
> I saw that it was beautiful, and I see that
>   what is not the earth is beautiful.

[P. 425.]

Earlier he sees the sleepers, hovers "a few inches from them"; now he "becomes the other dreamers." Earth, "body," the sleepers he has seen to be beautiful; now he discovers a new world that also is beautiful—the darkness-world of soul ("what is not the earth") and the inhabitants of that world, dream creatures, the "nimble ghosts" of the sleepers' dreams. The discovery is overwhelmingly exciting. If at the beginning of the poem the speaker is depressed, now he is manic—caught up in the wild, mad whirl of the imagination: "I am a dance—play up there! the fit is whirling me fast!" His mood changes abruptly from calm contentment to a reckless joy:

> I am the ever-laughing—it is new moon and
>   twilight,
> I see the hiding of douceurs, I see nimble
>   ghosts whichever way I look,
> Cache and cache again deep in the ground and sea,
>   and where it is neither ground nor sea.
>
> Well do they do their jobs those journeymen
>   divine,
> Only from me can they hide nothing, and would
>   not if they could,
> I reckon I am their boss and they make me a
>   pet besides,
> And surround me and lead me and run ahead when
>   I walk,
> To lift their cunning covers to signify me
>   with stretch'd arms, and resume the way;
> Onward we move, a gay gang of blackguards!
>   with mirth-shouting music and wild-flapping
>   pennants of joy!

[P. 426.]

Dream creatures—and beings who are more than that, the spirits of the universe—reveal themselves to him, leaving the places of their secret work. As they lift "their cunning covers," the hero meets

144

them by throwing off his different, stylistic restraints—his syntax loosens, he uses fewer repetitions, and he breaks laughingly into slang.

Suddenly, as suddenly as it begins, the excitement is over. The speaker's joyous celebration of the "gay gang of blackguards" is complemented by a sober listing of them, the dreamers he has "become." Together the different kinds of statements—one ecstatic, the other reflective—create a kind of symbolic atmosphere, a long view of the mood of the journey. The celebrations and the list both suggest comprehensiveness: the celebration simply by referring to the whole gang of phantoms; the list, short in comparison to Whitman's usual catalogues, in two ways—by emphasizing opposites ("the actor, the actress," "the voter, the politician," "the immigrant and the exile") and by being deliberately miscellaneous, including figures who are markedly unusual ("the criminal that stood in the box," "the stammerer"). Thus the speaker makes a backdrop against which he plays out particular adventures: it is as if he intuits, in these first moments of involvement in the night within his night, the mixed nature of the journey. For us, standing outside the action and waiting to begin our own action of discovery, the backdrop serves a different, public purpose. Even as we become involved in the separate images and scenes that follow, and even as we trace the "leading idea" that connects them, we remember that these particular instances are symbolic of all the dream experiences the poet could be telling us about and that the "leading idea" too is symbolic of the large experience of a hypothetical journey through life, not just the piece of the journey we can see.

So the actor starts his journey twice, as it were: the second beginning demonstrates the drama of transition in particular. His first adventure is his identification with a woman receiving her lover:

> I am she who adorn'd herself and folded her
>   hair expectantly,
> My truant lover has come, and it is dark.
>   [P. 426.]

The setting of the woman's dream readies us for the important ambiguity of the hero's experience. The woman waits in the dark,

145

and the speaker is moving into darkness; the "truant lover" is recognizably male, but the ambiguous "it is dark" raises the possibility that the lover is the "dark" itself. Thus the voice that describes its love affair is at once the woman's and the speaker's; the merging hero tries on a new identity, but still clings to his own:

> Double yourself and receive me darkness,
> Receive me and my lover too, he will not
>   let me go without him.

> I roll myself upon you as upon a bed, I
>   resign myself to the dusk.
>   [P. 426.]

The first line, echoing the hero's "I pierce the darkness," suggests the male movement, the movement of the speaker into the darkness, which must "Double [it]self" like a woman to receive him. In the next moment, however, the voice is female: the woman *and* her lover are sinking into the darkness. The same swift change of identities is dramatized in the single line following. First the voice expresses male aggressiveness ("I roll myself upon you"), then female passivity ("I resign myself"); the darkness, conversely, is first the passive party, then the active party, while being at the same time what it has been from the start of the episode—the place of love, the setting for the love affairs of both hero and woman. Finally the transformation of hero into woman is completed. The speaker has made the claim earlier, but now he really does "become" the other dreamers. To the end of Section 1, the identity of the male hero is subsumed into the identity of the woman: his journey through the night becomes her journey with the new lover darkness, which is striking out for a "shadowy shore." His actions no longer struggle with hers, but lie just beneath them: her reaching hands are his, and when she "fade[s] away" into and with the darkness, which is now the old lover as well as the new, he too fades away.

He fades, that is, into the next adventure. Section 2 seems to grow naturally out of Section 1—its first words, "I descend my western course," follow directly upon the last words of Section 1, "I fade away." But the "I" is a different self from the one that finished the first section: the woman is gone, and the voice is clearly the hero's again. This transformation is like the previous ones. As earlier we are half-way into the statement of the new voice before we realize it is different from the voice of the paragraph, the line, or even the phrase before, so here we are carried swiftly into a new section, introduced to the speaker's new identity as if by a magician's sleight-of-hand. The transformations are sudden, yet in various ways the poet blurs the edges of the break. He repeats key phrases ("Double yourself and receive me darkness, / Receive me and my lover too"), casually joins opposite movements with a bare comma ("I roll myself . . . , / I resign myself"), picks up one of the two threads and follows it ("He whom I call answers me"). The total effect is of the weird reasonableness of a dream: one body exchanges itself for another as if it must.

If the speaker "fade[s] away" into a new identity and a new section of the poem, the identity itself is a fading away and the new section indicates a new aspect of the hero who experiences all the identities. Piercing the darkness, putting the self to the test, results first in a heavy rush of hot love; but now, at the start of Section 2, the speaker moves from young to old, from active to passive, from a preoccupation with love to a preoccupation with death. He travels through a lifetime, and a lifetime through him, in two lines:

> I descend my western course, my sinews are
> flaccid,
> Perfume and youth course through me and I
> am their wake.
> [P. 427.]

He is an old woman, "yellow and wrinkled"; he is "the sleepless widow" looking onto a "winter midnight"; and finally he is the thing of death itself—"A shroud I see and I am the shroud." For a moment death seems to be simply another state of existence—a blankness that cannot be evaluated: "It is dark here under ground, it is not evil or pain here, it is blank here, for reasons." But then death takes on a gloomier look:

> (It seems to me that every thing in the light
> and air ought to be happy,
> Whoever is not in his coffin and the dark
> grave let him know he has enough.)
> [Pp. 427–28.]

147

Darkness—first a setting for perplexity, then a place of joyful discovery—is now itself a danger.

We follow this new turn of the speaker's mind into the third section of the poem, where the hero is a type of the man Whitman himself dreamed of being: a beautiful and courageous giant, in the "prime of . . . middle age." This "gigantic swimmer" is Whitman's ideal man put to the sternest test of experience; his struggles represent the struggles in which, having challenged his calmness by penetrating the darkness, the speaker himself is now engaged. Whereas at the start of the dream journey the speaker can feel exhilarated by the possibility of new experiences, can imagine himself borne along by them to the tune of "mirth-shouting music," now he not only senses the danger in those experiences but even hates them:

> I see his white body, I see his undaunted eyes,
> I hate the swift-running eddies that would dash
>   him head-foremost on the rocks.

> What are you doing you ruffianly red-trickled
>   waves?
> Will you kill the courageous giant? will you
>   kill him in the prime of his middle age?
>   [P. 428.]

What had been a whirling dance of discovery ("I am a dance—play up there! the fit is whirling me fast!") is now a grim dance of death:

> The slapping eddies are spotted with his blood,
>   they bear him away, they roll him, swing him,
>   turn him,
> His beautiful body is borne in the circling eddies,
>   it is continually bruis'd on rocks,
> Swiftly and out of sight is borne the brave corpse.
>   [P. 428.]

Yet, if the swimmer's buffeting represents the speaker's internal turmoil, if both swimmer and speaker are "baffl'd, bang'd, bruis'd," the speaker's response to the difficult experiences of the dream-world is somewhat different from the swimmer's response to the "slapping eddies." Even as the speaker admires the "courageous arms" and "undaunted eyes" of the swimmer, his holding out "while his strength holds out," the speaker's own strength has not held out. The swimmer is defeated by experience, borne "swiftly and out of sight" by the end of this episode; but the speaker's own defeat—his retreat from experience or conquering by experience— is indicated from the beginning of the episode, by his manner of telling it. From the moment when he first "pierce[s] the darkness," the speaker insists that he "becomes" the dreamers or the figures in the dreams, lives their lives as if they are his own; but in the description of the swimmer's struggle he retreats to a position outside the experience—he "sees," he does not "become." This removal from the experience is the speaker's first step toward extricating himself from the darkness: never again in the poem does he "become"; instead, he "sees" from distances further and further removed from the intensity of the experience.

Thus the stance of the speaker throughout Section 3, an implied statement of his psychological situation, prepares us for the overt statement that begins Section 4:

> I turn but do not extricate myself,
> Confused, a past-reading, another, but
>   with darkness yet.
>
> [P. 428.]

The confusion here is very different from the confusion in which he begins his journey. Then he is "lost to [him]self" because he has not yet entered into the long night of experience—cannot, in fact, escape from himself and "connect" to other life. Now, on the other hand, he is "baffl'd" because he has seen too much, has learned that darkness holds death as well as love, and is therefore at once committed to the revelations of this new world and fearful of that commitment. So different is this new confusion, in fact, that it is questionable that the hero's retreat is only a defeat. Becoming the woman, becoming the shroud, he tastes of both love and death, and the experience of death makes apparent the element of self-destruction that is also in love, and in all experience. Sensing that he is the swimmer who will be destroyed by the buffets of experience, he saves his own identity by placing the swimmer

149

outside himself. The retreat from direct participation in experience
may be in one sense a denial of self, but it is also an affirmation.

The retreat becomes even more apparent as the speaker proceeds
in Section 4. Both the scene itself and the attitude of the speaker
indicate the increasing helplessness Whitman feels in his journey
of experience. Here many men die, instead of one, and the emphasis is not on the struggle, the "holding out," but on the
"howls of dismay" and the drowning. The ship, the men on the
ship, the speaker who looks on—all are helpless before the tempest,
the "razory ice-wind," and the pounding surf:

> The beach is cut by the razory ice-wind, the
>   wreck-guns sound,
> The tempest lulls, the moon comes floundering
>   through the drifts.
>
> I look where the ship helplessly heads end on,
>   I hear the burst as she strikes, I hear the
>   howls of dismay, they grow fainter and fainter.
>
> I cannot aid with my wringing fingers,
> I can but rush to the surf and let it
>   drench me and freeze upon me.
>   [Pp. 428–29.]

Like the darkness, the sea, as we have seen hinted in "Cradle," is
endlessly rich with possibility but at the same time full of danger
and death. To protect himself, Whitman retreats to the position of
the boy at the start of his experience in "Cradle," "cautiously
peering, absorbing"—but because he has already visited the night,
he has more than that boy's sense of the wealth and the horror of
experience, of how much there is for him to do and of how little he
can.

Section 5 represents a further attempt at extrication from the
darkness. In it the actor changes his role: his voice is no longer
dramatic, the voice of a being passing through action at the
moment he describes it, but that of a narrator, telling about a past
action. The scene described in Section 4 is a scene from Whitman's
own life, "a past-reading," as he calls it, but it is represented as
happening in the present time of the dreamworld. In contrast, the
description of Washington's farewell to his men, a story that

Whitman himself had been told, is represented openly as a story: Whitman begins it with "Now of the older war-days, the defeat at Brooklyn." The speaker who is helpless in Section 4 is now almost invulnerable to experience, for he is fast becoming a detached observer and reporter, removed from the dreamers' night that lies within his own poetic night. The result is a scene much less private and dreamlike than any since he first entered the dreamers' darkness: the beginning, "Now of . . . ," is an invitation to the public. The scene itself is again concerned with cold, weeping, and death; but it moves in the end toward peace and comradeship, restating Whitman's typical movement toward comradeship when he is wounded by experience:

> Now of the older war-days, the defeat at Brooklyn,
> Washington stands inside the lines, he stands on
>   the intrench'd hills amid a crowd of officers,
> His face is cold and damp, he cannot repress the
>   weeping drops,
> . . . .
> He sees the slaughter of the southern braves
>   confided to him by their parents.
>
> The same at last and at last when peace is declared,
> He stands in the room of the old tavern, the
>   well-belov'd soldiers all pass through,
> The officers speechless and slow draw near in
>   their turns,
> The chief encircles their necks with his arm
>   and kisses them on the cheek,
> He kisses lightly the wet cheeks one after
>   another, he shakes hands and bids good-by
>   to the army.
>
> [P. 429.]

It is an upward turn of the imagination. Even as Whitman is retreating from the perplexities and dangers of the night journey, the play of his mind indicates that he can find love as well as death, "light and air" within the darkness. It may be, in fact, that a retreat from experience is necessary before experience can be felt as something other than assault.

The next section is even more openly a narrative. Whitman gives the story of Washington's farewell a certain dramatic immediacy by telling it in the historical present tense, but in describing this episode of his mother and a squaw he uses the most familiar of narrative techniques:

> Now what my mother told me one day as we sat
>   at dinner together,
> Of when she was a nearly grown girl living home
>   with her parents on the old homestead.
>
> [P. 429.]

Finally the speaker is well out of the especially strange night within the night—facing the reader directly, no longer hidden by the subtle shields of indirection. The object of his attention is correspondingly closer to "light and air." The story of the relationship between his mother and the squaw is a story of love and loss ("She remembered her many a winter and many a summer, / But the red squaw never came nor was heard of there again"); but the emphasis is strongly on beauty and love. The squaw sounds like a character out of the Children of Adam group, although Whitman allows her more particularity than the woman of those conceptual poems:

> Her hair, straight, shiny, coarse, black, profuse,
>   half-envelop'd her face,
> Her step was free and elastic, and her voice
>   sounded exquisitely as she spoke.
>
> My mother look'd in delight and amazement at the
>   stranger,
> She look'd at the freshness of her tall-borne
>   face and full and pliant limbs,
> The more she look'd upon her she loved her,
> Never before had she seen such wonderful beauty
>   and purity, . . .
>
> [P. 430.]

This "beauty and purity" is lost to Whitman's mother in the past but is central now to Whitman's imagination, the play of which has enabled him to find in himself not only the sadness and perplexities of "Autumn and winter," but also "love and summer" —"O love and summer, you are in the dreams and in me" (p. 430).

152

Still, remembering his mother's "amour of the light and air" is not quite having it himself:

> A show of the summer softness—a contact of some-
>   thing unseen—an amour of the light and air,
> I am jealous and overwhelm'd with friendliness,
> And will go gallivant with the light and air myself.
>
> [P. 430.]

The dreamworld of imagination is, for Whitman, not quite the world of reality. He has saved himself from drowning, and even has worked himself back to the notion that involvement in experience can be self-fulfilling as well as self-destructive; but he is not content. He would "gallivant with the light and air" even as he once had gallivanted into darkness with "a gay gang of black-guards."

Thus in Sections 7 and 8 the speaker, already removed from the dreamer's darkness, leaves even his own dreamworld: "I too pass from the night," he says in Section 8, but he really has "passed" before he says so. Once an experiencer, concerned primarily with himself, living through an action as he describes it, next a narrator, turning toward the reader to the degree that he removes himself from the action he describes, he now becomes a teacher, no longer *in* his "vision" but telling about it—turned directly toward the reader to issue didactic statements about dreaming and sleepers in general.

The first statement simply identifies dreaming as an act of the imagination, involved with merging and wish-fulfillment, in which everyone participates:

> Elements merge in the night, ships make tacks in
>   the dreams,
> The sailor sails, the exile returns home,
>
> . . . .
>
> The Dutchman voyages home, and the Scotchman and
>   Welshman voyage home, and the native of the
>   Mediterranean voyages home, . . .
>
> [Pp. 430–31.]

But the movement of the poem to this point forces us to doubt the suggestion that dreaming is all wish-fulfillment, all a pleasant escape:

> The poor Irishman lives in the simple house of
>   his childhood with the well-known neighbors
>   and faces,
> They warmly welcome him, he is barefoot again,
>   he forgets he is well off, . . .
>
>   [P. 431.]

Actually, as we have seen at almost every turn of the journey described by the speaker himself, the dream is terrifyingly capable of being a nightmare.

If the speaker's summary statement is not true to his own experience, in what sense can we believe in it and him? Only when we remember the speaker's present psychological situation and his present relationship to his dream—only, that is, when we conceive of the didactic statement not as an overt statement but as an act dramatically appropriate to the speaker at this point in the poem—does this blandly optimistic description of the dream begin to make sense. For the speaker has emerged from the sea of difficulties; safe on the shore, he looks at the sea with different eyes. His situation is analogous to that of the survivors in Stephen Crane's "The Open Boat," who, from their perspective on the beach, can see the meaningless hell from which they have just escaped as "white waves [which pace] to and fro in the moonlight."

Yet, if we must be skeptical of these visions from the shore, if we must remember that they are perceptions of experience from men no longer involved in experience, we must at the same time accept the visions as true to the journey. For these men have after all been through experience: they all have dared the sea and the night, and in a sense have thereby earned the right to see order and harmony. Whitman is not blind to what he has experienced: he remembers the wildness and the bloodiness, and sounds something like a man who is trying to convince himself of his own argument:

> I swear they are all beautiful,
> Every one that sleeps is beautiful, every
>   thing in the dim light is beautiful,
> The wildest and bloodiest is over, and
>   all is peace.
>
>   [P. 431.]

This grasping for peace and beauty is revealed all through the last two sections. It is expressed in Whitman's assurance that "the antipodes . . . are averaged now—one is no better than the other, the night and sleep have liken'd them and restored them" (p. 431); in his argument that "the soul is always beautiful, the universe is duly in order, every thing is in its place" (p. 432); and in the familiar proclamation of a universal democracy of health and purity:

> The sleepers are very beautiful as they lie
> unclothed,
> They flow hand in hand over the whole earth
> from east to west as they lie unclothed,
> The Asiatic and African are hand in hand, the
> European and American are hand in hand,
> Learn'd and unlearn'd are hand in hand, and
> male and female are hand in hand,
> The bare arm of the girl crosses the bare
> breast of her lover, they press close
> without lust, his lips press her neck,
>
> . . . .
> The felon steps forth from the prison, the
> insane becomes sane, the suffering of
> sick persons is reliev'd,
>
> . . . .
> Stiflings and passages open, the paralyzed
> become supple,
> The swell'd and convuls'd and congested
> awake to themselves in condition,
> They pass the invigoration of the night and
> the chemistry of the night, and awake.
>
> [Pp. 432–33.]

Denying Whitman the statement of this vision would be like denying him his reaching for a comrade's hand in "Of the Terrible Doubt of Appearances"; it would be like requiring Whitman to be always the central Whitman, struggling between alternatives, refusing him the right to be either of the polar Whitmans, who adopt clear and uncomplicated positions. Finding the comrade's hand and taking the sure stance are necessary tactics, which in their way order the chaos of "flashes and specks."

In the last eight lines of the poem, Whitman abandons didacticism and manages a true summary, a passage that incorporates the various ambiguities of the speaker's situation. The long didactic passages have accomplished their purpose: they are the final retreat of the speaker, and their calming influence finally allows him to express the complexity of his situation, if not really to be at peace. First he tells us what we have known since early in Section 7: "I too pass from the night." Then he addresses the night in tones that express exactly the contradictory attitudes he has toward the night —his fear of its wildness and bloodiness, his fear, that is, of being destroyed by too much experience, and his gratitude for the fullness and strength that the night has given him, his sense that the night has not drowned him but has made him grand:

> I stay a while away O night, but I return to you
>   again and love you.
>
> Why should I be afraid to trust myself to you?
> I am not afraid, I have been well brought for-
>   ward by you,
> I love the rich running day, but I do not desert
>   her in whom I lay so long,
> I know not how I came of you and I know not where
>   I go with you, but I know I came well and shall
>   go well.
>
> I will stop only a time with the night, and rise
>   betimes,
> I will duly pass the day O my mother, and duly
>   return to you.
>
> [P. 433.]

Why, we wonder, has the speaker "extricated" himself, if he is so eager to return? Why bother to question himself about fear, if he is in fact not half afraid? Thus the contradictory promises: "I stay a while away O night, but I return to you again," as against "I will stop only a time with the night, and rise betimes." The night journey has been in no sense an easy cure, a sure progression toward an ideal world of order. The speaker has begun in perplexity—"ill-assorted, contradictory, lost to [him]self"; and he has been "well brought forward" not into peace, but into a more profound perplexity, that of knowing his contradictions and himself.

That same perplexed hero, still somewhat shy about admitting his confusion, addresses us at the beginning of "Song of Myself."

Although "The Sleepers" and "Song of Myself" were probably written at about the same time, since they both make their first appearance, as untitled poems, in the original edition of *Leaves of Grass*, there is no hint from Whitman that the two poems are meant to be read together. In contrast to his later practice with "Out of the Cradle Endlessly Rocking" and "As I Ebb'd with the Ocean of Life," Whitman does not place "The Sleepers" next to "Song of Myself" even in the first edition; and afterwards, in one of the most clumsy of his arrangements, he puts even more distance between the two poems, assigning "The Sleepers" to a spot directly following "Passage to India" and "Prayer of Columbus," those poems of the 1870's. It is nevertheless helpful to think of "Song of Myself" and "The Sleepers" as companion pieces. If "The Sleepers" begins with Whitman about to enter his poetic vision and presents his entry and withdrawal, "Song of Myself" starts when the poet has returned from his vision, and dramatizes his gradual approach to another poetic vision, his startlingly similar adventures, and a withdrawal significantly different.*

* Some recent criticism of "Song of Myself"—Rountree, "Indirect Expression"; Adams, "Revaluation"; and Roy Harvey Pearce, *The Continuity of American Poetry*, pp. 69–83—has, in trying to account for the "openness" of the poem, concerned itself with the opportunities it makes possible for readers. This welcome movement away from earlier readings of the poem, which by and large either see it as formless or impose rather mechanical structures upon it, is essentially an attempt to resist the traditional definition of form. It is best summarized by Pearce, pp. 74–75: "The structure of *Song of Myself* . . . evinces little of that internal-external sense of necessity (in its most extreme forms, an Aristotelian beginning, middle and end; or a New Critical paradox, tension, ambiguity, or irony) which we tend to demand of an achieved literary work. True enough, the argument of the poem centers on points of psychic intensity; nonetheless, there is no fixed rational or affective scheme whereby we may decide that a given section should or should not have begun where it begins and ended where it ends, or contains what it contains. It is this 'formal' difficulty which has most often disturbed readers of Whitman and sent them to a poem like 'Out of the Cradle . . .' with its tight, firm internal design. But this is a specious difficulty; and the argument of the poem is, in its own way, entirely meaningful and quite of a piece with its epic (or must one now say, proto-epic?) intention. There is, in fact, a specific form and content for such insight as the poem makes possible, even though the specificity is entirely a matter of a private transaction between the poet and his world. For since that world contains the poet's readers as well as the poet, his is an insight which, if his readers are bold enough, will move them to transform themselves as he has transformed himself. All that he demands of them is that they yield to his poem, as has the world. This done, the 'procreant urge' will be spontaneously released and the readers will be on their way to their own private transformations. Yielding to the poem, in short, they will release in themselves the creative energies which will make them nothing less than heroic."

My own view is that even Whitman's monodramas, while they are more open

157

Laying claim to perfect internal contentment, the speaker at the start of "Song of Myself" seems to stand in contrast to the one at the very end of "The Sleepers," who demonstrates, by his contradictory statements, a sense of disparity between what he actually is and what he thinks he should be. That latter speaker's sense of internal division is described specifically in a notebook jotting, and, greatly magnified, in "As I Ebb'd with the Ocean of Life," where Whitman admits to feeling a distinction between "the real Me," the ideal self, and the self in the actual pettiness of its particularity. In the words of the notebook entry, ". . . *behind* all the faculties of the human being, as the sight, the other senses and even the emotions and the intellect, stands the real power, the mystical identity, the real I or Me or You." [3] Whereas the "real Me" appears here and in "As I Ebb'd" as a kind of phantom, distant from the particular body, it seems at the start of "Song of Myself" to be together with the "I": as Whitman says in Section 3, "I and this mystery here we stand." That even here the "mystery" is not actually at one with the "I," suggests that the speaker may not be as healthy and relaxed as he seems.

The first section of "Song of Myself" promises a beautifully harmonious relationship among poet, Nature, and reader:

> I celebrate myself, and sing myself,
> And what I assume you shall assume,
> For every atom belonging to me as good belongs to you.
>
> I loafe and invite my soul,
> I lean and loafe at my ease observing a spear of summer grass.
>
> My tongue, every atom of my blood, form'd from this soil,
>   this air,
> Born here of parents born here from parents the same, and
>   their parents the same,
> I, now thirty-seven years old in perfect health begin,
> Hoping to cease not till death.
>
> [Pp. 28–29.]

---

than the usual poem because they make the activity of the reader a part of their story, are not as open as Whitman liked to claim: that they do have "beginning, middle and end," which are based on the speaker's shifts of position and on certain responses that Whitman requires the reader to make.

The poet, it seems, is a "divine medium": he will let Nature speak through him "without check with original energy" (p. 29). If he sets himself off from his audience by insisting that he is a fourth-generation American who is thirty-seven years old and in perfect health, it is only because he can best celebrate the individuality of each reader and the perfection of Nature by celebrating his own individuality.

Whitman's image for entering the world of imagination, we recall, is the heterosexual act of love: in the Children of Adam poems, he pours his seed into a waiting world; in "The Sleepers," he "pierce[s]" the darkness. The speaker we meet at the start of "Song of Myself" has already experienced the sexual, imaginative act, although in a passive role:

> I mind how once we lay such a transparent summer
>   morning,
> How you settled your head athwart my hips and
>   gently turn'd over upon me,
> And parted the shirt from my bosom-bone, and plunged
>   your tongue to my bare-stript heart,
> And reach'd till you felt my beard, and reach'd till
>   you held my feet.
>
> [Section 5, p. 33.]

He remembers himself as passive because these lines describe not his plunging into the imaginative vision, the subject of the next lines, but the first stage of the imaginative act—his discovery of the imaginative world into which he will plunge, his seizure by his soul, the spirit of the imagination. The man who speaks to us in the present time, who says, "I lean and loafe at my ease observing a spear of summer grass," has returned from both the discovery and the plunge and is enjoying the "wholesome relief, repose, content" that he anticipates at the end of "Spontaneous Me." The repose, like the activity, is imaginative as well as physical: after withdrawing from his poetic vision, Whitman rests in the didactic form. But, as at the end of "The Sleepers," the harmony is precarious: the speaker is actually concealing the "struggle and turmoil" out of which he speaks.

In Section 2 the wonderfully relaxed and harmonious bard we meet in Section 1, reveals some kind of inner split:

159

Houses and rooms are full of perfumes, the shelves
    are crowded with perfumes,
I breathe the fragrance myself and know it and like it,
The distillation would intoxicate me also, but I shall
    not let it.

The atmosphere is not a perfume, it has no taste of
    the distillation, it is odorless,
It is for my mouth forever, I am in love with it,
I will go to the bank by the wood and become undisguised
    and naked,
I am mad for it to be in contact with me.

                                   [Section 2, p. 29.]

In the first section he loafs on the grass and, claiming to be "form'd from this soil, this air," is condescending toward "Creeds and schools." But now he confesses that he has a powerful tendency toward "Houses and rooms," an inclination he controls only with effort ("I shall not let it"); and on the other hand, although he professes an overwhelming love for the essential odor that is the odorlessness of the atmosphere, he indicates at the same time that he cannot now "go to the bank by the wood and become undisguised and naked." So his actions, if not his speech, check Nature on two fronts at once. He is impelled to be both in the rooms and on the bank in the wood, but he resists both the wholly mechanistic and the wholly organic impulse, and is left sprawled lazily on the grass, within eyeshot of both rooms and woods.

    The two modes of talk with which Whitman closes the section indicate his opposite loyalties:

The smoke of my own breath,
Echoes, ripples, buzz'd whispers, love-root,
    silk-thread, crotch and vine,
My respiration and inspiration, the beating of my
    heart, the passing of blood and air through my lungs,
The sniff of green leaves and dry leaves, and of the
    shore and dark-color'd sea-rocks, and of hay in
    the barn,
The sound of the belch'd words of my voice loos'd to
    the eddies of the wind,
A few light kisses, a few embraces, a reaching around
    of arms,

160

The play of shine and shade on the trees as the
    supple boughs wag,
The delight alone or in the rush of the streets,
    or along the fields and hill-sides,
The feeling of health, the full-noon trill, the
    song of me rising from bed and meeting the sun.

Have you reckon'd a thousand acres much? have you
    reckon'd the earth much?
Have you practis'd so long to learn to read?
Have you felt so proud to get at the meaning of poems?

Stop this day and night with me and you shall
    possess the origin of all poems,
You shall possess the good of the earth and sun,
    (there are millions of suns left,)
You shall no longer take things at second or third
    hand, nor look through the eyes of the dead, nor
    feed on the spectres in books,
You shall not look through my eyes either, nor take
    things from me,
You shall listen to all sides and filter them from
    your self.

                              [Section 2, pp. 29–30.]

The lively catalogue of images is the speech of the naked, woodsy
poet who reels off his list in "Spontaneous Me." Unconnected
logically to the rest of the section, having no argumentative
purpose, it seeks simply to evoke the mystery of things, and would
therefore seem to be the true expression of the man whom
Whitman, in Section 3 as in Section 1, represents himself as being:

To elaborate is no avail, learn'd and unlearn'd
    feel that it is so.

Sure as the most certain sure, plumb in the uprights,
    well entretied, braced in the beams,
Stout as a horse, affectionate, haughty, electrical,
I and this mystery here we stand.

                              [Section 3, p. 31.]

Yet part of him insists on voicing didactic elaborations. The
didactic portion of the passage that closes Section 2, although it
scorns "the spectres in books," recalls the speech of the professor in

"The Base of All Metaphysics"; despite his denial, Whitman tries to make the reader look through his eyes.

Section 4 continues the pattern of alternation in which Whitman first poses as completely harmonious (Sections 1 and 3) and then hints at an inner struggle (Section 2). Now he admits the existence of a separate "Me myself," which stands "Apart from the pulling and hauling," "amused, complacent, compassionating, idle, unitary." The admission reveals that the poet is more like the hero of "The Sleepers" or "As I Ebb'd" than he has wanted to say, and our suspicions are confirmed by his demonstration, even as he takes his harmonious stand, that he is indeed bothered by the "pulling and hauling":

> Trippers and askers surround me,
> People I meet, the effect upon me of my early life
>   or the ward and city I live in, or the nation,
> The latest dates, discoveries, inventions, societies,
>   authors old and new,
> My dinner, dress, associates, looks, compliments, dues,
> The real or fancied indifference of some man or woman
>   I love,
> The sickness of one of my folks or of myself, or ill-
>   doing or loss or lack of money, or depressions or
>   exaltations,
> Battles, the horrors of fratricidal war, the fever of
>   doubtful news, the fitful events;
> These come to me days and nights and go from me again,
> But they are not the Me myself.
>
> [Section 4, p. 32.]

A gap has suddenly appeared between the ideal self and the actual self—the same gap hinted at in "The Sleepers" and described in "As I Ebb'd" and the notebook entry. The gap, of course, has been there all the time, disguised by the pose of harmony. The man who promises in Section 1 that he will "harbor for good or bad" is, it turns out, only too eager to reject the bad. He remembers that he "sweated through fog with linguists and contenders" and confesses that even now worries and fears "come to [him] days and nights"; but he would dismiss from his identity, "what I am," the sweat and the tripping and asking.

162

The first four sections present, then, a portrait of a man torn between celebration of his ideal self, the self harmonious with readers and all the world, and acknowledgment of his "actual self," the self that must contend with the "pulling and hauling" of everyday difficulties. The rest of the poem records the speaker's long struggle to modify his attitudes toward those warring selves, thereby to reconcile them and make a whole identity.

The struggle takes particular form as a drama of the speaker's shifting relationships to readers and to a poetic vision of the sort we have seen enacted in "The Sleepers." At the start of Section 5, having introduced himself and his purpose, the speaker is ready to move toward the real center of his interest. He has suggested from the beginning that the really important action he will present is an act of the poetic imagination:

> I celebrate myself, and sing myself,
> . . . .
> I loafe and invite my soul, . . .
> [Section 1, p. 28.]

His characteristic act, that with which he can best celebrate his individuality, is singing, or so he says: his "tongue" in particular is "form'd from this soil, this air," and he will permit Nature to "speak." Now, in Section 5, he fulfills his promise. Still posing as the harmonious man—emphasizing, as he does in Section 3, the equality of his body and soul—he invokes his poetic muse:

> I believe in you my soul, the other I am must
>   not abase itself to you,
> And you must not be abased to the other.
>
> Loafe with me on the grass, loose the stop from
>   your throat,
> Not words, not music or rhyme I want, not custom
>   or lecture, not even the best,
> Only the lull I like, the hum of your valvèd voice.
> [Section 5, pp. 32–33.]

He wants his soul to sing through his mouth a special kind of song: a song without music or rhyme, as we could have predicted after reading the 1855 Preface; a song free of didacticism, "even the

163

best"; a song, in fact, that has no words but simply provides the
kind of lulling accompaniment suitable for the story that follows:

> I mind how once we lay such a transparent summer
> morning,
> How you settled your head athwart my hips and
> gently turn'd over upon me,
> And parted the shirt from my bosom-bone, and
> plunged your tongue to my bare-stript heart,
> And reach'd till you felt my beard, and reach'd
> till you held my feet.
>
> Swiftly arose and spread around me the peace and
> knowledge that pass all the argument of the
> earth,
> And I know that the hand of God is the promise
> of my own,
> And I know that the spirit of God is the brother
> of my own,
> And that all the men ever born are also my brothers,
> and the women my sisters and lovers,
> And that a kelson of the creation is love,
> And limitless are leaves stiff or drooping in the
> fields,
> And brown ants in the little wells beneath them,
> And mossy scabs of the worm fence, heap'd stones,
> elder, mullein and poke-weed.
>
> [Section 5, p. 33.]

Whitman never wrote more beautiful lines. The passage is pointed
to with pride by all lovers of his poetry—and in particular by critics
who want either to demonstrate Whitman's mysticism or to
celebrate him as a prophet of universal peace. Certainly it does
evoke a sense of everlasting harmony. But we must still wonder
whether this re-creation in tranquillity is true to the moment as it
really was, or whether we must disbelieve this singer even as we love
his song. For this account of the imaginative vision is remarkably
like the account at the end of "The Sleepers," a re-creation that, as
a kind of protective device, represents as peaceful a journey filled
with horror and suffering. The existence of "The Sleepers" requires
us at least to entertain the notion that the vision described from
outside is quite different from what it is in the living of it, and that

Whitman's truly characteristic act of the imagination is not to sing a song about a past experience but to go through the vision and describe it as he goes.

If we must wait to find out what the vision and the speaker are really like, so must the speaker himself. He spends a good half of the poem, until the end of Section 32, working himself up to take the plunge into the merging vision that, in his perplexity and innocence, he has taken so quickly in "The Sleepers." Sections 5–7 are the first stage in his approach to the vision. He edges toward it by recalling the previous vision of merger; and then, picking up from the last words of his story ("heap'd stones, elder, mullein and poke-weed"), tries another approach:

> A child said *What is the grass?* fetching it to me
> with full hands;
> How could I answer the child? I do not know what
> it is any more than he.
>
> I guess it must be the flag of my disposition, out
> of hopeful green stuff woven.
>
> Or I guess it is the handkerchief of the Lord,
> A scented gift and remembrancer designedly dropt,
> Bearing the owner's name someway in the corners,
> that we may see and remark, and say *Whose?*
>
> Or I guess the grass is itself a child, the pro-
> duced babe of the vegetation.
>
> Or I guess it is a uniform hieroglyphic,
> And it means, Sprouting alike in broad zones
> and narrow zones,
> Growing among black folks as among white,
> Kanuck, Tuckahoe, Congressman, Cuff, I give them
> the same, I receive them the same.
>
> And now it seems to me the beautiful uncut hair
> of graves.
>
> [Section 6, pp. 33–34.]

What starts out to be another story turns into a poetic exercise in the present time. Whitman lets his mind run easily over a thing: he makes metaphors before our eyes. Like the vision in "The Sleep-

165

ers," this different kind of poetic flight comes to rest on an image having to do with death. But here, consciously playing the poet, Whitman is more in control of his flight: instead of being lacerated by new experience, he "uses" the image to turn toward happier thoughts:

> Tenderly will I use you curling grass,
> It may be you transpire from the breasts
>   of young men,
> It may be if I had known them I would have
>   loved them,
> It may be you are from old people, or from
>   offspring taken soon out of their mothers'
>   laps,
> And here you are the mothers' laps.
>
> . . . .
>
> I wish I could translate the hints about the
>   dead young men and women,
> And the hints about old men and mothers, and
>   the offspring taken soon out of their laps.
>
> What do you think has become of the young and
>   old men?
> And what do you think has become of the women
>   and children?
>
> They are alive and well somewhere,
> The smallest sprout shows there is really
>   no death,
> And if ever there was it led forward life, and
>   does not wait at the end to arrest it,
> And ceas'd the moment life appear'd.
>
> All goes onward and outward, nothing collapses,
> And to die is different from what any one supposed,
>   and luckier.
>
> [Section 6, pp. 34–35.]

To use the grass tenderly means also, of course, to lie on it gently: we are reminded that the speaker is leaning and loafing, "observing a spear of summer grass." Therefore we are reminded also that he is part descriptive poet and part didactic poet. On the one hand, the

166

grass makes its own meanings (the blades, or leaves, are "uttering tongues") and the poet, to pass along its hints to readers, need only record the different shapes it takes; on the other hand, he must "translate" its hints in direct statements like, ". . . to die is different from what any one supposed, and luckier."

Thus the poetic exercise, the closest Whitman has been yet to engaging in the poetic vision of merging, leads away from the vision and toward didacticism. Section 7 continues the didacticism that closes Section 6 and adds an aggressive tone:

> I am not an earth nor an adjunct of an earth,
> I am the mate and companion of people, all just
>   as immortal and fathomless as myself,
> (They do not know how immortal, but I know.)
>
> Every kind for itself and its own, for me
>   mine male and female,
> For me those that have been boys and that love
>   women,
> For me the man that is proud and feels how it
>   stings to be slighted,
> For me the sweet-heart and the old maid, for
>   me mothers and the mothers of mothers,
> For me lips that have smiled, eyes that have
>   shed tears,
> For me children and the begetters of children.
>
> Undrape! you are not guilty to me, nor stale
>   nor discarded,
> I see through the broadcloth and gingham whether
>   or no,
> And am around, tenacious, acquisitive, tireless,
>   and cannot be shaken away.
>   [Section 7, p. 35.]

Of course, in this speaker who wavers between the rooms and the woods, the didactic mood too can turn toward its opposite poetic mood. The final didactic thrust—"Undrape!"—leads into the second stage of Whitman's approach toward his poetic vision, Sections 8–15. We find him acting out his tenacious acquisitiveness, fulfilling the promise of the descriptive catalogues that have been alternating with didactic statements. He is moving very close to the vision of merger:

> The little one sleeps in its cradle,
> I lift the gauze and look a long time, and
>   silently brush away flies with my hand.
>
> The youngster and the red-faced girl turn
>   aside up the bushy hill,
> I peeringly view them from the top.
>
> The suicide sprawls on the bloody floor of
>   the bedroom,
> I witness the corpse with its dabbled hair, I
>   note where the pistol has fallen.
>
> The blab of the pave, tires of carts, sluff of
>   boot-soles, talk of the promenaders,
> The heavy omnibus, the driver with his interrogating
>   thumb, the clank of the shod horses on the granite
>   floor,
> . . . .
> Arrests of criminals, slights, adulterous offers
>   made, acceptances, rejections with convex lips,
> I mind them or the show or resonance of them—I
>   come and I depart.
>   [Section 8, pp. 35–36.]

Three imagistic scenes, moving from birth through lusty young life to death, from peace to excitement to suffering; then a catalogue, a rush of particulars, as if to fill up that range of life and mood. But even this flood of interest in the things around him is not quite the wild dance of merger: Whitman is careful to say that he sees, does not "become"—"I lift," "I peeringly view," "I witness," "I mind."

This cautious position outside the life he describes is typical of the hero's stance in Sections 8–15. Except for four incidents on which he does not spend much time—when he becomes a loader of hay (Section 9), a hunter, a sailor, and a clam-digger (Section 10) —the speaker's adventures in this group of sections are vicarious only. He sees the marriage of a trapper and an Indian girl (Section 10), is host to a runaway slave (Section 10), watches a lonesome

168

woman watch "Twenty-eight young men bathe by the shore" (Section 11), loiters by a butcher-boy (Section 12), follows the movements of blacksmiths (Section 12), admires the proud driving of a negro carriageman (Section 13), rambles past wood-drake and wood-duck, jay, and bay mare (Section 13), "listen[s] close" to the cry of the wild gander and stops by animals wild and domesticated, the moose, the cat, the "litter of the grunting sow" and "brood of turkey-hen" (Section 14). Section 15 is a catalogue over sixty lines long that "completes" Sections 9–14 in the way that the catalogue in Section 8 completes the preceding separate pictures. In it the speaker travels everywhere, recording "all the changes of city and country"; but always, as indicated by parenthetical remarks carefully worded and placed, he makes clear that he is spectator to the action and not participant.

The didactic statement that closes Section 15 is an apt summary of what has been happening in this stage of Whitman's movement toward the poetic vision of his most intense involvement:

> The city sleeps and the country sleeps,
> The living sleep for their time, the dead sleep
> for their time,
> The old husband sleeps by his wife and the young
> husband sleeps by his wife;
> And these tend inward to me, and I tend outward
> to them,
> And such as it is to be of these more or less I am,
> And of these one and all I weave the song of myself.
> [Section 15, p. 44.]

His imagination has waked enough to describe the things outside of himself; but it has not, except in a few instances, become identified with them. Unlike the child and the beings of the child's world in "There Was a Child Went Forth," this perceiver and the things around him do not immediately "become" each other; rather, they "tend" toward each other.

The didactic explanation itself, of course, is a sign that the speaker's involvement is less than complete. It is part of a pattern of didacticism that emerges gradually toward the end of Sections 8–15:

169

In me the caresser of life wherever moving, backward
    as well as forward sluing,
To niches aside and junior bending, not a person or
    object missing,
Absorbing all to myself and for this song.

Oxen that rattle the yolk and chain or halt in the
    leafy shade, what is that you express in your eyes?
It seems to me more than all the print I have read in
    my life.

[Section 13, p. 40.]

The press of my foot to the earth springs a hundred
    affections,
They scorn the best I can do to relate them.

. . . .

What is commonest, cheapest, nearest, easiest, is Me,
Me going in for my chances, spending for vast returns,
Adorning myself to bestow myself on the first that
    will take me,
Not asking the sky to come down to my good will,
Scattering it freely forever.

[Section 14, p. 41.]

If the sense that "the body balks account" can lead on the one
hand, as in "I Sing the Body Electric," to singing a list of names, it
can lead also to didacticism—the attempt, made even as its
probable failure is acknowledged, to say directly just why the thing
is important. Print may not serve to "relate" things or man's
responses to things, but the poet must try anyhow, with all the
different kinds of talk available to him.

Thus the urge toward didacticism, which appears briefly in
Sections 8–15 as Whitman grows dissatisfied with his strings of
pictures, becomes dominant in Sections 16–25. The speaker explains the significance of the voyage he has just reported, giving us
categories for the experiences that he has made seem miscellaneous:

I am of old and young, of the foolish as much as
    the wise,
Regardless of others, ever regardful of others,

170

> Maternal as well as paternal, a child as well
>   as a man,
> Stuff'd with the stuff that is coarse and stuff'd
>   with the stuff that is fine, . . .
>   [Section 16, p. 44.]

Again, as in Sections 5–7 and sometimes in Sections 1–4, he insists that he is perfectly in harmony with the flow of the universe:

> I know I am solid and sound,
> To me the converging objects of the universe
>   perpetually flow,
> All are written to me, and I must get what the
>   writing means.
>
> I know I am deathless,
> I know this orbit of mine cannot be swept by a
>   carpenter's compass,
> I know I shall not pass like a child's carlacue
>   cut with a burnt stick at night.
>
> I know I am august,
> I do not trouble my spirit to vindicate itself
>   or be understood,
> I see that the elementary laws never apologize,
> (I reckon I behave no prouder than the level I
>   plant my house by, after all.)
>
> I exist as I am, that is enough,
> If no other in the world be aware I sit content,
> And if each and all be aware I sit content.
>   [Section 20, pp. 47–48.]

> I am the poet of the Body and I am the poet of the Soul,
> The pleasures of heaven are with me and the pains of
>   hell are with me,
> The first I graft and increase upon myself, the latter
>   I translate into a new tongue.
>   [Section 21, p. 48.]

He is content, claims this man in whom body and soul are a unity, whether or not we are "aware." But this is only the voice of the *poseur* talking, that part of the speaker which pretends that the poet is beautifully harmonious. Murmuring protests, hinting that

171

all is not quite what it seems, is the other part, which would acknowledge a separation between the actual self and the ideal self. The things of the universe do not after all flow so easily to the speaker; for he "must get what the writing means," and he does want readers to know him:

> This is the meal equally set, this the meat for
>   natural hunger,
> It is for the wicked just the same as the righteous,
>   I make appointments with all,
> I will not have a single person slighted or left away,
> The kept-woman, sponger, thief, are hereby invited,
> The heavy-lipp'd slave is invited, the venerealee is
>   invited;
> There shall be no difference between them and the rest.
>
> . . . .
>
> This hour I tell things in confidence,
> I might not tell everybody, but I will tell you.
> > [Section 19, pp. 46–47.]
>
> All I mark as my own you shall offset it with your own,
> Else it were time lost listening to me.
> > [Section 20, p. 47.]

The hero pretends to be like a natural phenomenon, available to all who want him. But he is too insistent to be really so spontaneous ("I will not have a single person slighted"); so that his promise to "tell things in confidence," which seems to contradict the preceding lines, actually is spoken out of the same spirit that produces the expansive invitation. As at the start of the poem, Whitman means to give himself away: his protest that he is content without listeners follows hard upon his singling out a listener, each of his readers, for special attention. The result, as in Sections 1–4, is the picture of a man at war with himself.

We are therefore not surprised when, a few pages later, we find our supposedly harmonious hero clearly split into two:

> My voice goes after what my eyes cannot reach,
> With the twirl of my tongue I encompass worlds
>   and volumes of worlds.

172

Speech is the twin of my vision, it is unequal to
    measure itself,
It provokes me forever, it says sarcastically,
Walt you contain enough, why don't you let it out then?

Come now I will not be tantalized, you conceive too
    much of articulation,
Do you not know O speech how the buds beneath you are
    folded?
Waiting in gloom, protected by frost,
The dirt receding before my prophetical screams,

. . . .

My final merit I refuse you, I refuse putting from
    me what I really am,
Encompass worlds, but never try to encompass me,
I crowd your sleekest and best by simply looking
    toward you.

                    [Section 25, p. 55.]

Knowing that he does not know the limits of his speech, he stifles, for the moment, his tendency toward didactic utterance. The man who in "Scented Herbage of My Breast" scorns the blades that "remain down there so ashamed," swearing that he "will say what [he has] to say by itself" (p. 96), here refuses to uproot the buds of hidden meaning with his "prophetical screams." Rejecting his didacticism because of the limits it places upon him, he ends this stage of his development with the end of Section 25:

Writing and talk do not prove me,
I carry the plenum of proof and every thing
    else in my face,
With the hush of my lips I wholly confound the skeptic.

                    [Section 25, p. 55.]

Thus Whitman returns, in Sections 26–32, to the descriptive voice of Sections 8–15. There he "witnesses"; here he begins by listening:

Now I will do nothing but listen,
To accrue what I hear into this song, to let sounds
    contribute toward it.

I hear bravuras of birds, bustle of growing wheat,
  gossip of flames, clack of sticks cooking my meals,
I hear the sound I love, the sound of the human voice,
I hear all sounds running together, combined, fused
  or following,
Sounds of the city and sounds out of the city, . . .
                              [Section 26, pp. 55–56.]

The shift finally occurs, as we have seen, after a specific rejection of
didacticism; but, just as the didacticism of Sections 16–25 is
prepared for gradually in the previous group of sections, so has the
descriptive voice grown steadily toward this position of dominance.
In Sections 21 and 22, for instance, the didactic voice is interrupted
by lyric addresses to the earth and sea, addresses that almost
become catalogues of natural glories; and Section 24 contains one
of Whitman's wittiest catalogues, in "worship" of "the spread of
[his] own body." These exceptions to a passage heavily didactic
imply the impatience of the hero's poetic imagination with the
limitations imposed by didacticism: "Writing and talk do not
prove [him]," and he must get on to the vision of merging.

    In this new group of sections, then, the speaker is far more
involved in the things around him than ever before in "Song of
Myself." He has risked "becoming," briefly, in Sections 9 and 10;
but the power of those imaginative involvements is feeble compared to what seizes him now:

I hear the violoncello, ('tis the young man's
  heart's complaint,)
I hear the key'd cornet, it glides quickly in
  through my ears,
It shakes mad-sweet pangs through my belly and breast.

I hear the chorus, it is a grand opera,
Ah this indeed is music—this suits me.

A tenor large and fresh as the creation fills me,
The orbic flex of his mouth is pouring and filling me full.

I hear the train'd soprano (what work with hers
  is this?)
The orchestra whirls me wider than Uranus flies,

174

It wrenches such ardors from me I did not know I
    possess'd them,
It sails me, I dab with bare feet, they are lick'd
    by the indolent waves,
I am cut by bitter and angry hail, I lose my breath,
Steep'd amid honey'd morphine, my windpipe throttled
    in fakes of death,
At length let up again to feel the puzzle of puzzles,
And that we call Being.

[Section 26, p. 56.]

This is the mad whirl of the imagination, and it almost destroys
him. Like the speaker in "The Sleepers" but unlike the giant
swimmer, he is "let up," and, retreating to the safe limits of his
own identity, reverts briefly to didacticism, an exploration of the
"puzzle of puzzles":

To be in any form, what is that?
(Round and round we go, all of us, and ever
    come back thither,)
If nothing lay more develop'd the quahaug in
    its callous shell were enough.

[Section 27, p. 57.]

But his long growth since the beginning of the poem, the
alternation of didacticism and imagistic description that has gradually brought him closer to the merging vision, serves him well. He is
able to move from thoughts of the "quahaug" into speculation
about his sense of touch, and from there into new adventures:

Is this then a touch? quivering me to a new identity,
Flames and ether making a rush for my veins,
Treacherous tip of me reaching and crowding to
    help them,
. . . .
On all sides prurient provokers stiffening my limbs,
Straining the udder of my heart for its withheld drip,
Behaving licentious toward me, taking no denial,
. . . .
I am given up by traitors,
I talk wildly, I have lost my wits, I and nobody
    else am the greatest traitor,

175

> I went myself first to the headland, my own hands
>   carried me there.

> You villain touch! what are you doing? my breath
>   is tight in its throat,
> Unclench your floodgates, you are too much for me.
>   [Section 28, pp. 57–58.]

Once more, however, he cannot quite manage the full flight: led into "a new identity" by his senses, he feels himself endangered. We have seen this supposedly unified man argue with his didactic speech, which wants to limit him; now he quarrels with the touch that destroys limitations. The result is another retreat to didacticism (Section 30) and then, as in Sections 8–15, a description of things from the safety of a position outside of things:

> In vain the buzzard houses herself with the sky,
> In vain the snake slides through the creepers and logs,
> In vain the elk takes to the inner passes of the woods,
> In vain the razor-bill'd auk sails far north to Labrador, . . .
>   [Section 31, p. 59.]

> I think I could turn and live with animals, they are
>   so placid and self-contain'd,
> I stand and look at them long and long.
>   [Section 32, p. 60.]

But again, this late in the poem, the retreat is only momentary. The imagined sight, and then the feel, of a stallion lifts the speaker out of his role as spectator. He finally achieves the vision of merging, the most intense activity of his imagination:

> His nostrils dilate as my heels embrace him,
> His well-built limbs tremble with pleasure as
>   we race around and return.
> I but use you a minute, then I resign you, stallion,
> Why do I need your paces when I myself out-gallop them?
> Even as I stand or sit passing faster than you.
>   [Section 32, pp. 60–61.]

Thus are we brought into the climactic scenes of the mono-drama. Even though the speaker's growth and our preparation have been accomplished gradually, the opening lines of Section 33 both record excitement and create it:

Space and Time! now I see it is true, what I
  guess'd at,
What I guess'd when I loaf'd on the grass,
What I guess'd while I lay alone in my bed,
And again as I walk'd the beach under the paling
  stars of the morning.

My ties and ballasts leave me, my elbows rest in
  sea-gaps,
I skirt sierras, my palms cover continents,
I am afoot with my vision.
[Section 33, p. 61.]

The approaches to imaginative flight presented from the start of
the poem have been, compared to this true flight, "guesses," merely
tentative: loafing on the grass, like lying awake at night or walking
the beach, is a gesture not of harmonious wholeness, but of
incompletion, a certain perplexity.* Now the hero finally goes
naked "to the bank by the wood"; he is "in contact" with the
atmosphere and with all other beings:

By the city's quadrangular houses—in log huts,
  camping with lumbermen,
Along the ruts of the turnpike, along the dry
  gulch and rivulet bed,
Weeding my onion-patch or hoeing rows of carrots
  and parsnips, crossing savannas, trailing in forests,
Prospecting, gold-digging, girdling the trees of a
  new purchase,
Scorch'd ankle-deep by the hot sand, hauling my boat
  down the shallow river,
Where the panther walks to and fro on a limb overhead,
  where the buck turns furiously at the hunter, . . .
[Section 33, p. 61.]

So it goes for some eighty lines, and then Whitman "anchor[s]
his ship for a little while" (p. 65) to make sure that we know the
significance of his vision:

* See Whitman's reproduction of his phrenological table and Fowler's accompanying notes, in *Leaves of Grass* (Brooklyn, 1856), p. 362: "Leading traits appear to be Friendship, Sympathy, Sublimity, and Self-Esteem, and markedly among his combinations the dangerous faults of Indolence, a tendency to the pleasures of Voluptuousness and Alimentiveness, and a certain reckless swing of animal will." I am especially interested, in connection with the image of loafing on the grass, in the "dangerous fault" of "Indolence."

177

I fly those flights of a fluid and swallowing soul,
My course runs below the soundings of plummets.

I help myself to material and immaterial,
No guard can shut me off, no law prevent me.
[Section 33, p. 65.]

But immediately he is off again, and now the journey is so much like the one enacted in "The Sleepers" that it is almost as if we are spectators at a revised version of the play. An early adventure with a bride—"I tighten her all night to my thighs and lips"—yields suddenly to scenes of death and suffering: in quick succession, the speaker is a drowned man, a man suffering at a ship-wreck, and a mother "condemn'd for a witch." Whereas in Section 10 he shields a runaway slave, now he is "the hounded slave" (Section 33, p. 66), and then "the mash'd fireman with breast-bone broken." As in "The Sleepers," deep imaginative involvement is accompanied by images of pain, as if what the hero "becomes" is conditioned by his sense of doom, a fear that his individual identity cannot survive such experiences of new identities.

And his response to the pain is like his response in "The Sleepers." There he settles upon the comradeship between Washington and his soldiers; here he assuages his pain by imagining that the fireman's suffering is eased by the presence of "White and beautiful . . . faces," faces like those that serve as emblems of peace in the Drum-Taps poems. Then, also as in "The Sleepers," the gradual withdrawal from imaginative experience is signaled by changes in his approach to the reader. Descriptive poetry, in which the speaker is involved in the things around him and careless of his reader, gives way to narrative:

I am an old artillerist, I tell of my fort's
    bombardment,
I am there again.
[Section 33, p. 67.]

"I take part," he says; but he says also, "I see and hear the whole"; and it is fitting, for a speaker in this somewhat removed position, that the man suffering is not himself, but "my dying general." In Section 34 the use of the narrative is even more open: "Now I tell what I knew in Texas in my early youth," the speaker begins, and goes on to tell the story of the Alamo, "the tale of the murder of the four hundred and twelve young men" (p. 68). This is still grim stuff; but the speaker, turned toward readers rather than inward, is not in personal danger. And the next narrative, split between Sections 35 and 36, stresses the serenity of the captain almost as much as the suffering of the sea-flight, although it does end with images of horror.

Only when he is almost out of his vision can the speaker voice explicitly the fear that has been implied by his withdrawal:

> You laggards there on guard! look to your arms!
> In at the conquer'd doors they crowd! I am possess'd!
> Embody all presences outlaw'd or suffering,
> See myself in prison shaped like another man,
> And feel the dull unintermitted pain.
>
> [Section 37, p. 71.]

If he has been flying "those flights of a fluid and swallowing soul," he himself has almost been swallowed: he is "possess'd" in both senses of the term. "I resist any thing better than my own diversity," he has said early in the poem (Section 16, p. 45); and now he cries for help to energies long ignored, the guardians of the private self.

Their answer comes promptly, making possible the long final movement of the speaker, enacted in Sections 38–52.

> Enough! enough! enough!
> Somehow I have been stunn'd. Stand back!
> Give me a little time beyond my cuff'd head,
>   slumbers, dreams, gaping,
> I discover myself on the verge of a usual mistake.
>
> That I could forget the mockers and insults!
> That I could forget the trickling tears and the
>   blows of bludgeons and hammers!
> That I could look with a separate look on my own
>   crucifixion and bloody crowning.
>
> [Section 38, p. 72.]

The hero, having worked himself up to his most intense poetic vision, has been speaking since the start of Section 33 with the voice of his soul, which, passionate rather than lulling, seizes the whole self and carries it off on what Whitman, talking of Blake, calls a "wild teetotum." [4] The protest comes, then, in the voice of what I have called the "aesthetic body," which resists the poet's loss of his particularity and, fulfilling the functions of Coleridge's "talent," restrains the soul's flight through page after page of this poem.

This enactment of an inner struggle demonstrates openly, more so even than the earlier debates (Sections 25 and 28), what Whitman has hinted at from the start. There is not one Whitman, who unifies body and soul and is harmonious with all the world, but two: the "mystical identity," the "real power," which is beyond particular body and is haughty or loving as the spirit moves it; and the actual identity, conscious of its internal split between body and soul and plagued by the presence of "seekers and askers." The "usual mistake" is to stay too long in the poetic night—to assume that the self is so healthy and whole that it can exchange identities endlessly, without injuring itself or the process. The preoccupation with scenes of suffering and death suggests that Whitman senses the mistake even as he commits it; but his triumph now is to state that mistake, as he does only ambiguously in "The Sleepers." And beyond the statement lies another triumph, which the hero of "The Sleepers" does not even approach. This speaker corrects his mistake —not by withdrawing into a world without the problem, but by acting in the situation itself. Before the "pains of hell" can be "translate[d] into a new tongue," they must be confronted in all their original hellishness. They must, that is, be confronted in the arena of the private identity. The old way, the suffering with other sufferers, is too easy; there is something offhanded about "Agonies are one of my changes of garments" (Section 33, p. 67). Thus the hero vows that he will no longer deny his own, private torment, his fear of mocking and insults: he will no longer stand "amused, complacent" (Section 4, p. 32), will no longer affect unconcern at the sight of his "own crucifixion and bloody crowning," the blows rained upon him by "Trippers and askers."

The self is born anew. Whitman, seeing himself as a secular Christ, gives the story of Jesus a humanistic meaning:

180

I remember now,
I resume the overstaid fraction,
The grave of rock multiplies what has been
    confided to it, or to any graves,
Corpses rise, gashes heal, fastenings roll from me.
                    [Section 38, p. 72.]

To insist upon private identity is to define "the Me myself" as *everything* one is. Body and soul are reconciled, their unity dependent upon the separate functions of each; ideal self and actual self are reconciled, and the *poseur* pricked by his own questions disappears. Withdrawal to the smallest, most private room of all, the "grave of rock," results in an outward movement free from the perils of the poetic flight because the voyager has confronted them:

I troop forth replenish'd with supreme power,
    one of an average unending procession,
Inland and sea-coast we go, and pass all
    boundary lines,
Our swift ordinances on their way over the
    whole earth,
The blossoms we wear in our hats the growth
    of thousands of years.

Eleves, I salute you! come forward!
Continue your annotations, continue your
    questionings.
                [Section 38, p. 72.]

"Trippers and askers," once ignored or feared, now are faced squarely and even welcomed. The result—the rest of the poem—is a masterpiece of didactic poetry; the hero, once preoccupied with achieving his private poetic vision, now turns outward toward readers in a dazzling display of versatility.

All the techniques that make "To You" a successful didactic poem are in this last movement of "Song of Myself": rapid changes of tone, posings as stern prophet and understanding comrade, intimate addresses and pronouncements for the group, and, what "To You" cannot boast, comic uses of the language.

181

As in "To You," this teacher saves his moral lesson for last. Sections 39–43 introduce the speaker, almost as if the poem is beginning again. In a sense, of course, it is; for the speaker, having "pass'd his prelude on the reeds within" (Section 42, p. 76), has shifted his interest from vision to idea. Section 39 defines a type, the "friendly and flowing savage." Sections 40 and 41 are more personal: we are shown that the description of the "savage"— "Behavior lawless as snow-flakes, words simple as grass, uncomb'd head, laughter, and naivetè" (Section 39, p. 73)—applies to our particular hero. And more besides, for with bewildering speed he is frontier braggart, whisperer, sober promiser, angry prophet, universal lover, saviour—and all the while ironic toward himself:

> Flaunt of the sunshine I need not your bask—lie over!
> You light surfaces only, I force surfaces and depths also.
>
> Earth! you seem to look for something at my hands,
> Say, old top-knot, what do you want?
>
> Man or woman, I might tell how I like you, but cannot,
> And might tell what it is in me and what it is in you,
>   but cannot,
> And might tell that pining I have, that pulse of my
>   nights and days.
>
> Behold, I do not give lectures or a little charity,
> When I give I give myself.
>
> You there, impotent, loose in the knees,
> Open your scarf'd chops till I blow grit within you,
> Spread your palms and lift the flaps of your pockets,
> I am not to be denied, I compel, I have stores plenty and to spare,
> And any thing I have I bestow.
> . . . .
>
> On women fit for conception I start bigger and
>   nimbler babes,
> (This day I am jetting the stuff of far more
>   arrogant republics.)
> . . . .

182

I seize the descending man and raise him with re-
    sistless will,
O despairer, here is my neck,
By God, you shall not go down! hang your whole
    weight upon me.

                        [Section 40, pp. 73–74.]

I heard what was said of the universe,
Heard it and heard it of several thousand years;
It is middling well as far as it goes—but is
    that all?

Magnifying and applying come I,
Outbidding at the start the old cautious hucksters,
Taking myself the exact dimensions of Jehovah,
Lithographing Kronos, Zeus his son, and Hercules
    his grandson,
Buying drafts of Osiris, Isis, Belus, Brahma, Buddha,
In my portfolio placing Manito loose, Allah on a
    leaf, the crucifix engraved,
With Odin and the hideous-faced Mexitli and every
    idol and image,
Taking them all for what they are worth and not
    a cent more,
. . . .
The supernatural of no account, myself waiting my
    time to be one of the supremes,
The day getting ready for me when I shall do as
    much good as the best, and be as prodigious;
By my life-lumps! becoming already a creator,
Putting myself here and now to the ambush'd womb
    of the shadow.

                        [Section 41, pp. 75–76.]

There have been touches of this witty ingenuity in the didactic
passages of Sections 16–25; but here, coming in the voice of the
prophet who has found himself, it is sustained and livelier. We are
anything but set off from this teacher: we may think him a little
mad, but he is exciting to watch and good fun—and he has not
preached at us. We are prepared by indirect approaches for
direction, Whitman's "call":

183

A call in the midst of the crowd,
My own voice, orotund sweeping and final.
[Section 42, p. 76.]

So we are warned explicitly, and even now it does not come. The
speaker must make a few more preparatory points, while we
wonder what the ultimate message is, about himself and his
conception of poetry:

I know perfectly well my own egotism,
Know my omnivorous lines and must not write any less,
And would fetch you whoever you are flush with myself.

Not words of routine this song of mine,
But abruptly to question, to leap beyond yet nearer
bring;
This printed and bound book—but the printer and the
printing-office boy?
The well-taken photographs—but your wife or friend
close and solid in your arms?
[Section 42, pp. 77–78.]

And, most important, about his attitude toward readers:

Ever myself and my neighbors, refreshing,
wicked, real,
Ever the old inexplicable query, ever that
thorn'd thumb, that breath of itches and thirsts,
Ever the vexer's *hoot! hoot!* till we find where
the sly one hides and bring him forth, . . .
[Section 42, pp. 76–77.]

Down-hearted doubters dull and excluded,
Frivolous, sullen, moping, angry, affected,
dishearten'd, atheistical,
I know every one of you, I know the sea of
torment, doubt, despair and unbelief.

How the flukes splash!
How they contort rapid as lightning, with
spasms and spouts of blood!

Be at peace bloody flukes of doubters and
sullen mopers,
I take my place among you as much as among any,

184

The past is the push of you, me, all, precisely
   the same,
And what is yet untried and afterward is for you,
   me, all precisely the same.

I do not know what is untried and afterward,
But I know it will in its turn prove sufficient,
   and cannot fail.
                    [Section 43, p. 79.]

Now the speaker not only admits but affirms that he is discontent
when we are not "aware." Yet he wants more than to bring us
"flush" with himself and his "omnivorous lines." There is a good
that lies beyond "This printed and bound book"—the good simply
of "leap[ing] beyond." Thus he both challenges "vexers" and
doubters, the "Trippers and askers" who have once so bothered
him, and accepts them as members of his band. He would convince
them, but must also admit that in doubting him they are already
practicing the first part of his lesson.

Finally, these last remarks having strongly suggested the lesson,
we are ready for the direct statement:

It is time to explain myself—let us stand up.

What is known I strip away,
I launch all men and women forward with me into
   the Unknown.
. . . .

I am an acme of things accomplish'd, and I am
   encloser of things to be.

My feet strike an apex of the apices of the stairs,
On every step bunches of ages, and larger bunches
   between the steps,
All below duly travel'd, and still I mount and mount.
             [Section 44, pp. 80–81.]

It is the truth of the central Whitman, the truth of gradual
development. It is imaged, we remember, by the march of procession: the rough edges of existence must be confronted and turned
to new purposes; accepting what we are, we must proceed unknow-
ing but with faith that we will discover further meaning. The

lesson is taught, in one or another of its aspects, all through the last
sections of the poem:

> There is no stoppage and never can be stoppage,
> If I, you, and the worlds, and all beneath or
>   upon their surfaces, were this moment reduced
>   back to a pallid float, it would not avail in
>   the long run,
> We should surely bring up again where we now stand,
> And surely go as much farther, and then farther
>   and farther.
>
> [Section 45, p. 82.]
>
> I tramp a perpetual journey, (come listen all!)
> My signs are a rain-proof coat, good shoes, and
>   a staff cut from the woods,
> No friend of mine takes his ease in my chair,
> I have no chair, no church, no philosophy,
> I lead no man to a dinner-table, library, exchange,
> But each man and each woman of you I lead upon a knoll,
> My left hand hooking you round the waist,
> My right hand pointing to landscapes of continents
>   and the public road.
>
> Not I, not any one else can travel that road for you,
> You must travel it for yourself.
>
> [Section 46, p. 83.]
>
> I am the teacher of athletes,
> He that by me spreads a wider breast than my own
>   proves the width of my own,
> He most honors my style who learns under it to destroy
>   the teacher.
>
> [Section 47, p. 84.]

It is taught also by means less direct: by implying the contrast
between this speaker and the one in "The Sleepers." Whereas at
the end of "The Sleepers" Whitman averts his eyes from the
"wildest and bloodiest," here he accepts the "pains of hell" and
looks beyond them:

> And as to you Death, and you bitter hug of mortality,
>   it is idle to try to alarm me.
>
> . . . .

Of the turbid pool that lies in the autumn forest,
Of the moon that descends the steeps of the sough-
   ing twilight,
Toss, sparkles of day and dusk—toss on the black
   stems that decay in the muck,
Toss to the moaning gibberish of the dry limbs.
                   [Section 49, p. 87.]

He knows the "bitter hug"—he has been in the "grave of rock"—
but having faced it, he is not alarmed; he knows the decaying
things in the twilit pool, but he knows also the "sparkles of day and
dusk," which, glinting off "the black stems," make life out of
death. So we are brought to understand, when for a moment at the
end of "Song of Myself" Whitman sounds much the way he does
in "The Sleepers," that he has reached his place by a very different
route:

> There is that in me—I do not know what it is—
>   but I know it is in me.
>
> Wrench'd and sweaty—calm and cool then my body
>   becomes,
>
> . . . .
>
> Perhaps I might tell more. Outlines! I plead
>   for my brothers and sisters.
>
> Do you see O my brothers and sisters?
> It is not chaos or death—it is form, union,
>   plan—it is eternal life—it is Happiness.
>   [Section 50, p. 88.]

In "Song of Myself" Whitman does not deny "chaos or death": he
insists upon them, but denies that they are final. Whereas in "The
Sleepers" he achieves his vision of peace by leaving the "Wrench'd
and sweaty" world, in "Song of Myself" he confronts and accepts
his sweatiness, and thus becomes "calm and cool."

The difference between the two speakers can also be measured
by the difference in what and how they teach. The lesson in "The
Sleepers," about a beautiful universal comradeship, reveals a
teacher clinging to a rock of certainty; the lesson in "Song of
Myself," which concerns "advancing" or "pressing on," reveals a
speaker who knows the dangers of the unknown but is "a bold

187

swimmer, [jumping] off in the midst of the sea" (Section 46, p. 84). The teaching at the end of "The Sleepers" is mild but wholly direct: the teacher holds to his position and keeps the student in his. The teaching at the end of "Song of Myself," on the other hand, is as indirect as didacticism can be. We laugh with Whitman, and work our way with him toward his lesson, learning it, almost, before he has said it directly—the teacher does not keep the student in his place, but allows him to be almost an equal.

Thus the final charge to readers:

> I concentrate toward them that are nigh, I wait
> on the door-slab.
>
> Who has done his day's work? who will soonest
> be through with his supper?
> Who wishes to walk with me?
>
> Will you speak before I am gone? will you prove
> already too late?
>
> The spotted hawk swoops by and accuses me, he
> complains of my gab and my loitering.
>
> I too am not a bit tamed, I too am untranslatable,
> I sound my barbaric yawp over the roofs of the world.
>
> The last scud of day holds back for me,
> It flings my likeness after the rest and true
> as any on the shadow'd wilds,
> It coaxes me to the vapor and the dusk.
>
> I depart as air, I shake my white locks at the
> runaway sun,
> I effuse my flesh in eddies, and drift it in
> lacy jags.
>
> I bequeath myself to the dirt to grow from the
> grass I love,
> If you want me again look for me under your
> boot-soles.
>
> You will hardly know who I am or what I mean,
> But I shall be good health to you nevertheless,
> And filter and fibre your blood.

Failing to fetch me at first keep encouraged,
Missing me one place search another,
I stop somewhere waiting for you.
[Sections 51 and 52, p. 89.]

The hero no longer "loafes" on the grass and is no longer caught in a wild flight of the imagination; he is, instead, setting out on the "perpetual journey" of development, the never-ending discovery of himself and everything that is. In the course of the poem he has made the first "cycle" of that journey, for he has traveled from idler to voyager, has learned before our eyes the lesson that he states directly at the end. He leaves as a guide for us not himself but the spirit of what he has done: it will "filter and fibre" our blood as do the air, the earth, and the sea. He will "stop somewhere" for us only in the sense that some time we will recognize his truth. Yet even as he takes his leave, committing himself to the process of time, we know, if we have come this far with him, that he has stopped long enough with us to do his work. For if he has learned his lesson as he moves through the poem, we have learned it too: the manner of his telling, the form of his poem, has made us travel a long and winding road toward meaning.

The image of the road is even more important in "Song of the Open Road" than in "Song of Myself," for "Open Road" dramatizes Whitman's experience on the road itself rather than his experience in moving from the grass to the road. As at the end of "Song of Myself," Whitman in Section 1 of "Open Road" is "Done with indoor complaints, libraries, querulous criticism"; he is "Afoot and light-hearted" (p. 149). The new problem is, What now? Unlike Adam and Eve, who like Whitman have "the world . . . all before them" but who enter it heavyhearted, having to learn what to do with their new facts of pain and hard work, Whitman must learn what to do with the facts of health and freedom.

There is another problem too, the existence of which makes it not wholly accurate to say that "Song of the Open Road" begins where "Song of Myself" leaves off. At the end of "Song of Myself" Whitman is challenging his readers to join him on his journey; at the start of "Open Road" he thinks of readers as "burdens" rather than as companions in an exploration:

(Still here I carry my old delicious burdens,
I carry them, men and women, I carry them with me
    wherever I go,
I swear it is impossible for me to get rid of them,
I am fill'd with them, and I will fill them in return.)

                                                    [P. 149.]

"Delicious" burdens they may be, and burdens of the mind and heart rather than of the back, but carrying of any sort is far different from urging into action. If Section 1 of "Open Road" rings a change on the end of *Paradise Lost*, it also serves to remind us of Aeneas, whose new beginning is somewhat qualified by his particular burden, his father, the weight of the past. The speaker's problems, then, in "Open Road," are two: what to do on the road, and how to deal with the burden of readers. The response to each problem involves the response to the other.

The arena of discovery, the place where the responses are worked out, is the road itself, which, now that Section 1 has introduced us to the "I," is presented to us in Sections 2 and 3. Our exploration of the road, which has heretofore been called simply "the open road" and "the long brown path," waits upon the speaker's first discovery, which has to do with both the soul of the road, that which lies unseen behind its particularities, and the body of the road, its various objects. The soul of the road, the truth testified to by the black, the birth, the fop, and the hearse, is "the profound lesson of reception"—or, beyond that, the truth of crossing, or passing: "They pass, I also pass, any thing passes, none can be interdicted" (p. 150). This understanding gives meaning to Whitman's various encounters; in turn, the particular experiences give shape to the meanings Whitman carries with him:

    You air that serves me with breath to speak!
    You objects that call from diffusion my meanings
        and give them shape!
    You light that wraps me and all things in delicate
        equable showers!
    You paths worn in the irregular hollows by the roadsides!
    I believe you are latent with unseen existences, you are
        so dear to me.

                                                    [P. 150.]

190

It is not clear whether meaning is made by the operation of subject upon object or of object upon subject: what is clear is the interrelatedness of things, the "crossing" between subject and object that is at once the act of seeing and the discovery of meaning. Thus the images of Section 3, like the lessons of Section 2, concentrate on crossing and passing:

> You flagg'd walks of the cities! you strong curbs
>   at the edges!
> You ferries! you planks and posts of wharves! you
>   timber-lined sides! you distant ships!
> You rows of houses! you window-pierc'd façades!
>   you roofs!
> You porches and entrances! you copings and iron guards!
> You windows whose transparent shells might expose so much!
> You doors and ascending steps! you arches!
> You gray stones of interminable pavements! you trodden
>   crossings!
>
> [P. 150.]

The result of this new perception, Whitman's simultaneous awareness of meaning and shapes, is, as expressed in Section 4, a sense of the earth as expanding, alive, and proportioned in its parts. So far has the road come from being a mere "brown path" that the speaker can imagine a conversation with it:

> O highway I travel, do you say to me *Do not leave me?*
> Do you say *Venture not—if you leave me you are lost?*
> Do you say *I am already prepared, I am well-beaten
>   and undenied, adhere to me?*
>
> O public road, I say back I am not afraid to leave you,
>   yet I love you,
> You express me better than I can express myself,
> You shall be more to me than my poem.
>
> [P. 151.]

Now that Whitman has committed himself to the road, and in so doing has expanded both his world and himself, will the road end by limiting him? Though he asserts his independence of it, he also reaffirms his commitment to it; he seems, indeed, in this echo of his address to the night at the end of "The Sleepers," to express his

191

need of the road. Yet, it may be that the speaker's deferral to the road, his exalting of its powers of expression over his own, is not after all a surrender, but rather a new way of looking at the road, in which he and the road are again expanded. This possibility is hinted at in the closing part of Section 4, in which, far from diminishing himself, Whitman sees himself as a miracle worker and speaks of "heroic deeds" and "free poems." Significantly, in the light of later developments, he emphasizes not the open road, although he has just celebrated its power of expression, but "the open air" (p. 151).

What has happened becomes clearer in Section 5, where Whitman declares himself "loos'd of limits and imaginary lines" and his "own master total and absolute." He has, it would seem, somehow divested himself of the hold of the road:

> I inhale great draughts of space,
> The east and the west are mine, and the north
> and the south are mine.
>
> I am larger, better than I thought,
> I did not know I held so much goodness.
>   [P. 151.]

What he has shaken loose of, really, is the road as a limited symbol, the road that has particular objects and a particular meaning. He has already raised the road beyond its aspect as "a long brown path"; now he has taken it even further. By committing himself in Section 4 to the road's power of expression, the speaker has given the road a life beyond that which it has in Sections 2 and 3; he has given it the life of an expanding symbol. That is why he stresses the open air in Section 4, and fails even to mention the road in Sections 5 through 11, talking instead of the earth, the air, and the "pathless and wild seas"; he is working out, in various shapes, the *principle* of the road. Having had his own shape brought forth out of his "diffuse meanings," he is bringing meanings, and new shapes, out of the shape that was "the long brown path." In expanding the road he of course expands himself: the road expresses him better than he can express himself, but only because he grows in order to express the road.

192

Whitman achieves, in Section 5, not only a discovery of the road and of himself, but also a discovery of readers:

> All seems beautiful to me,
> I can repeat over to men and women You have done such
>   good to me I would do the same to you,
> I will recruit for myself and you as I go,
> I will scatter myself among men and women as I go,
> I will toss a new gladness and roughness among them,
> Whoever denies me it shall not trouble me,
> Whoever accepts me he or she shall be blessed and
>   shall bless me.
>
> [Pp. 151–52.]

He has said as early as Section 1 that he will "whimper no more, postpone no more," but the attitude toward readers in Section 5 is no more a mere repetition than his declaration of independence in Section 5 is a repetition of his claim of lightheartedness. For he is treating readers not as "delicious burdens" but as companions—"I will recruit for myself and you as I go"—and he sees himself as seeding recruits, starting them on their own lives, rather than carrying them. Having freed himself of the "well-beaten" road, having left the road by insisting on its symbolic significance, Whitman is able to free himself of his own inclinations to be a rigid guide; he releases himself of his burdens by loosing them to their own roads.

Those men and women made new, seen as full beings instead of as the speaker's burdens, spring to life in the next section, grown from the seeds of Whitman's faith:

> Now if a thousand perfect men were to appear it
>   would not amaze me,
> Now if a thousand beautiful forms of women appear'd
>   it would not astonish me.
>
> Now I see the secret of the making of the best persons,
> It is to grow in the open air and to eat and sleep
>   with the earth.
>
> [P. 152.]

Having discovered that the way to make "the best persons" is to let them grow in the open air—having established, that is, that his job

193

is to scatter himself among men and women, to seed them, not to carry them—the speaker uses that knowledge in a turn toward direct contact with readers. He scatters among them his various thoughts—on great personal deeds, on wisdom, on philosophies and religions, and on "realization." The last part of the section moves very close indeed to readers; the tone is muted, not yet one of exclamatory urging:

> Here is realization,
> Here is a man tallied—he realizes here what he has in him,
> The past, the future, majesty, love—if they are vacant
>   of you, you are vacant of them.
>
> Only the kernel of every object nourishes;
> Where is he who tears off the husks for you and me?
> Where is he that undoes stratagems and envelopes for
>   you and me?
>
> Here is adhesiveness, it is not previously fashion'd,
>   it is apropos;
> Do you know what it is as you pass to be loved by strangers?
> Do you know the talk of those turning eye-balls?
>   [Pp. 152–53.]

First a quiet warning—"if they are vacant of you, you are vacant of them"; then further instruction, followed by questions. Not yet the "Undrape!" of "Song of Myself": Whitman asks questions about tearing off the husk, but does not yet actually tear it; in fact, as in "To You," he seems to be using stratagems to undo "stratagems and envelopes." Thus the manner of his talk and its content, especially his reference to adhesiveness, cooperate to nurture the developing relationship between speaker and reader.

In this context the questions of Section 7—which seem, when the section is read by itself, to be private wonderings about the nature of "interchange"—represent not only a pause in the speaker's outward movement, a consolidation of gains and a further inward exploration, but also a posing of fundamental questions for readers he wants to put on their own.

> What is it I interchange so suddenly with strangers?
> What with some driver as I ride on the seat by his side?

194

What with some fisherman drawing his seine by the shore
    as I walk by and pause?
What gives me to be free to a woman's and man's good-will?
    what gives them to be free to mine?

                     [P. 153.]

These wonderings, provoked by the "efflux of the soul," are not to
be confused with the perplexed questions that mark the last part of
"There Was a Child Went Forth." For if the "efflux" provokes the
questions, it also provides a ready answer:

The efflux of the soul is happiness, here is happiness,
I think it pervades the open air, waiting at all times,
Now it flows unto us, we are rightly charged.

Here rises the fluid and attaching character, . . .
                [Pp. 153–54.]

Since the principle of happiness is to be associated with "the
cheerful voice" and "gay fresh sentiment" mentioned in Section 4,
it can be thought of as the principle of being alive, expanding, and
whole. Whitman says he now "becomes charged with it," now
gives off the glow of "attaching character" that is the product of
happiness; but he has in fact, by shifting his relationship with
readers, already demonstrated his "attaching character," his willingness to cross and his ability to be crossed to. Even as he speaks
in Section 8, he demonstrates it again—"Now it flows unto *us, we*
are rightly charged."

We realize from Whitman's appeal in Sections 7 and 8 to
images of vegetation, that the speaker's "attaching character" is not
so much a quality learned as a quality latent that has grown to
fullness:

Why are there trees I never walk under but large and melodious
    thoughts descend upon me?
(I think they hang there winter and summer on those trees and
    always drop fruit as I pass;)

                     [P. 153.]

The fluid and attaching character is the freshness and sweet-
    ness of man and woman,

(The herbs of the morning sprout no fresher and sweeter
  every day out of the roots of themselves, than it sprouts
  fresh and sweet continually out of itself.)

[P. 154.]

When Whitman says at the end of "Song of Myself," "I stop
somewhere waiting for you," he means that he will be like this tree,
ripe and full, giving of himself to whoever is ready for his
"melodious thoughts." When he speaks here of herbs sprouting
from roots, he is suggesting that ripeness, which he achieves in
"Song of Myself" and toward which he is moving at this point in
"Song of the Open Road," grows out of readiness: that his
metamorphosis on the road, his discovery of the fullness of the road
and the largeness of himself and of his readers, is a natural growth
whose seed was his willingness to enter the road at all.

The measure of his transformation is that this readiness to
journey, to suffer new experience, is at the start of the poem
thought of as lightheartedness; here, at the end of Section 8, it is
called "the shuddering longing ache of contact."

Toward the fluid and attaching character exudes the sweat
  of the love of young and old,
From it falls distill'd the charm that mocks beauty and
  attainments,
Toward it heaves the shuddering longing ache of contact.

[P. 154.]

Happiness, then, even in this dramatization of a day journey, is not
the simplemindedness with which Whitman is often associated; to
be full and alive, charged with the efflux of the soul that is
happiness, is to ache.

The long last line of Section 8, imitating the movement it
describes, carries Whitman into Section 9, and into a new kind of
contact with the reader:

Allons! whoever you are come travel with me!
Traveling with me you find what never tires.

[P. 154.]

Now the speaker has found his full voice. The open air, as he first
recognizes in Section 3, has indeed served him "with breath to
speak": his journey in it has brought him to the point where, in

196

naming his aching impulse toward others, he has uncovered his own kernel, and to the point where he can fulfill the promise of Section 5—"I will recruit for myself and you as I go"—by calling frankly upon readers to join him in developing their worlds.

The remaining seven sections form one long movement, the second part of the poem. With six of them beginning with "Allons!" and the other with "Listen!," they create a didactic mood much like that of the last part of "Song of Myself." Rhythms of argument play throughout the part, working across section divisions. The didactic statement has three aspects: criticism of the life not on the road, celebration of life on the road, and warning of the difficulties of life on the road. Instead of taking consistent, logical positions in relation to each other, these aspects weave together into one telling alogical argument. A tracing of the design would look like this: extended celebration (Sections 9–10), criticism (Section 10), warning (Sections 10–11), criticism (Section 11), extended celebration (Sections 12–13), criticism (Section 13), warning (Section 14), celebration (Section 15), and criticism (Section 15).

But such a description does disservice to Whitman's art, for his arrangement of the aspects of his statement is less significant than the pattern of tones and stresses. The quiet promises and almost affectionate description of life off the road in Section 9 yield, for instance, to the excitement and anger of Section 10:

> Allons! the inducements shall be greater,
> We will sail pathless and wild seas,
> We will go where winds blow, waves dash, and the
>   Yankee clipper speeds by under full sail.
>
> Allons! with power, liberty, the earth, the elements,
> Health, defiance, gayety, self-esteem, curiosity;
> Allons! from all formules!
> From your formules, O bat-eyed and materialistic priests.
>   [Pp. 154–55.]

As in the movement from Section 8 to Section 9, the communication between speaker and reader is raised to a new intensity. In Section 11 there is new urgency in the call, and new confidence that the call will bear fruit:

Listen! I will be honest with you,
I do not offer the old smooth prizes, but offer rough new prizes,
These are the days that must happen to you:
You shall not heap up what is call'd riches,
You shall scatter with lavish hand all that you earn
   or achieve,
You but arrive at the city to which you were destin'd,
   you hardly settle yourself to satisfaction before you
   are call'd by an irresistible call to depart, . . .

[P. 155.]

Whitman's enthusiasm spills out in Section 12 in the form of a catalogue of the "great Companions" whom the speaker and reader will join. The "great Companions" are journeyers of every sort— sailors, walkers, even "kissers of brides, tender helpers of children, bearers of children," and "Trusters of men and women." They are all "on the road" in the sense that they are all "Forth-steppers from the latent unrealized baby-days," and all are "as with companions, namely their own diverse phases." (p. 156)

   The journey, that is, is one of self-discovery and self-development:

To see nothing anywhere but what you may reach it and pass it,
To conceive no time, however distant, but what you may reach
   it and pass it,
To look up or down no road but it stretches and waits for you,
   however long but it stretches and waits for you,
To see no being, not God's or any, but you also go thither,
. . . .
To take your lovers on the road with you, for all that you
   leave them behind you,
To know the universe itself as a road, as many roads, as
   roads for traveling souls.

[Pp. 156–57.]

Just so does the speaker play out a journey of self-exploration, his being a journey of voice. Even after having attained the elevated area of the didactic call to readers, he begins "superior journeys," exploring the possibilities of didacticism. As indicated by the passage just quoted, the first part of Section 13 in a sense continues the catalogue begun in Section 12: listing what journeyers do

198

instead of who they are, it builds upon the enthusiasm expressed in Section 12 and concentrates our attention upon travel itself. The speaker travels, in the rest of Section 13, first to a philosophic summary about progress, a kind of resting place in the center of the section, composed of two long sentences, and then to a passionate indictment of life off the road:

> Whoever you are, come forth! or man or woman come forth!
> You must not stay sleeping and dallying there in the house,
>   though you built it, or though it has been built for you.
>
> Out of the dark confinement! out from behind the screen!
> It is useless to protest, I know all and expose it.
>
> Behold through you as bad as the rest,
> Through the laughter, dancing, dining, supping, of people,
> Inside of dresses and ornaments, inside of those wash'd
>   and trimm'd faces,
> Behold a secret silent loathing and despair.
>
> No husband, no wife, no friend, trusted to hear the confession,
> Another self, a duplicate of every one, skulking and hiding
>   it goes,
> Formless and wordless through the streets of the cities,
>   polite and bland in the parlors,
> In the cars of railroads, in steamboats, in the public
>   assembly,
> Home to the houses of men and women, at the table, in the
>   bedroom, everywhere,
> Smartly attired, countenance smiling, form upright, death
>   under the breast-bones, hell under the skull-bones,
> Under the broadcloth and gloves, under the ribbons and
>   artificial flowers,
> Keeping fair with the customs, speaking not a syllable of itself,
> Speaking of any thing else but never of itself.
>
> [Pp. 157–58.]

Like Whitman's naming of his own "ache of contact," this is an uncovering of a kernel of reality. It is as different from the description of the "indoor" world in Section 1—"indoor complaints, libraries, querulous criticisms"—as the ache is different from lightheartedness and the developed symbol of the road from the "long brown path."

199

The kernel uncovered is not simply that of life off the road; it is also that of the speaker's own voice—the indictment is something that has to be worked up to, discovered. Yet the mood is not immediately pressed; in a familiar movement, Section 14 is a retreat of sorts, a gathering of force before the final great push. In place of the exclamatory urgings of Section 13 ("Out of the dark confinement! out from behind the screen!") there are questions ("Have the past struggles succeeded?/ What has succeeded? yourself? your nation? Nature?"—p. 158), and in place of striking imagery there is lengthy abstraction:

> Now understand me well—it is provided in the essence
>   of things that from any fruition of success, no
>   matter what, shall come forth something to make
>   a greater struggle necessary.
>
> [P. 158.]

If this were another poet, we would suspect him of self-irony, for this seems like rather stuffy talk for a man on the open road. As it is, we are tempted to write it off as one of Whitman's failures of taste. Perhaps, however, we can save this language for the poem by thinking of Whitman as trying to save it, to vivify it by taking it out of the lecture hall, to demonstrate its relevance to life on the road by surrounding it with language more usually associated with the spirit of the road. For he precedes the passage with the challenging questions about success and follows it with a "call of battle":

> My call is the call of battle, I nourish active rebellion,
> He going with me must go well arm'd,
> He going with me goes often with spare diet, poverty, angry
>   enemies, desertions.
>
> [P. 158.]

The total language of Section 14 thus examines struggle from several perspectives. Though the tone is moderate in comparison to that of Section 13, and the section therefore a consolidation rather than a pressing forward into further urgency, the section does contribute to the whole movement of exploration and discovery by revealing that the journey is a struggle, not a lighthearted excursion.

200

The speaker suffers the "ache of contact"; the indoor world has "death under the breast-bones, hell under the skull-bones"; the journey is a kind of war. All this knowledge, worked out in the course of the poem, is used in Section 15, which returns to the mood of urgency, finding in it possibilities of tone previously unexplored by the poem:

> Allons! the road is before us!
> It is safe—I have tried it—my own feet have tried it well—
>   be not detain'd!
> Let the paper remain on the desk unwritten, and the book
>   on the shelf unopen'd!
> Let the tools remain in the workshop! let the money remain
>   unearn'd!
> Let the school stand! mind not the cry of the teacher!
> Let the preacher preach in his pulpit! let the lawyer
>   plead in the court, and the judge expound the law.
>
> Camerado, I give you my hand!
> I give you my love more precious than money,
> I give you myself before preaching or law;
> Will you give me yourself? Will you come travel with me?
> Shall we stick by each other as long as we live?
>
> [Pp. 158–59.]

The list of indoor activities has special significance because we associate them, now, with "a secret silent loathing and despair"; the claim that the journey is safe is especially rewarding because we know that it is a struggle. The "ache of contact" manifests itself more directly. Didacticism, Whitman's call to action, at the last moment of the poem shows its other face, the face we have grown to recognize from reading the Calamus group and "The Sleepers." The challenge—"Will you give me yourself? will you come travel with me?"—is also a plea: the reader, suddenly, is not being urged into his own path but is being asked to remain as companion—to travel, but to travel with Whitman.

But why not? We realize, eventually, that the final turn is not really a turn—that Whitman has been saying this by implication all along. For the reader whom the speaker has come to see as a man in his own right, not a burden to be carried, has been necessary to the speaker's discoveries, which have been made not by

201

means of a lonely meditation, but in a monologue to readers on the road. Speaker and reader support each other. In the indoor world men cannot really talk—there is "No husband, no wife, no friend, trusted to hear the confession"; on the road one can be a "Truster of men and women," and talk of himself.

Learning to speak to readers, discovering the possibilities of his voice, Whitman has discovered himself and his world. Yet discovery is also creation. In the sense that his uncovering of the kernels of reality is dependent upon his journey with readers in the open air, Whitman has been formed by the road; but in another sense he has formed it, for his complicated journey toward himself and toward readers is testimony to the richness of the symbol. The road, by the time Whitman has worked with it, is not merely the "long brown path," nor the open air or sea, nor even the principle of openness. It is these things but more than these, for if Whitman's poem is the "song of the open road," then the road itself takes on all the complications of his song—its light-heartedness and pain, its hesitations and bravado, its abstractions and imagery, its frankness and its stratagems. The road is each man's way of "crossing"—his avenue, however idiosyncratic, toward knowledge of himself, Nature, and other men.

Our own road through Whitman's monodramas has another bend to turn, "As I Ebb'd with the Ocean of Life." As in "Song of Myself," the speaker is torn between his suffering "actual" self and his conception of what he should be, the "mystical identity" or ideal self, here called "the real Me." Again the reconciliation of the two selves, the making of a whole identity, depends on Whitman's taking a new look at separateness and involvement.

As the poem begins, we overhear an address from the speaker to Paumanok, the "fish-shaped island"—an address that, since it tells a story instead of recording a movement in the poetic voice, is as much narrative as lyric. The story is about a time in the recent past:

> As I ebb'd with the ocean of life,
> As I wended the shores I know,
> As I walk'd where the ripples continually wash
>   you Paumanok,
> Where they rustle up hoarse and sibilant,

Where the fierce old mother endlessly cries for
  her castaways,
I musing late in the autumn day, gazing off southward,
Held by this electric self out of the pride of which
  I utter poems,
Was seiz'd by the spirit that trails in the lines
  underfoot,
The rim, the sediment that stands for all the water
  and all the land of the globe.

[Section 1, pp. 253–54.]

The island Paumanok, "fish-shaped," is at once part of and
separate from the "measureless float" that surrounds it: Whitman
uses the original name because it means, he says, "the island with
its breast long drawn out, and laid against the sea." [5] In a like
manner, of course, the ocean, "mother" to the man of whom
Paumanok is "father," is wedded to the land even as it is separate
from it. The spirit of "The rim, the sediment," the place where
water and land are indistinguishable, is the spirit of the organic
vision—the sense of the inseparability of "all the water and all the
land of the globe." "Even as a boy," Whitman tells us, he "had the
fancy, the wish, to write a piece, perhaps a poem, about the sea-
shore—that suggesting, dividing line, contact, junction, the solid
marrying the liquid—that curious, lurking something, (as doubtless every objective form finally becomes to the subjective spirit,)
which means far more than its mere first sight, grand as that is—
blending the real and ideal, and each made portion of the other." [6]

The "rim," therefore, can suggest either the glories or the horrors
of the organic vision, depending upon the observer's frame of
mind. A notebook entry, at which we have looked in another
context, records the rim's suggestion of glory—Whitman's seizure
by the notion that he can be one with all the world: "When I
walked at night by the sea shore and looked up at the countless
stars, I asked of my soul whether it would be filled and satisfied
when it should become god enfolding all these, and open to the life
and delight and knowledge of everything in them or of them; and
the answer was plain to me at the breaking water on the sands of
my feet; and the answer was, No, when I reach there, I shall want
to go further still." [7] Section 1 does not report Whitman's seizure

by a sense of his own pettiness. If he is "Fascinated" by "Chaff, straw, splinters of wood, weeds, and the sea-gluten," he has also been fascinated, with no sense of his own diminution, by "mossy scabs of the worm fence, heap'd stones, elder, mullein and poke-weed" (Section 5, "Song of Myself," p. 33).

It is Section 2 that records the shift in attitude:

> As I wend to the shores I know not,
> As I list to the dirge, the voices of men
> and women wreck'd,
> As I inhale the impalpable breezes that set in
> upon me,
> As the ocean so mysterious rolls toward me closer
> and closer,
> I too but signify at the utmost a little wash'd-up drift,
> A few sands and dead leaves to gather,
> Gather, and merge myself as part of the sands
> and drift.
>
> [P. 254.]

It is *now* that his sense of identity with the drift makes him feel small: he has "move[d] his hand or foot an inch," and it is as Ishmael warns:

. . . lulled into such an opium-like listlessness of vacant, unconscious reverie is this absent-minded youth by the blending cadence of waves with thoughts, that at last he loses his identity; takes the mystic ocean at his feet for the visible image of that deep, blue, bottomless soul, pervading mankind and nature. . . . In this enchanted mood, thy spirit ebbs away to whence it came; becomes diffused through time and space. . . .

There is no life in thee, now, except that rocking life imparted by a gently rolling ship; by her, borrowed from the sea; by the sea, from the inscrutable tides of God. But while this sleep, this dream is on ye, move your foot or hand an inch; slip your hold at all; and your identity comes back in horror. Over Decartian vortices you hover. And perhaps, at mid-day, in the fairest weather, with one half-throttled shriek you drop through that transparent air into the summer sea, no more to rise for ever. Heed it well, ye Pantheists! [8]

In the notebook entry and Section 33 of "Song of Myself," Whitman, seized by his "electric self" and leaping into the vision

204

of merger, feels himself "diffused through time and space": his "ties and ballasts" leave him, and he is everywhere. In "Out of the Cradle Endlessly Rocking" he is strongly attracted to the "rocking life," but also, having shifted from the perspective of Section 33, feels threatened by it. Now, in Section 2 of "As I Ebb'd," the shift has become total and we see him at his low ebb. "There and then," in the scene reported in Section 1, he may have been ebb*ing* ("As I ebb'd with the ocean of life"), but he was still "Held by this electric self out of the pride of which I utter poems." Now, however, as the ocean flows again ("the ocean so mysterious rolls toward me closer and closer"), he feels like the drift, a "castaway" who will not be bathed by the ocean, as in "Cradle," but drowned by it, engulfed again by the waves that have cast him on the shore.

The pull of the electric self is gone, and Whitman is overwhelmed by what has merely nagged at him in "Song of Myself," his sense of the distance between his actual self and his ideal self:

> O baffled, balk'd, bent to the very earth,
> Oppress'd with myself that I have dared to open
>   my mouth,
> Aware now that amid all that blab whose echoes
>   recoil upon me I have not once had the least
>   idea who or what I am,
> But that before all my arrogant poems the real Me
>   stands yet untouch'd, untold, altogether unreach'd,
> Withdrawn far, mocking me with mock-congratulatory
>   signs and bows,
> With peals of distant ironical laughter at every word
>   I have written,
> Pointing in silence to these songs, and then to the
>   sand beneath.
>   [P. 254.]

Whitman has accomplished, as the climactic action of "Song of Myself," a reconciliation of the actual self and the ideal self, and he has built upon that reconciliation in "Song of the Open Road"; but now, in "As I Ebb'd," he shows us the reconciliation come undone. He is conscious more intensely than ever of the split between what he actually is—a man anchored to the ground, physically petty, and a poet who must deal in words inadequate to express the hidden

205

meanings of life—and what he is ideally, his own hidden meaning, the "mystical identity" that is harmonious both inwardly and with all the world and that therefore is no size and needs no words. Whitman hovers indeed over "Descartian vortices": at the end of Section 2, he fears Nature, condemns himself as he identifies himself with the drift, and rejects his poems.

Yet even here he is not completely at ebb. Even in this moment of terrible despair and loneliness, the poet is beginning to move outside himself. The discovery of his own pettiness in the drift is inseparable from the familiar movement of "Song of Myself," the merging and gathering:

> A few sands and dead leaves to gather,
> Gather, and merge myself as part of the
> sands and drift.
>
> [P. 254.]

And for the first time in the poem he becomes concerned with the larger implications of his problem: "I perceive I have not really understood any thing, not a single object, and that no man ever can." If that statement is self-pitying, and to some extent an attempt at self-justification, it is also the faint stirring of an outward tendency, the turning away from the separate world of the private self toward the community of men and Nature.

Section 3 begins with a change of tone that testifies to the quickening of the outward, healing tendency:

> You oceans both, I close with you,
> We murmur alike reproachfully rolling sands
> and drift, knowing not why,
> These little shreds indeed standing for you
> and me and all.

> You friable shore with trails of debris,
> You fish-shaped island, I take what is underfoot,
> What is yours is mine my father.
>
> [P. 255.]

Earlier he has admitted woefully his identity with "the sediment": now, "clos[ing] with" the ocean of water and the ocean of rolling sand, he insists upon his identity with "the sediment," which marks the meeting place of the two oceans.* He accepts himself, that is, as a drowned man—a role he has avoided in "The Sleepers":

> I too Paumanok,
> I too have bubbled up, floated the measureless
> float, and been wash'd on your shores,
> I too am but a trail of drift and debris,
> I too leave little wrecks upon you, you fish-
> shaped island.
>
> [P. 255.]

The acceptance is made as an existential act of faith: "knowing not why" he is what he is, he embraces what he is. Yet that kind of commitment is not sufficient for this hero. Also behind the acceptance, at first merely suggested but then emerging as a desperate cry, is a drive for the security of certainty:

> . . . I take what is underfoot,
> What is yours is mine my father.
>
> . . . .
>
> I throw myself upon your breast my father,
> I cling to you so that you cannot unloose me,
> I hold you so firm till you answer me something.
>
> Kiss me my father,
> Touch me with your lips as I touch those I love,
> Breathe to me while I hold you close the secret
> of the murmuring I envy.
>
> [P. 255.]

When the boy in "Cradle" calls out in the same way for ultimate answers, we put it down to youthful recklessness as well as fear and note that the mature poet does not seem wholly sympathetic to the call. Yet here the speaker's cry is a welcome sign of life. When the

---

* This is the best I can do with the puzzling line—"You oceans both, I close with you." It is possible, and I once thought, that the two oceans are the ebbing water and the water which is now flowing—but that does not make very striking sense in context. It is perhaps more likely that the oceans are his own flowing ocean, as represented by his "electricity" in the episode described in Section 1, and his own presently ebbing ocean. But I cannot figure why he would now "close" with his flowing ocean. The movement here, rather, is an insistence on himself as petty —which seems to me to suggest that he is "closing" with the sediment, closing with "You oceans both" by closing with the meeting place of the ocean of water and the ocean of sand, which Whitman here for the only time calls "rolling sands," as if to suggest a wavelike movement.

"drowned man" calls for help and clings for safety to a comrade-father, we are not inclined to give him up.

Somewhere the poet gets his answer, for the first lines of Section 4 demonstrate that he has come as far since his last words as he does between Sections 2 and 3:

> Ebb, ocean of life, (the flow will return,)
> Cease not your moaning you fierce old mother,
> Endlessly cry for your castaways, but fear not,
>   deny not me,
> Rustle not up so hoarse and angry against my
>   feet as I touch you or gather from you.
>
> [P. 255.]

So far is the poet from fearing the ocean now, that he no longer counts himself a "castaway" and even tells the ocean not to fear *his* outward movement. And in a faint echo of the "gab" he earlier rejects, he assures the flowing ocean that it has nothing to fear from ebbing—for he, Whitman, has ebbed and come to life again! We can speculate, I think, that the new confidence results from his embrace of the land. We never hear the word from the land; but the secret of Paumanok, it seems to me, is simply the opposite of the sea's secret in "Cradle." It is the truth of separateness, the truth of an island, which holds itself apart from "the measureless float." To keep from drowning in "Descartian vortices," Whitman must embrace the Cartesian split: just as in "Song of Myself" he must insist on loneliness and mortality in order to pass beyond them, so here he must embrace matter and separateness, in order to join them again, in a living relationship, to spirit and involvement.

So Whitman begins by seeing the blending, the inseparability, of land and sea, but finds himself petty by the light of that truth; in fear, he embraces land, separateness, as a truth in and of itself, and finds that he can once more love the sea. And finally, having found his "father" and "mother," he comes to find himself, the issue of matter and spirit, separateness and endless involvement:

> I mean tenderly by you and all,
> I gather for myself and for this phantom
>   looking down where we lead, and following
>   me and mine.
>
> [P. 256.]

The distance between himself and "the real Me," the phantom, has been radically reduced: if he is incapable of the glorious reconciliation of "actual self" and "ideal self" that he achieves in "Song of Myself," at least he manages to heal his wound. He is no longer the debris itself but a gatherer of debris; and he gathers "for myself and for this phantom" the poems that the phantom scorns and he rejects in Section 2. Thus he says "me and mine"—himself and his poems—and ends the poem with a passage that is as much a defense of the poems as an apology for them:

> Me and mine, loose windrows, little corpses,
> Froth, snowy white, and bubbles,
> (See, from my dead lips the ooze exuding at last,
> See, the prismatic colors glistening and rolling,)
> Tufts of straw, sands, fragments,
> Buoy'd hither from many moods, one contradicting
>   another,
> From the storm, the long calm, the darkness, the
>   swell,
> Musing, pondering, a breath, a briny tear, a dab
>   of liquid or soil,
> Up just as much out of fathomless workings fer-
>   mented and thrown, . . .
>   [P. 256.]

He is not really a drowned man at all, for, just as the dead limbs in "Song of Myself" give off "sparkles," his "dead" lips exude an ooze with the "prismatic colors" of life—the "ooze" of poetry. He is, in fact, the ocean itself, for he casts up "fragments," poems, out of his own "fathomless workings"—his own contradictory moods.

In the last moments of the poem, the haunting presence of "the real Me" fades away, its place "up there" taken by the reader, Whitman's familiar "Whoever you are":

> We, capricious, brought hither we know not
>   whence, spread out before you,
> You up there walking or sitting,
> Whoever you are, we too lie in drifts at
>   your feet.
>   [P. 256.]

209

The subtle disappearance of the phantom signals the last, subtle turn of the poet: in this final outward movement, his reaching toward readers, he demonstrates for once and all his reawakening. He does not, of course, take the lofty place of the didactic poet at the end of "Song of Myself"; nor will he ever match the flood of great dramatic poems appearing between 1855–60—"The Sleepers," "Song of Myself," "Crossing Brooklyn Ferry," "Song of the Broad-Axe," "From Pent-up Aching Rivers," "Scented Herbage of My Breast," and "As I Ebb'd." But neither is he dead to us. If we can think of the imagistic and didactic poems, which appear increasingly in 1860 and afterward, as Whitman's attempts to have things all one way or another, to gain surcease from the struggle he plays out in each dramatic poem, at the same time they have their own importance. They may be, in fact, "debris," "fragments" that Whitman shores against his ruins; but they are fragments well made, which do as much as they can within the limitations of their forms.

Yet, important as they are, we have come, as readers of monodramas, a long way from the roles they made us play. Like imagistic poems, monodramas make us come to the poet's world, but, focusing on action instead of thing, they are necessarily less private; the action—beginning, turning, and end—gives us direction, but not the oppressive direction of the worst didactic poems, which join mask and focus against us in a conspiracy of preaching. So we are asked, by the dramatic poems, neither too much nor too little, and thus have much to do and gain. Although our interviews on the grass and road with Whitman and our glimpse of him on the shore are not so strange as our night meeting with him in "The Sleepers," they are strange enough. As it is in the dream poem, we are given few guides into the meaning of the actions: like the hero of "Song of Myself," we "must get what the writing means." Above all, despite the disclaimer of that idler in disguise, we are required to be "aware." In being conscious of shifts in mood, changes in imagery, modifications of stance—in suspending our disbelief till we can get what the action means—we yield our separate identities; but at the same time, of course, we affirm them and make them new.

VII INDIRECTION: READER ENGAGEMENT

WHITMAN'S "INDIRECTION" or "suggestiveness" is, he claims, an attempt to urge readers into their own free journey: "I round and finish little, if anything; and could not, consistently with my scheme. The reader will always have his or her part to do, just as much as I have had mine. I seek less to state or display any theme or thought, and more to bring you, reader, into the atmosphere of the theme or thought—there to pursue your own flight."[1] But if he wants us to involve ourselves, he also, as we have seen, wants to control our involvement: he would send us on a journey, but along a road of his making, a poem with an action we must trace. He would, moreover, prepare us for the journey, and demand that we be in good shape along the way:

> About this business of Democracy & human rights &c,
> often comes the query—as one sees the shallowness
> and miserable selfism of these crowds of men, with
> all their minds so blank of high humanism and as-
> piration—. . . . Is not Democracy of human rights
> humbug after all—Are these flippant people with
> hearts of rags and souls of chalk, are these worth
> preaching for & dying for upon the cross? May be
> not—may be it is indeed a dream—yet one thing
> sure remains—but the exercise of Democracy, equality,

211

to him who, believing preaches, and to the people who
work it out—*this* is not a dream—to work for Democracy
is good, the exercise is good—strength it makes &
lessons it teaches—gods it makes, at any rate, though
it crucifies them often.[2]

One's self—you, whoever you are, pour'd into whom
all that you read and hear what existent is in
heroes or events, with landscape, heavens, and
every beast and bird, becomes so only then with
play and interplay. For what to you or me is the
round universe, . . . except as feeding you and me?
May-be indeed it is by us created in winking of our
eyes. Or may-be for preparing us, by giving us
identity—then sailing us with winds o'er the great
seas, the apparent known, steadily to the harbors
of the really great unknown.[3]

For Whitman, being a good democrat and being a good reader
require the same "exercise"; only by "work[ing] it out" will we become strong; only by "play and interplay" between us and the reality outside, including the reality that is a poem, will we find our
"identity." Thus he is "the teacher of athletes"; and his favorite
sport, as suggested earlier, is wrestling:

"Don't read my books" I heard Walt. Whitman . . . say one day. . . :
"You want something good in the usual sense; a plot, a love story—
something based on the accepted principles and on precedent. You
don't want something to wrestle with you and puzzle you, you want one
of the good English poets' books—or the good and pleasing Long-
fellow, or such. I have written no such books. I have attempted to
construct a poem on the open principles of nature. . . . The whole
drift of my books is to form a race of fuller athletic, yet unknown
characters, men and women for the United States to come.[4]

If we wrestle with the poem, Whitman says in this note for one of
his self-advertisements, if we struggle to find the meaning of that
"*furtive* . . . old hen" * the poet, then we will be something like
poets ourselves, for we will have helped to make the poem.

* Edward Carpenter, *Days*, p. 43, quotes Whitman: "What lies behind 'Leaves
of Grass' is . . . concealed, studiedly concealed; some passages left purposely obscure. There is something in my nature *furtive* like an old hen! You see a hen
wandering up and down a hedgerow, looking apparently quite unconcerned, but

To urge us into this kind of involvement, Whitman writes poems like the monodramas just discussed—poems that do not have plot "in the usual sense," that are not stories told by a narrator about more or less typical characters, but that demonstrate "the open principles of nature" by showing us, without guides into the action, the private struggles and development of a distinctly individual hero. And he writes poems even more indirect than those—poems that, because their main purpose seems to be the involvement of the reader, I call "poems of reader engagement." The involvement or "engagement" Whitman requires can be either intellectual or imaginative—or, at its best, both intellectual and imaginative.

In "Respondez!," whose title makes obvious its concern with the reader, the involvement demanded is intellectual. In this rejected poem, a longer version of a three-line poem called "Transpositions" (pp. 433–34), Whitman presents a list of propositions that seem at first glance to be ironic inversions, bitter indictments of a sleeping, decadent America:

> RESPONDEZ! Respondez!
> (The war is completed—the price is paid—the title
>   is settled beyond recall;)
> Let every one answer! let those who sleep be waked!
>   let none evade!
> Must we still go on with our affectations and sneaking?
> Let me bring this to a close—I pronounce openly for a
>   new distribution of roles;
> . . . .
> Let men and women be mock'd with bodies and mock'd
>   with Souls!
> Let the love that waits in them, wait! let it die, or
>   pass still-born to other spheres!
> . . . .
> Let the people sprawl with yearning, aimless hands!
>   let their tongues be broken! let their eyes be
>   discouraged! let none descend into their hearts
>   with the fresh lusciousness of love!

presently she finds a concealed spot, and furtively lays an egg, and comes away as though nothing had happened! That is how I felt in writing 'Leaves of Grass.' Sloan Kennedy calls me 'artful'—which about hits the mark. I think there are truths which it is necessary to envelop or wrap up."

213

(Stifled, O days! O lands! in every public and
    private corruption!
Smother'd in thievery, impotence, shamelessness,
    mountain-high;
Brazen effrontery, scheming, rolling like ocean's waves
    around and upon you, O my days! my lands!
For not even those thunderstorms, nor fiercest lightnings
    of the war, have purified the atmosphere;)
—Let the theory of America still be management, caste,
    comparison! (Say! what other theory would you?)
                         [Pp. 591–92.]

But a few of the propositions, we realize on closer inspection,
double back on the poem—are not ironic at all:

Let that which stood in front go behind! and let that
    which was behind advance to the front and speak;
                         [P. 591.]

Let contradictions prevail! let one thing contradict
    another! and let one line of my poems contradict
    another!
                         [P. 591.]

Let the cow, the horse, the camel, the garden-bee
    —let the mud-fish, the lobster, the mussel,
eel, the sting-ray, and the grunting pig-fish
    —let these, and the like of these, be put on
a perfect equality with man and woman!
                         [P. 592.]

These lines, published in 1856, agree so closely with some of the
most famous of Whitman's assertions in the 1855 edition—for one,
"Do I contradict myself? Very well then . . . I contradict myself"
—that we have no choice but to take them as sober statements of
belief, and then to wonder about "Respondez!" as a whole.
Whitman, with a parenthetical hint, encourages our wrestling:

Let judges and criminals be transposed! Let the
    prison-keepers be put in prison! let those
    that were prisoners take the keys! (Say! why
    might they not just as well be transposed?)
                         [P. 593.]

The poem, it turns out, is a test of our wits. What are we to make, for instance, of the proposition, "Let him who is without my poems be assassinated!" (p. 592)? If we are not alert, we find ourselves tricked, exposed by Whitman's irony as one who is still asleep.

In "Crossing Brooklyn Ferry," on the other hand, it is the reader's imagination, not his alertness, that is exercised. For good reason: imagination, the poem suggests, is what allows the private self to participate in the external world, and two private selves, poet and reader, to join experiences in the world of the poem.*

In his first lines the speaker, personifying the things of nature, reveals himself as an imaginative man:

> Flood-tide below me! I see you face to face!
> Clouds of the west—sun there half an hour high—
>   I see you also face to face.

> [P. 159.]

At the same time, these lines, and of course the title, introduce the speaker as a "crosser"—a rider of the ferry from Brooklyn to Manhattan, and a man fascinated by the turn of the tide and the crossing of day into night. This double impression, of the speaker as a "crosser" and as an imaginative man, is reinforced by the remainder of Section 1:

> Crowds of men and women attired in the usual costumes,
>   how curious you are to me!
> On the ferry-boats the hundreds and hundreds that cross,
>   returning home, are more curious to me than you suppose,
> And you that shall cross from shore to shore years hence
>   are more to me, and more in my meditations, than you
>   might suppose.

> [Pp. 159–60.]

Now the crossing is to the speaker's companions on the ferry as well as to the things of Nature, and even to a man of the future, the reader, who is reached by "meditations," exercises of the imagination.

* Although Coffman, "Catalog Technique," *Modern Philology*, II, 225–32, approaches "Crossing Brooklyn Ferry" from an angle somewhat different from mine, my reading touches his at several points. See also Miller, " 'Brooklyn Ferry' and Imaginative Fusion," *Guide*, pp. 80–89.

As we recognize that the physical act of "crossing Brooklyn ferry" is analogous to the crossings achieved by the imagination, we are encouraged to accept ourselves as proper subjects of the poem, as much a part of Whitman's universe as the present things and people he describes. If the clouds and tide can be looked on "face to face," so can we, whose faces the poet never saw; if even the "usual" crowds are special, "curious," to this speaker, we can certainly believe ourselves worthy of his attention; if the speaker is himself special, different from what we ordinarily "might suppose," and still interested in us, surely we too are special. Whitman would cultivate our sense of individual identity, our sense of specialness, so that we might more willingly enter the world of his poem, all of whose inhabitants are "curious." The keenness of his psychological awareness is matched by the subtlety of his rhetoric. Shifting his direct address from the tide and clouds to his companions on the ferry and finally to ourselves as readers, he brings us into the poem almost without our realizing it. Accepting ourselves as special, we also accept ourselves as part of the communal "you."

As early as Section 1, then, the barriers have begun to fall. Whitman is teaching us how to cross, or encouraging our tendencies to cross: only by asserting self, using the special quality that is imagination, will we be able to join his harmonious community. This relationship between individual and community, rendered implicitly in Section 1, is given explicit statement in Section 2:

> The impalpable sustenance of me from all things at all
>   hours of the day,
> The simple, compact, well-join'd scheme, myself disin-
>   tegrated, every one disintegrated yet part of the scheme,
> The similitudes of the past and those of the future,
> The glories strung like beads on my smallest sights and
>   hearings, on the walk in the street and the passage
>   over the river,
> The current rushing so swiftly and swimming with me
>   far away,
> The others that are to follow me, the ties between me
>   and them,
> The certainty of others, the life, love, sight, hearing
>   of others.

[P. 160.]

216

The passage begins and ends in abstraction, but its core is made of images, and together the two kinds of expression "explain" Section 1. Given the phrase "every one disintegrated yet part of the scheme," we realize that the community created in Section 1—a world in which Natural forces and present and future human beings are all involved with one another—is an imitation of what Whitman takes to be a total "scheme"; and we realize also that the association he is attempting to create between the reader and that community, in which the reader would assert his identity yet become part of the whole, represents the relationship he thinks to be proper between whatever individual and the external world. The concept is enriched by the form of the passage, which moves not logically but associatively, from idea to image and back to idea, and by the images themselves. The beads emphasize the separateness, the "disintegration," of the various parts of the whole, and the aloofness of the perceiver, who can think of his senses as the string that passes through experiences, unifying them but essentially unchanged by them; whereas the current emphasizes unity, and the involvement of the perceiver, who is caught up by waters so intimate to him that they can be thought of as "swimming." The closing abstraction thus is charged by the images. Whitman can return to "the others that are to follow" in confidence that we who follow in time will also, enticed by the rich possibilities of relationship, follow in spirit. He stresses our "other-ness," including *others* in six consecutive lines, only in order to heighten his insistence on the "similitudes" of the future. He is on safe enough ground, for he concentrates not on the specific experience of the ferry-crossing, though he begins there, but on universal phenomena:

> A hundred years hence, or ever so many hundred years
>   hence, others will see them,
> Will enjoy the sunset, the pouring-in of the flood-tide,
>   the falling-back to the sea of the ebb-tide.
>   [P. 160.]

In Section 3 he is more daring. "Similitude" becomes "identity," for Whitman, shifting tense in order to emphasize his status as a man of the present, claims not just to be like us, but to be with us:

217

It avails not, time nor place—distance avails not,
I am with you, you men and women of a generation, or ever
  so many generations hence,
Just as you feel when you look on the river and sky,
  so I felt,
Just as any of you is one of a living crowd, I was one
  of a crowd,
Just as you are refresh'd by the gladness of the river
  and the bright flow, I was refresh'd,
Just as you stand and lean on the rail, yet hurry with the
  swift current, I stood yet was hurried,
Just as you look on the numberless masts of ships and the
  thick-stemm'd pipes of steamboats, I look'd.

[Pp. 160–61.]

He seems to assume that we have precisely the experiences he has had, the specific sensations of the ferry ride, and therefore are at one with him. This would be a dangerous position indeed to take, for if sensing unity with the poet depends on identical physical experience, then the erection of Brooklyn Bridge, though allowing us Hart Crane's great poem, would have seriously damaged this one. But Whitman is cunning enough to avoid the danger. Although we have not experienced the ferry crossing, our sense of unity with the poet is enhanced rather than disturbed, for in the guise of predicting our experiences, Whitman is actually introducing us to his, allowing us further to appreciate his world by describing it in minute detail.

The long list of sights that closes Section 3, one of the most successful of Whitman's catalogues, includes scenes from winter and summer, from midday, twilight, and night. The eye focuses almost always on motion—sailors at work, vessels arriving, hulls swinging—and often on the evanescence of things: "the gradual edging toward the south" of the "Twelfth-month sea-gulls,". the "shimmering track of beams," the changing patterns of waves, the falling of flags at sunset, the flicker of light cast over the city by foundry chimneys. The effect is to capture both the particularities of Whitman's ferry crossing—the special action, the life, of each thing—and its universal quality, the participation of the crossing in the eternal round, the turn of the year, the turn of the day, the

218

delicate turn of each thing toward shadow, haze, and darkness. Presented with these pictures, we experience imaginatively what the speaker claims to have enjoyed through the senses. His assertion that we have had his experiences may be false at the start, but by the end he has made it true. Brooklyn Bridge or no, he has his way: he is with us—not because he knows what we are doing, but because he has brought us to his world.

The nature of this relationship between poet and reader, demonstrated in Section 3, is stated openly in Section 4, which draws together the first three sections, briefly summarizing the first movement of the poem:

> These and all else were to me the same as they are to you,
> I loved well those cities, loved well the stately and
>   rapid river,
> The men and women I saw were all near to me,
> Others the same—others who look back on me because
>   I look'd forward to them,
> (The time will come, though I stop here to-day and to-night.)
> [P. 162.]

We look back on Whitman, experience his cities and his river, because he looked forward to us, presenting his world so as to encourage our participation in it.

In Sections 5–7, the second movement, he brings us even closer to him, for now, having introduced us to his world, he confronts us with his private self. He has been describing "the float forever held in solution"; now he begins a description of the self that has been "struck from the float":

> What is it then between us?
> What is the count of the scores or hundreds of years
>   between us?
>
> Whatever it is, it avails not—distance avails not,
>   and place avails not,
> I too lived, Brooklyn of ample hills was mine,
> I too walk'd the streets of Manhattan island, and bathed
>   in the waters around it,
> I too felt the curious abrupt questionings stir within me,
> In the day among crowds of people sometimes they came upon me,

219

In my walks home late at night or as I lay in my bed
    they came upon me,
I too had been struck from the float forever held in solution,
I too had receiv'd identity by my body,
That I was I knew was of my body, and what I should be I knew
    I should be of my body.

[P. 162.]

Earlier, in Section 3, he has said that he is "one of a crowd," refreshed by the scenes of the night; now he shows himself lying awake in the night, separated from the crowd by his "curious abrupt questionings." Yet, in repeating the crucial line "it avails not—distance avails not," Section 5 is an echo of Section 3: knowledge of the separate self, represented by *body*, is as important for communication between poet and reader as knowledge of the external world.

This special quality of the speaker, the sense of separateness that is as important to life as the harmony described in Section 3, has several aspects. As presented in Section 6, it is self-doubt; the tendency toward evil—the "cheating look, the frivolous word, the adulterous wish"; and secretiveness in the presence of comrades. The life of the individual is "the same old laughing, gnawing, sleeping": like the external life depicted in Section 3, it gleams but also has its "dark patches," frolics and shimmers but also recedes and grows dim. The individual lives a life, but plays a part—"The same old role, the role that is what we make it. . . ." As in the Calamus group, the reader is warned that the speaker may be different from what he seems, but that very confession makes their relationship more intimate. Section 7, summarizing the second movement as Section 4 does the first, states what has already become true—"Closer yet I approach you . . ." (pp. 162–63).

Larger summaries yet are provided by Sections 8 and 9, both of which bring together the previous two movements, testifying in different ways to the importance of the external world and of the private self. At the same time these sections end the story of the reader's imaginative entrance into Whitman's double world, for, proceeding from the assumption that the entrance is already accomplished, they close the poem in celebration.

Section 8 is composed entirely of rhetorical questions that praise

220

the special life, the "curiousness," of all the various inhabitants whom Whitman has described: the sunset, the waves, and other sights of the ferry crossing; the comrades attracted by the speaker; the speaker himself; and finally the reader:

> What is more subtle than this which ties me to the woman
>   or man that looks in my face?
> Which fuses me into you now, and pours my meaning into you?
>
> We understand then do we not?
> What I promis'd without mentioning it, have you not accepted?
> What the study could not teach—what the preaching could
>   not accomplish is accomplish'd, is it not?
>
> [P. 164.]

What the reader has accepted, through an act of the imagination, is the importance, the reality for him, of the speaker's environment and private self. Whitman is thus enabled to go beyond a simple description of the scenes of the ferry crossing. Section 9 begins with a long series of exclamations, which serve as tonal complements, responses of a sort, to the rhetorical questions of Section 8. Almost all the sights listed in Section 3 are reviewed, and their activity insisted upon: they are "appearances," "film"—but necessary, for, like the individual who plays a part, they are the guises of the soul, expressions of the vital force that can be sensed best in shimmering, haze, and shadow. As such symbolic expressions of the soul, they are "dumb, beautiful ministers"—the stuff through which men travel to the soul, and therefore to each other.

> You have waited, you always wait, you dumb, beautiful
>   ministers,
> We receive you with free sense at last, and are insatiate
>   henceforward,
> Not you any more shall be able to foil us, or withhold
>   yourselves from us,
> We use you, and do not cast you aside—we plant you permanently
>   within us,
> We fathom you not—we love you—there is perfection in you also,
> You furnish your parts toward eternity,
> Great or small, you furnish your parts toward the soul.
>
> [P. 165.]

221

The poem ends, in a sense, where it begins—in praise of the things of the external world. But there is a difference: at the end the speaker is saying *We*. A connection has been made between man and man as well as between man and Nature, and that "crossing," born of the speaker's concern and the reader's imaginative faith, testifies as much as any sensory experience to the fullness and richness of life.

Intellectual alertness and imaginative faith together are demanded from us by "When Lilacs Last in the Dooryard Bloom'd." It seems, at first, that "Lilacs" can be read in the same way as "The Sleepers": it has the same dreamlike quality, for we are witness to the drama of a mind's working with the peculiarly private problem of grief. "Lilacs" provides, however, not even the occasional overt guidance that we find in "The Sleepers"; its pauses, turnings, and radical shifts require even more from our awarenesses.

"Lilacs" deals with Whitman's exploration of images all of which are bound up with the problem of mourning—his gradual, half-conscious explanation, to himself and to readers, of their origins and meanings. Since each image carries with it a particular mood and even a certain conception of life and death, the largest action of "Lilacs" is what we have come to expect of Whitman's dramatic poems: the poet's movement among different moods and ideas in an attempt to come to terms with the outside world and finally with himself.

Two of the images, the lilac and the star, appear in the first lines of the poem, where they have the importance only of natural facts, the setting for that time in the recent past when the poet "mourn'd":

> When lilacs last in the dooryard bloom'd,
> And the great star early droop'd in the
>   western sky in the night,
> I mourn'd, and yet shall mourn with ever-
>   returning spring.
> [Section 1, p. 328.]

These lines are spoken as if from a time somewhat after the spring of Lincoln's death (the spring when the star "droop'd" and the lilacs last bloomed) and before the following spring; but in the next lines, the speaker loses his descriptive objectivity and, caught up by his own talk of mourning, begins to mourn right now:

> Ever-returning spring, trinity sure to me you bring,
> Lilac blooming perennial and drooping star in the west,
> And thought of him I love.
>
> [Section 1, p. 328.]

He turns away from readers and addresses the "spring," and as he loses his detachment from that terrible April it is apparent that he cannot separate the physical setting of the original mourning from the continuing "thought of him I love"—that images and thought are fused, a "trinity," in his one act of mourning.

This fusion of image and "thought of him" is a phenomenon Whitman notes also in "Death of Abraham Lincoln," the speech he delivered for years on the anniversary of Lincoln's death: "I remember where I was stopping at the time, the season being advanced, there were many lilacs in full bloom. By one of those caprices that enter and give tinge to events without being at all a part of them, I find myself always reminded of the great tragedy of that day by the sight and odor of these blossoms. It never fails." [5] Here "ever-returning spring" does indeed impose a symbol upon the poet; but in "Lilacs" Whitman at least partly makes the spring return and therefore helps to bring the "trinity" to himself. An interplay between the spring and the speaker, a cooperative creation in which each party is active and passive, brings into being the symbolic complex of star, lilac, and thought. The spring provides the original images and, being the time of Lincoln's death, in a sense causes the original mourning and therefore triggers subsequent mourning; the speaker, talking about his mourning, himself triggers new mourning and thus fills his own mind with the "trinity." Thus Whitman's movement for the rest of the poem is both an automatic acting-out of his pattern of grief, a yielding to the "caprice" that "give[s] tinge to events," and an active response to the pressure from Nature and himself, an attempt to explain the "caprice" and therefore to articulate the meaning of the "trinity," the meaning of his own grief.

His relationship to the star, in Section 2, is a case in point. On the one hand, he concentrates his attention on the star alone, as if he means to explore one by one the components of the trinity. But on the other hand, he is paralyzed with grief when he meets the star that he himself has brought forth:

> O powerful western fallen star!
> O shades of night—O moody, tearful night!
> O great star disappear'd—O the black murk
>   that hides the star!
> O cruel hands that hold me powerless—O
>   helpless soul of me!
> O harsh surrounding cloud that will not
>   free my soul.
>   [Section 2, p. 329.]

When he turns to the lilac, he is exploring the second component of the trinity, but he is also, as if by self-preserving reflex, trying to counter the desperate mood and the idea of love and loss that are suggested by the star:

> In the dooryard fronting an old farm-house
>   near the white-wash'd palings,
> Stands the lilac-bush tall-growing with
>   heart-shaped leaves of rich green,
> With many a pointed blossom rising delicate,
>   with the perfume strong I love,
> With every leaf a miracle—and from this
>   bush in the dooryard,
> With delicate-color'd blossoms and heart-
>   shaped leaves of rich green,
> A sprig with its flower I break.
>   [Section 3, p. 329.]

As the speaker moves his concentration from the fallen, hidden star to "the lilac-bush tall-growing," far forward in the composition, the psychic scene shifts from "the black murk" to the open air. The lilac suggests the idea of continuing life and the mood of quiet joy: calm celebration replaces the wild wailing of Section 2, and the speaker sees himself as active ("A sprig with its flower I break") instead of paralyzed. The light and activity suggest release from the intense grief of his sudden fall into mourning in Section 2, and also a growing assertion of himself against the symbols that have seized him: his struggle to live with his grief is inseparable from his struggle for expression.

Then, unannounced, two more symbols appear: the "shy and hidden" thrush, "warbling a song," and the coffin passing through country and city, "Carrying a corpse to where it shall rest in the grave." The hero wanders blindly, yet he is making a path to travel. Searching for a way out of his grief, he happens upon symbols that contain new values of mood and idea; but his movement also is deliberate—turning to the third component of his "trinity," he finds that to explore his "thought," he must give it symbolic shape. The resulting symbols, found or made, deal much more specifically than the lilac and star with the poet, the man mourned, and the relationship between them. There are striking analogies between the bird and the speaker's role in that relationship—though, as we shall see, far from a complete identity. The bird sings; it is hidden in "secluded recesses," which can refer not only to a swamp but also to the recesses of the speaker's mind; and it is the speaker's "dear brother":

> Solitary the thrush,
> The hermit withdrawn to himself, avoiding the
> settlements,
> Sings by himself a song.
>
> Song of the bleeding throat,
> Death's outlet song of life, (for well dear
> brother I know,
> If thou wast not granted to sing thou
> would'st surely die.)
> [Section 4, p. 330.]

The coffin, of course, is associated with the other party to the relationship, the dead "him." Thus the hero sees it as more public than the bird: no hider in a swamp, it "passes" everywhere; and it has reality not just for one listener but for a "sea" of silent onlookers. The symbol of the bird fuses the idea of love and loss with a sense of life; and the mood of desperate joy suggested by the bird's "bleeding throat" shows how different this new entity is from either star or lilac, those simpler symbols whose values it borrows. The coffin also suggests loss, but dominant is a new value—the

225

sense it carries of death as rest after a long journey ("Carrying a corpse to where it shall rest in the grave"), a sense of death accompanied by a mood of peace and quiet.

By the end of Section 6, then, four symbols have appeared in the poem, all of them having to do with the hero's mourning. The first two, the star and the lilac, have been brought to the speaker out of the unconscious, natural workings of himself and the spring; his probing for meaning in these *données*, or his stumbling upon other alternatives, results in his creation, or discovery within himself, of two other symbols, more complex. He is poised among four alternate conceptions of life and death: that death is final and life painful (his attitude in the context of the star), that death and life are part of one continuous process (the lilac), that life is transitory and death the final goal, a place of rest; and a fourth possibility, not made clear thus far in the poem, barely hinted at by the tone of the bird's song. Thus the speaker's attitude toward life and death is at this point in suspension; but in the other area of the poem's concern, the relationship between himself and the symbols that seize his imagination, he is becoming steadily more assertive.

His movement in one area will decide his direction in the other. In the last lines of Section 6, the complementary dramas take an important turn:

> Here, coffin that slowly passes,
> I give you my sprig of lilac.
> [Section 6, p. 331.]

The gift of a sprig of lilac is a simple act of reverence, but it has large implications: Whitman has, it seems, chosen to sacrifice the principle of continuing life to the principle of life as preparation for the long peace of death. At the same time, however, the gift is important for Whitman's movement toward expression—and the drive of that drama will prove to be more powerful than his inclination to sacrifice life to death. Until now, he has chosen to respond separately, or has been forced to respond separately, to each part of the symbolic complex that grips his mind. Now, however, he takes a long step: to give lilac to a coffin is to break the boundaries that exist around each symbol, to articulate the meaning of the symbols by placing them in relation to each other and himself in relation to them. Doing so, he moves closer to his own freedom, for he is now not just a responder to images which come unbidden to him, nor even a maker of symbols, but a maker of scenes that include symbols. To give away the lilac is to give away life, but to *see* himself as a giver of lilacs is to be the very figure of life.

The speaker and we ourselves are ready for the next turn of the speaker's mind. Section 7, a long parenthesis expanding on the scene invented at the end of Section 6, changes significantly the emphasis of that scene:

> (Nor for you, for one alone,
> Blossoms and branches green to coffins
>   all I bring,
> For fresh as the morning, thus would I
>   chant a song for you O sane and sacred death.
>
> All over bouquets of roses,
> O death, I cover you over with roses and
>   early lilies,
> But mostly and now the lilac that blooms
>   the first,
> Copious I break, I break the sprigs from
>   the bushes,
> With loaded arms I come, pouring for you,
> For you and the coffins all of you O death.)
> [Section 7, p. 331.]

The gift of a sprig of lilac is a sorrowful sacrifice of life to the memory of one dead man. But now Whitman, building upon the creativity implied by his scene-making, thinks for the first time that he will sing a song—a song about life, "fresh as the morning," which he images as a pouring forth of flowers. In one sense, the song, dedicated not to Lincoln but to "sane and sacred death," will simply multiply the act of reverence: it will be a copious breaking of sprigs, a breaking "for" death. But the hero also thinks of his song in a different way, as an assertion of life in the face of death. His song will "break . . . sprigs" only figuratively: the "tossing of lilacs" is really a creation of new life, an outpouring of words which will "cover . . . over" death. The symbols still grip him—thus his

227

use of "lilacs" as a metaphor for song and of "coffins" as a metaphor for death—but he has new vitality.

So when in Section 8 the hero returns to his exploration of those symbols, he does so with fresh confidence. Now he does not respond helplessly to them—is not controlled by them, but uses them to know himself. Compare this response to the star with the automatic frenzy of Section 2:

> O western orb sailing the heaven,
> Now I know what you must have meant as a
>   month since I walk'd,
> As I walk'd in silence the transparent
>   shadowy night,
> As I saw you had something to tell as you
>   bent to me night after night,
> As you droop'd from the sky low down as if
>   to my side, (while the other stars all
>   look'd on,)
> As we wander'd together the solemn night, (for
>   something I know not what kept me from sleep,)
> As the night advanced, and I saw on the rim of
>   the west how full you were of woe,
> As I stood on the rising ground in the breeze
>   in the cool transparent night,
> As I watch'd where you pass'd and was lost in
>   the netherward black of the night,
> As my soul in its trouble dissatisfied sank, as
>   where you sad orb,
> Concluded, dropt in the night, and was gone.
>   [Section 8, p. 331.]

"A month since," a short while before Lincoln's death, the speaker has had premonitions of evil ("something I know not what kept me from sleep"), and has had those premonitions aggravated by the star's bending and disappearance. Since that time, the premonitions have been justified and the star's meaning made clear by the actual falling of the "western star" that was the President from Illinois. The speaker has known from the start of the poem, of course, that Lincoln is dead; but he has had only a vague sense of the connection between the star's warning and Lincoln's death—

he knows that the star is fused with his thought of Lincoln, but he does not know why. This vague sense that the western star is also Lincoln is what makes him grieve so wildly in Section 2, whereas "a month since," as he tells us, his soul had been merely "dissatisfied" when the star "dropt." Now, in Section 8, he does not respond unconsciously to a vague sense of the star's meaning, but is actually able to tell the story that articulates that meaning—the truth that "drooping" must be "dropping," that love is followed inevitably by loss.

Knowing what the star meant, he knows also what the star means: he realizes why it has been fused in his mind with the "thought of him I love." Earlier he thinks in terms of symbols, producing the bird and coffin to represent the "thought"; but he has also, all the while, been thinking *about* symbols. His ability to articulate the meaning of the symbol demonstrates both his continuing growth away from paralyzing grief and his gradual discovery of the life within himself, for the articulation of meaning has come in the form of a reminiscence. First a maker of images, then a maker of scenes, he is now a maker of images, scene, and action—the teller of a story.

The hero has articulated the meanings of lilac and coffin by placing them in new relation to each other; as symbols they have all but departed the poem, having done their work and having had the hero's work done to them. Now in its turn the star will leave, and the speaker will move on to the most private of his symbols, the bird. But not just yet:

> Sing on there in the swamp,
> O singer bashful and tender, I hear your
>   notes, I hear your call,
> I hear, I come presently, I understand you,
> But a moment I linger, for the lustrous star
>   has detain'd me,
> The star my departing comrade holds and
>   detains me.
>   [Section 9, p. 332.]

Just as the lilac and coffin retain enough force to be used as metaphors in Section 7, the star "holds and detains" the speaker

229

even as it is "departing." The speaker will prove to himself that he "understand[s]" the bird, just as he has proved that he knows what the star means; but he is not quite ready for the final test.

He is ready, however, to delve more deeply into the problem of his own song. The somewhat wistful desire for song expressed in Section 7 ("thus would I chant a song for you O sane and sacred death") becomes in Section 10 a pattern of question and answer, challenge and confident response:

> O how shall I warble myself for the dead one
>   there I loved?
> And how shall I deck my song for the large
>   sweet soul that has gone?
> And what shall my perfume be for the grave of
>   him I love?
>
> Sea-winds blown from east and west,
> Blown from the Eastern sea and blown from the
>   Western sea, till there on the prairies
>   meeting,
> These and with these and the breath of my chant,
> I'll perfume the grave of him I love.
>
> [Section 10, p. 332.]

Again the hero makes new metaphors: his song will not be, as in Section 7, the tossing of lilacs upon a coffin, but a fusion of his breath with the breath of "Sea-winds." Nor does he practice only this new-found genius for image-making; he is, after all, a maker of scenes as well:

> O what shall I hang on the chamber walls?
> And what shall the pictures be that I hang
>   on the walls,
> To adorn the burial-house of him I love?
>
> Pictures of growing spring and farms and homes,
> With the Fourth-month eve at sundown, and the
>   gray smoke lucid and bright,
> With floods of the yellow gold of the gorgeous,
>   indolent, sinking sun, burning, expanding
>   the air,

> With the fresh sweet herbage under foot, and
>   the pale green leaves of the trees prolific,
> In the distance the flowing glaze, the breast
>   of the river, with a wind-dapple here and
>   there,
> With ranging hills on the banks, with many a
>   line against the sky, and shadows,
> And the city at hand with dwellings so dense,
>   and stacks of chimneys,
> And all the scenes of life and the workshops,
>   and the workmen homeward returning.
>   [Section 11, pp. 332–33.]

The "pictures" he would hang are rich in the detail of life and land, capturing with Impressionist accuracy a specific moment of a specific day—notably, a day in the month of Lincoln's assassination. The growth and action of country and city, embodied in insistent and swelling present participles, almost bursts from the framework of Whitman's reminders, in the opening and closing lines of the passage, that these are after all just "pictures," "scenes."

The hero is brimful of life, and the joy and urgency of his answers finally spill over into Section 12. Gone are "perfume," "pictures," "scenes"—all the metaphors standing between the speaker and song; gone is the need to give a reason for the song; gone is the singer's questioning, testing, challenging of himself. He simply sings:

> Lo, body and soul—this land,
> My own Manhattan with spires, and the spar-
>   kling and hurrying tides, and the ships,
> The varied and ample land, the South and the North
>   in the light, Ohio's shores and flashing Missouri,
> And ever the far-spreading prairies cover'd with
>   grass and corn.
>   [Section 12, p. 333.]

Having tried his voice and found it strong, Whitman moves even closer to a confrontation with the bird, the only symbol remaining unexplained. And still he pauses:

231

Sing on, sing on you gray-brown bird,
Sing from the swamps, the recesses, pour
    your chant from the bushes,
Limitless out of the dusk, out of the
    cedars and pines.

Sing on dearest brother, warble your reedy song,
Loud human song, with voice of uttermost woe.

O liquid and free and tender!
O wild and loose to my soul—O wondrous singer!
You only I hear—yet the star holds me, (but
    will soon depart,)
Yet the lilac with mastering odor holds me.
                  [Section 13, p. 333.]

He is fascinated by the bird's song, but seems fearful of his fascination. Protesting that he is held by the star and lilac, he really holds to them, as if the values they represent will protect him from the delicious danger close to his heart.

What the danger is we do not yet know, but as Section 14 begins we realize that Whitman has made the leap and is about to articulate the meaning of the bird. The explanation comes, as it does for the star, in the form of a story—a story that is a continuation of the one told in Section 8, a story about how Whitman felt when his forebodings came true:

Now while I sat in the day and look'd forth,
In the close of the day with its light and
    the fields of spring, and the farmers pre-
    paring their crops,
In the large unconscious scenery of my land
    with its lakes and forests,
In the heavenly aerial beauty, (after the
    perturb'd winds and the storms,)
Under the arching heavens of the afternoon swift
    passing, and the voices of children and women,
The many-moving sea-tides, and I saw the ships how
    they sail'd,
And the summer approaching with richness, and the
    fields all busy with labor,
. . . .

Falling upon them all and among them all, envel-
oping me with the rest,
Appear'd the cloud, appear'd the long black trail,
And I knew death, its thought, and the sacred
knowledge of death.

Then with the knowledge of death as walking one
side of me,
And the thought of death close-walking the other
side of me,
And I in the middle as with companions, and as
holding the hands of companions,
I fled forth to the hiding receiving night that
talks not,
Down to the shores of the water, the path by the
swamp in the dimness,
To the solemn shadowy cedars and ghostly pines
so still.

And the singer so shy to the rest receiv'd me,
The gray-brown bird I know receiv'd us comrades
three,
And he sang the carol of death, and a verse for
him I love.
[Section 14, pp. 333–34.]

The importance of the speaker's shift in tense here cannot be
overemphasized: the consistent past tense signifies present time no
more than it does in Section 8, the reminiscence about "a month
since." Whitman does not travel to the swamp now, as critics have
invariably alleged; [6] rather, he comes now to the point of being able
to tell about his previous psychic journey, his awakening to death.
He uses *Now* in the same way that he uses the present tense in
Section 5 of "Song of Myself"—dramatically, to convey the
excitement of the moment in the past. That time in the past is a
day in mid-April, the day of Lincoln's death; and the appearance of
the cloud, "the long black trail" that throws its shadow on that
day, is the news of Lincoln's death (thus in Section 6 the coffin
passed "Through day and night with the great cloud darkening the
land"). With but one change, the time of day when the "cloud"

233

fell, Section 14 is a metaphorical statement of the scene Whitman describes naturalistically in his prose works:

The day, April 14, 1865, seems to have been a pleasant one throughout the whole land—the moral atmosphere pleasant too. . . . Early herbage, early flowers, were out.[7]

The day of the murder we heard the news very early in the morning. Mother prepared breakfast—and other meals afterward—as usual; but not a mouthful was eaten all day by either of us. . . . Little was said. We got every newspaper morning and evening, and the frequent extras of that period, and pass'd them silently to each other.[8]

Whitman's song of life in Sections 11 and 12, it turns out, is actually preparation for the story to follow—a loving description of the look of that "pleasant" April day before the news came of Lincoln's death. Section 14 starts from that description ("Now while I sat in the day"), repeats some of it, and goes on to describe Whitman's awakening to death.

The awakening consists really of three stages of awareness: the first represented by Whitman's holding the hands of two comrades, the "thought of death" and the "knowledge of death"; the second represented by his "tallying" of the bird's song; the third, by the "unclosing" of his sight to visions. The first stage, produced by the shock of Lincoln's death, comes as an instantaneous understanding:

> And the streets how their throbbings throbb'd,
>   and the cities pent—lo, then and there,
> Falling upon them all and among them all,
>   enveloping me with the rest,
> Appear'd the cloud, appear'd the long black
>   trail,
> And I knew death, its thought, and the sacred
>   knowledge of death.
>   [Section 14, p. 334.]

It becomes clear in Section 15 that the "thought of death" is the idea of death as pain and that the "knowledge of death" is the idea of death as deliveress from pain (". . . I saw they were not as was thought,/ They themselves were fully at rest, they suffer'd not"). These contradictory conceptions combine, on that April day, to send the hero fleeing into a dark and hidden corner of his own mind—a place that is at once a swamp and an exotic garden. It is a place of both despair and religious ecstasy, inhabited by a self that is imaged as a bird with "loud human voice."

The bird sings what Whitman in his sudden sorrow wants most to hear—an elegiac lament and consolation:

> Come lovely and soothing death,
> Undulate round the world, serenely arriving,
>   arriving,
> In the day, in the night, to all, to each,
> Sooner or later delicate death.
>
> Prais'd be the fathomless universe,
> For life and joy, and for objects and knowledge
>   curious,
> And for love, sweet love—but praise!
>   praise! praise!
> For the sure-enwinding arms of cool-enfolding
>   death.
>
> Dark mother always gliding near with soft feet,
> Have none chanted for thee a chant of fullest
>   welcome?
> Then I chant it for thee, I glorify thee above all,
> I bring thee a song that when thou must indeed
>   come, come unfalteringly.
>
> Approach strong deliveress,
> When it is so, when thou has taken them I
>   joyously sing the dead,
> Lost in the loving floating ocean of thee,
> Laved in the flood of thy bliss O death.
>
> From me to thee glad serenades,
> Dances for thee I propose saluting thee,
>   adornments and feastings for thee,
> And the sights of the open landscape and
>   the high-spread sky are fitting,
> And life and the fields, and the huge and
>   thoughtful night.
>
> The night in silence under many a star,
> The ocean shore and the husky whispering
>   wave whose voice I know,

And the soul turning to thee O vast and well-
veil'd death,
And the body gratefully nestling close to thee.

Over the tree-tops I float thee a song,
Over the rising and sinking waves, over the
myriad fields and the prairies wide,
Over the dense-pack'd cities all and the
teeming wharves and ways,
I float this carol with joy, with joy to
thee O death.

[Section 14, p. 335.]

The song celebrates the conception represented by the sea in "Out
of the Cradle Endlessly Rocking"—death as a "loving floating
ocean." Like the ocean that whispers "Death, death, death, death,
death" in "Cradle," the ocean of death in "Lilacs" is forever
"arriving, arriving," offering the individual a chance to lose himself
in the "measureless float." There is, however, a difference of
emphasis in the two conceptions—an important difference, for it
helps to clarify the nature of the visions urged forth by the song.
The ocean in "Cradle," if we can trust the narrator's imagery,
promises new life to the dead, albeit in a different form. The bird's
song, on the other hand, does not emphasize the continuance of
process, the coming of life out of death: lines like "the sure-
enwinding arms of cool-enfolding death" and "the soul turning to
thee O vast and well-veil'd death,/ . . . the body gratefully nestling close to thee," suggest that the individual will find rest in
death, a kind of permanence.

Whitman "tallie[s]" the bird's song—provides words for the
music of his secret spirit, his hope that the "thought" of death, the
conception of death as painful, is after all not true. He convinces
himself: as he stands holding the hands of his comrades, listening
to the song of himself and the bird, the "sight that was bound in
[his] eyes unclose[s]." He realizes that it is "not as was thought,"
that death is not pain but the deliveress from pain:

Loud in the pines and cedars dim,
Clear in the freshness moist and the
swamp-perfume,
And I with my comrades there in the night.

236

While my sight that was bound in my eyes
  unclosed,
As to long panoramas of visions.

And I saw askant the armies,
I saw as in noiseless dreams hundreds of
  battle-flags,
Borne through the smoke of the battles and
  pierc'd with missiles I saw them,
And carried hither and yon through the smoke,
  and torn and bloody,
And at last but a few shreds left on the
  staffs, (and all in silence,)
And the staffs all splinter'd and broken.

I saw battle-corpses, myriads of them,
And the white skeletons of young men, I
  saw them,
I saw the debris and debris of all the
  slain soldiers of the war,
But I saw they were not as was thought,
They themselves were fully at rest, they
  suffer'd not,
The living remain'd and suffer'd, the mother
  suffer'd,
And the wife and the child and the musing
  comrade suffer'd,
And the armies that remain'd suffer'd.
                    [Section 15, p. 336.]

As his love for Lincoln pushes him to the belief that Lincoln is at
rest, not in pain, he realizes that he, Whitman, the "musing
comrade," is the sufferer—that, in fact, life is war and all the living
are sufferers. Or perhaps it goes the other way. Hearing his song of
"praise! praise! praise!" for death, he realizes that it is a song of
"uttermost woe," as he calls it in Section 13. He sees himself as
desolate and life as fragmented, and responds to a sense of
desolation as he does in "The Sleepers" and in some of the
Calamus poems: concentrating on his vague feeling that death is
rest, stressing his own song's hints, he produces the vision of an
ideal world of peace. We cannot, of course, finally determine

237

which of these beliefs comes first, the sense of life as suffering or of death as rest: they are inseparable, for each feeds the other.

The Whitman who tells us how he discovered these various conceptions of life and death, the Whitman who sings to us in the present time of the poem, includes all these conceptions and pushes beyond them. He conceives of death as painful both for the dead and for those who "remain" (the "black murk that hides the star" is "harsh" to the star and "cruel" to himself); he conceives of death as restful (the coffin goes to "rest in the grave"); he praises restful death (he gives the coffin his sprig of lilac and sings, "O sane and sacred death"). But he knows also that the living must do more than suffer and more than praise death—that if the coffin "passes" beyond life to its place in the grave, then mourners must pass beyond their psychic night, their sense of desolation, and move into the life that remains to be lived.

Thus, though he is very much tempted by the consolation of the song and the visions in the swamp, he takes a harder way. He does not pile life at the feet of easeful death, but faces death for what it is and "cover[s] it . . . over," dissipating the wild frenzy of Section 2 with a gradual rise to the storytelling of Section 8, the songs of life in Sections 11 and 12, and finally the storytelling of Sections 14 and 15. That ultimate story, being about the roots of his grief, being a confrontation of the bird and an articulation of his dangerous tendency toward retreat from life, is a song grander even than his lyric ode to life in Sections 11 and 12. And it is grander than the bird's elegy, which may be "death's outlet song of life" but which allows the singer it keeps alive still to hide in the "receiving night." The speaker who tells us his story has grieved like the bird, but has risen out of his grief into a new day.

So the hero has found himself by making a song, the story of his own grief. The lilac and star, having been explained, are symbols no more, and return to their original function as natural facts. The various conceptions of death, having been explored, are no longer important. And the hero, who has become a poet in order to find himself, can relinquish his own hidden meaning, his role as poet, even as the star and lilac relinquish their hidden meanings:

> Passing the visions, passing the night,
> Passing, unloosing the hold of my comrades'
>   hands,

238

Passing the song of the hermit bird and the
  tallying song of my soul,
Victorious song, death's outlet song, yet varying
  ever-altering song,
As low and wailing, yet clear the notes, rising
  and falling, flooding the night,
Sadly sinking and fainting, as warning and
  warning, and yet again bursting with joy,
Covering the earth and filling the spread of
  the heaven,
As that powerful psalm in the night I heard
  from recesses,
Passing, I leave thee lilac with heart-shaped
  leaves,
I leave thee there in the door-yard, blooming,
  returning with spring.

I cease from my song for thee,
From my gaze on thee in the west, fronting
  the west, communing with thee,
O comrade lustrous with silver face in the
  night.
                              [Section 16, pp. 336–37.]

Yet, if the hero has found himself by making a song, at the same
time he has made a song by finding himself. The largest tribute to
Lincoln is Whitman's demonstration of the truth of continuing
life—his whole movement toward storytelling and beyond, his
grieving and recovery. The largest tribute, that is, is the whole
poem, "Lilac and star and bird twined with the chant of my soul,"
in which the symbols still have meaning:

Yet each to keep and all, retrievements out
  of the night,
The song, the wondrous chant of the gray-brown
  bird,
And the tallying chant, the echo arous'd in
  my soul,
With the lustrous and drooping star with the
  countenance full of woe,
With the holders holding my hand nearing the
  call of the bird,

239

> Comrades mine and I in the midst, and their
> memory ever to keep, for the dead I loved
> so well,
> For the sweetest, wisest soul of all my days and
> lands—and this for his dear sake,
> Lilac and star and bird twined with the chant
> of my soul,
> There in the fragrant pines and the cedars dusk
> and dim.
> [Section 16, p. 337.]

Section 16 is an apt summary not only of what Whitman has done but also of what we have done, and must do, to read the poem. The second part of the section, around which the first and third parts pivot, fuses Whitman's "mechanistic" and "organic" styles:

> I cease from my song for thee,
> From my gaze on thee in the west, fronting
> the west, communing with thee,
> O comrade lustrous with silver face in the night.

It is, in a sense, the norm of the section. A combination of regularity (subject-predicate construction) and flowingness (the present participles), it allows the reader to be both rationally and imaginatively comfortable: it satisfies his tendencies in either direction, yet does not require that he take risks in reading. The first and third sections demand more, and reward the reader with a more exciting kind of knowledge. The first part is an extended participial construction centering on two dependent subject-verb combinations—"I leave," "I leave"; the third, a conglomeration of nouns, prepositional phrases, and infinitives which promise to act as adverbial phrases but cannot, because of the absence of a controlling verb. Whitman creates two worlds here, one of which requires intellectual engagement, the other imaginative engagement. The world of the first part has a hidden order, with all things moving through an active self; the world of the third part is fragmented, for things exist next to each other rather than flowing toward and out of one point. The reader enters the first part through a grammatical construction that is inverted but becomes

240

orderly when he discovers the suspended subject and verb. In the third part, however, where things are joined by implication ("Yet each to keep and all" implies that "I" is the keeper), the reader can enter only if he is willing to accept implication rather than grammatical control, only if he is willing to make his own imaginative connections.

The two ways in which the reader must engage himself in the whole poem—the ways in which he must yield himself to "Lilacs" and assert himself in it—are analogous to the two kinds of entry necessary for Section 16. One way into "Lilacs" is intellectual, as in the first part of Section 16. It comprises a suspension of disbelief until the key to order is found (the subject and verb in Section 16, the story of the past in the whole poem) and a mental rearrangement of the "twisted" elements into a more regular pattern. In reading "Lilacs" the first time, we have discovered the history of the hero gradually, as he has been able to articulate it. Coming to the end of the poem, we have at last the material to explore a dimension of it that has heretofore been shrouded in mystery. Only when we have the part of the story told in Section 8, can we figure out that the frenzied grieving in Section 2 is an intensification of the disturbance Whitman suffered "a month since." Only when we have heard the bird's song can we recognize that for Whitman to see himself as giving the lilac to the coffin is for him to move, however moderately, toward the dangerous position represented by that song. And, most important, only when we have read Sections 14 and 15 can we understand the true relationship of Whitman to the bird with "loud human voice"—only then can we realize why he is so tempted by the bird and so afraid of it, and thus understand in all its subtlety his drama of self-discovery. The poet, withholding his story until the end of the poem, has required us to come to his work a second time: we have yielded to the poem by restraining our drive for regularity and comprehension, and we have asserted ourselves by hooking up discoveries we make late in the poem with things that have puzzled us before.

The second way into "Lilacs" is imaginative, as in the second part of Section 16. Like "The Sleepers" and especially "As I Ebb'd," "Lilacs" is full of breaks in tone and unexplained shifts in stance—gaps in the speaker's movement that we can bridge only by a kind of guessing, the exercise of our imagination. Section 2, where the hero grieves for the star, and Section 3, where he turns to the lilac in quiet celebration, are joined not by rational lines but by implication, the special logic of emotion and metaphor. And what rational connection is there between Sections 8 and 9, or Sections 9 and 10? We can make the necessary leaps only if we yield ourselves to the patterns of Whitman's imagination, and only if we are willing to act according to the intuitive sense that we acquire from the yielding.

So "Lilacs" can be said to be about an especially active kind of reading, activity at once intellectual and imaginative. The act of reading this poem is, as it were, a matter of death and life. Whitman yields his separateness in loving another man and mourning for him, and his mourning paralyzes and isolates him. He asserts his separateness by responding to that act of grief—by cultivating it, countering it, trying to understand it; and as he responds he is released from isolation. As Whitman yields to the "thought of him," so must the reader yield to *his* experience, the poem; as Whitman asserts himself to modify his experience, so must the reader assert himself to read the poem in the fullest way. If the reader does what he must—if he uses himself by self-denial and self-assertion—his solitary, static completion is made into incompletion, engagement in an entity outside himself, immersion in the flow of life.

When we read this way—when we travel the road of Whitman's best works, "Lilacs" and the barely less demanding monodramas—we can only hope that we will figure straight and leap true. The poet himself, his own best critic, is not so sure we will:

. . . Walt Whitman *is* a pretty hard nut to crack. His involved sentences, . . . his kangaroo leaps as if from one crag to another, his appaling catalogues, (enough to stagger the bravest heart,) his unheard of demand for brains in the reader as well as in the things read, and then his scornful silence, never explaining anything nor answering any attack, all lay him fairly open to be misunderstood, to slur, burlesque, and sometimes to spiteful innuendo; and will probably continue to do so.[9]

CONCLUSION

WITH TRAUBEL at his feet, Whitman poked with his cane in the litter of his room in Camden, reassuring himself about our generation of readers while searching for yet another letter of adulation from the decades past. Vain he had always been, and now, well past his poetic prime, he was uncertain of his powers; but his preoccupation with responses to his work was more than vanity and uncertainty. For from the start he had been fascinated by the problems of writing and reading, which served as foci for the psychological and political mysteries that stirred him.

The subject matter of Whitman's poems represents his explorations of these psychological and political mysteries, the problem of identity and the problem of government. Thus the "love" poems of the Children of Adam and Calamus groups are about two ways of knowing, two very different kinds of involvement, one of which also concerns separation; the "voyage" poems, like "Song of Myself" and "The Sleepers," are actually about merger and withdrawal, freedom and restraint; the "political" poems, like "By Blue Ontario's Shore," are about individuality and community; the "desolation" poems, like "As I Ebb'd with the Ocean of Life," "Out of the Cradle Endlessly Rocking," and "When Lilacs Last in the Dooryard Bloom'd," are about particularity and the cosmic fraternity, loneliness and release. And the forms of his poems play out his explorations of these problems in the special context of writing and reading, for, representing the relationships of both poet and reader to the poem instead of the relationship of one individ-

243

ual to another, they can be thought of as freezing into position the poet's attitudes of approach and withdrawal, of demand and heedlessness, and as requiring various modes of detachment and involvement from the reader.

It is because of this special relationship of Whitman's forms to his central interest in writing and reading that I have organized this book around his forms rather than, for instance, around certain repeated themes or images. Having done so, I find myself tempted to explore a little farther: to apply to other works, terms developed in the context of Whitman's poetry—to move from a thorough investigation of form in Whitman to speculations about the problem of form in general.

But to use Whitman's poems, however tentatively, as points of departure into quite different work, may not be altogether appropriate. For Whitman offers scanty material for investigation of several important forms. The didactic work, the descriptive work, the narrative, the lyric, the dramatic monologue, the mono-drama, the work of "reader engagement": when we list Whitman's forms, we recall that he tends to be autobiographical in the dramatic monologue; uncomfortable in the narrative—which is after all, when one thinks of epics, novels, and short stories as belonging to that category, probably the most widely used form; and, as in rudimentary efforts like "Song of the Banner at Daybreak," primitive in the written drama, a form in which there is no one poetic mask but a number of masks, colliding with each other and changing.

A full-dress statement about categories of form requires support by at least several examples of each genre established, which suggests an appeal to works from many hands. Perhaps, however, given Whitman's impressive if not comprehensive formal range, we can use his poems as vehicles toward a suggestive rather than a full-dress statement, toward "faint clews" about a system rather than the system itself.

Even such incomplete system-building will be worth the risk only if the categories have indeed demonstrated their usefulness in the context of Whitman's poems, and if, in the context of other literature, they seem able to suggest new combinations, stimulate new talk. The intention is not to subvert the more familiar categories—the novel, the poem, the epic, the elegy, the sonnet, the tragedy, which certainly have demonstrated their usefulness—but simply to suggest some new ones, which cut across the old. Obviously, then, these new categories are not meant to be exhaustive: there are important things they do not do. They do not, for instance, describe the special kind of stylistic surprise that allies Donne's "A Valediction: Forbidding Mourning" or Marvell's "To His Coy Mistress" to Pound's "In a Station of the Metro" or certain sections of "Song of Myself," or the special kind of subject matter that joins "Lycidas" to "Adonais" and "When Lilacs Last in the Dooryard Bloom'd," or the special kind of line that makes "Lilacs" father to *The Waste Land*. But then no set of categories can enclose or describe all the responses that we have as readers. All that we can ask of any one set is that it provide terms that can describe accurately how a particular work functions; that it comprise categories narrow enough to define a significant number of differences among various works, and broad enough to include a significant number of works in each category; that its approach be special enough to allow us to think of particular works in ways interestingly different from those in which we have thought of them before; and that it encourage us to do the critic's traditional and necessary job of historical and cultural comparison.

If my discussions of Whitman's poems have in fact done what they pretend, they will have demonstrated, enough to evoke at least conditional belief, the suitability of my categories for the first three of the functions just enumerated. The fitness of the categories for historical and cultural comparison, I can only hint at here.

We learn, from our experiences with Whitman's poems, certain techniques of reading. We find, for instance, that we cannot accept the speaker's statements in "The Sleepers" as we accept them in "Out of the Cradle Endlessly Rocking," for Whitman in "The Sleepers" says things that are true only for the dramatic instant in which he says them; and we find that in "Song of Myself" we can rest on his statements, accept them as true for the whole poem, only when he has become a whole "Identity." Thus we learn by analogy why we must wait in Wordsworth's "Ode: Intimations of Immortality" until Section 5 and again until Section 9 to become acquainted with the philosophic base on which the poem rests; not until those sections does the poet attain the kind of serenity necessary for him to provide us with that grounding. And, having had the experience of reading "Song of Myself," we are led to wonder whether Wordsworth's *The Prelude,* subtitled "The Growth of a Poet's Mind," is not a dramatization of growth as well as a story about growth: whether, that is, *The Prelude,* in which the speaker is shown shifting back and forth from meditation to narrative, is not as well called a monodrama as some new sort of epic. Taught to become aware of a dramatic speaker's shifts in tone and stance, we are less ready to condemn the "inconsistencies" in an essay by Emerson and more willing to test the whole essay for significance by tracing the course of the speaker's shifting: again, we ask ourselves whether a work like "Experience," which begins like an ode of dejection but ends on a note of affirmation, is not more appropriately called a monodrama than an "essay."

The discovery of difference as well as similarity is encouraged by the set of categories I propose; precisely because the definition of form I am using has nothing to do with verbal manner, specific subject matter, or the look of the work on the page, we can return for comparisons to the very idiosyncracies the set avoids. When we have defined didacticism, for example, and have speculated about ways of writing a didactic piece that is literature, not a call to action, we can learn something about the history of literature by comparing "An Essay on Man," "To You" or the last part of "Song of Myself," and one of Frost's short didactic poems; or, in the area of the dramatic monologue, by comparing "Prayer of Columbus" with examples of the form as written by Robert Browning and T. S. Eliot.

Or, to come at the problem of historical comparison from a different angle, we can notice the prevalence in one period of a certain form. The Age of Pope, for example, tends heavily toward didacticism, its moral epistles, satires, and philosophical essays testifying to the rich possibilities of the form. It is usually said that, in contrast, the Romantics are partial to the lyric, but for purposes of comparison it may be as significant to recognize, since the Renaissance too is much given to the lyric, that the Romantics are unusually fond of the monodrama, a form much freer, and more demanding for the reader, than the lyric. Coleridge's "Kubla

Khan," a narrative followed by a private meditation, and his "Dejection: An Ode"; Wordsworth's "Immortality Ode"; Keats's "Ode to a Nightingale"; Shelley's "Adonais"—all, and more, are monodramas, in which the speaker as the moment demands turns in toward himself, out toward a third person or object, or toward readers to tell a story or issue a didactic statement. And the modern world seems to produce works of reader engagement: *The Sound and the Fury, Ulysses, The Waste Land, The Bridge,* all, like "Lilacs," present the appearance of disorder, but contain order implied and ready to emerge, awaiting only the saving journey of the reader through the work.

The categories also provide us, finally, with terms to describe works not squarely in any category. It may, for instance, be useful to talk of a "narrative drama," a written play, like Shaw's *Pygmalion,* Williams' *Glass Menagerie,* or Miller's *Death of a Salesman,* in which the author is so liberal with "stage directions" or commentary that he might almost be an omniscient narrator. Complementing this subform could be a more familiar one, the "dramatic narrative," in which the teller is not a trustworthy guide giving us hints into the meaning of the action: *The Adventures of Huckleberry Finn* and *The Aspern Papers* would be dramatic narratives, but not *Great Expectations* or *The Heart of Darkness,* where the narrator is a character representative of, not separate from, the author's point of view.

We have been rewarded long and well by our discussions of Swift and Pope, Wordsworth and Coleridge, Hawthorne and Melville. It may prove interesting to talk also about the different ways in which Swift, Dickens, Whitman, and Williams tell their stories in *Gulliver's Travels, Great Expectations,* "Out of the Cradle Endlessly Rocking," and *Glass Menagerie;* or about the didactic utterances that are Dryden's "Religio Laici," Swift's "City Shower," and Whitman's "To You"; or about the efforts of Whitman, Eliot, and Faulkner, in their various works of reader engagement, to make their readers living men.

ABBREVIATIONS

Correspondence	*The Correspondence*, edited by Edwin Haviland Miller.
Critical Aids	*Walt Whitman's Poems, Selections with Critical Aids*, by Gay Wilson Allen and Charles T. Davis.
Days	*Days with Walt Whitman*, by Edward Carpenter.
Faint Clews	*Faint Clews and Indirections*, edited by Clarence Gohdes and Rollo G. Silver.
Guide	A *Critical Guide to Leaves of Grass*, by James E. Miller, Jr.
In Re	*In Re Walt Whitman*, edited by Horace Traubel.
N & F	*Notes & Fragments*, edited by R. M. Bucke.
Prose	*Prose Works 1892*, edited by Floyd Stovall.
Reader's Edition	*Leaves of Grass, Comprehensive Reader's Edition*, edited by Harold W. Blodgett and Sculley Bradley.
Singer	*The Solitary Singer*, by Gay Wilson Allen.
Symbolism	*Symbolism and American Literature*, by Charles N. Feidelson, Jr.
UPP	*The Uncollected Prose and Poetry of Walt Whitman*, edited by Emory Holloway.
WWWC	*With Walt Whitman in Camden*, by Horace Traubel.
Workshop	*Walt Whitman's Workshop*, edited by Clifton Joseph Furness.

NOTES

INTRODUCTION

1. Allen and Davis, *Walt Whitman's Poems, Selections with Critical Aids*; Miller, *A Critical Guide to Leaves of Grass*, pp. 3–160. Miller has another book on Whitman, *Walt Whitman*, that, in addition to discussing matters of style which the earlier book does not emphasize, condenses several of the close readings presented in *Guide* and offers some new ones.

2. F. O. Matthiessen, *American Renaissance*, pp. 549–77, examines the analogies of oratory, the opera, and the ocean. He is followed by Calvin S. Brown, "Musical Development of Symbols," *Music and Literature*, pp. 178–94, and Robert D. Faner, *Walt Whitman & Opera*.

3. "Whitman's Sense of Evil: Criticisms," *Walt Whitman Abroad*, edited by Gay Wilson Allen, p. 251.

4. "Walt Whitman, Impressionist Prophet," *Leaves of Grass One Hundred Years After*, edited by Milton Hindus, p. 117.

5. Allen and Davis, *Critical Aids*, pp. 27–32; Miller, *Guide*, pp. 3–160; and Fiedler, "Introduction," *Whitman*, p. 13.

6. Sutton, "The Analysis of Free Verse Form, Illustrated by a Reading of Whitman," *Journal of Aesthetics and Art Criticism*, XVIII (December, 1959), 241–54 (revision: "Whitman's Poetic Ensembles," *Whitman*, edited by Roy Harvey Pearce, pp. 119–45); Fussell, "Whitman's Curious Warble: Reminiscence and Reconciliation," *The Presence of Whitman*, edited by R. W. B. Lewis, pp. 28–51; Coffman, " 'Crossing Brooklyn Ferry,' Note on the Catalog Technique in Whitman's Poetry," *Modern Philology*, LI (May, 1954), 225–32, and "Form and Meaning in Whitman's 'Passage to India,' " *PMLA*, LXX (June, 1955), 337–49; Rountree, "Whitman's Indirect Expression and Its Application to 'Song of Myself,' " *PMLA*, LXXIII (December, 1958), 549–55; and Lovell, "Appreciating Whitman: 'Passage to India,' " *Modern Language Quarterly*, XXI (June, 1960), 131–41.

7. Adams, "Whitman: A Brief Revaluation," *Tulane Studies in English*,

V (1955), 11–49; Marks, "Whitman's Triadic Imagery," *American Literature*, XXIII (March, 1951), 99–126.

8. *The Evolution of Walt Whitman*, II, 257.

9. John Kinnaird, "The Paradox of an American Identity," *Partisan Review*, V (1958), 380–405 (revision: "Leaves of Grass and The American Paradox," *Whitman*, edited by Pearce, pp. 24–36), and Malcolm Cowley, "Walt Whitman's Buried Masterpiece," *Saturday Review*, XLII (October 31, 1959), 11–13, 32–34, defend the 1855 edition, whereas Roy Harvey Pearce, "Introduction," *Leaves of Grass, Facsimile Edition of the 1860 Text*, pp. vii–li, sees the truly significant Whitman as emerging in 1855 but not coming to maturity until 1860 (and as beginning to die with the 1867 edition).

CHAPTER I

1. Smith, *Whitman's Leaves of Grass: Style and Subject Matter with Special Reference to Democratic Vistas*, p. 24; Boatright, "Whitman and Hegel," *Studies in English*, IX, *The University of Texas Bulletin* (July 8, 1929), 134–50; Howard, "For a Critique of Whitman's Transcendentalism," *Modern Language Notes*, XLVII (February, 1932), 79–85; Stovall, "Main Drifts in Whitman's Poetry," *American Literature*, IV (March, 1932), 3–21; Marks, "Triadic Imagery"; Daiches, "The Philosopher" in *Walt Whitman: Man, Poet, Philosopher*, pp. 35–53; Chase, *Walt Whitman Reconsidered*.

2. Burroughs, *Walt Whitman, a Study*, pp. 14, 76, 120–21, 169, 172–73; Carpenter, *Days with Walt Whitman*, p. 113; Bradley, "The Fundamental Metrical Principles of Whitman's Poetry," *American Literature*, X (January, 1939), 437–59; Matthiessen, *Renaissance*, pp. 515–625; Gay Wilson Allen, *Walt Whitman Handbook*, pp. 292–302, 409–22, 428–37; Feidelson, *Symbolism and American Literature*, pp. 16–28, 235–40; Adams, "Revaluation."

3. *Symbolism*, p. 120.

4. *Ibid.*, p. 20.

5. *Ibid.*, p. 21.

6. *Ibid.*, p. 18.

7. *Ibid.*, p. 20.

8. *Whitman*, p. 63.

9. *Ibid.*, pp. 93–94.

10. "Revaluation," pp. 120–21.

11. "Meditation VI—Of the Existence of Material Things," *The Methods, Meditations, and Selections from the Principles of Descartes*, edited and translated by John Veitch, p. 86.

12. Meyer H. Abrams, *The Mirror and the Lamp*, p. 69.

13. *Ibid.*, p. 16.

14. *Ibid.*, p. 69.

15. *Ibid.*, pp. 20–21.

16. "Preface, 1855," *Prose Works 1892*, edited by Floyd Stovall, II, 438 —hereafter cited as *Prose*, II. Volume in *The Collected Writings of Walt Whitman*, edited by Gay Wilson Allen and Sculley Bradley.

17. "Coleridge," *Appreciations*, p. 80.

18. "Carlyle from American Points of View" in "Specimen Days," *Prose Works 1892*, edited by Floyd Stovall, I, 258—hereafter cited as *Prose*, I.

19. "A Song for Occupations," *Leaves of Grass, Comprehensive Reader's Edition*, edited by Harold W. Blodgett and Sculley Bradley, p. 216— hereafter cited as *Reader's Edition*, except in the case of direct quotations in my text, which will be followed only by page reference in parentheses.

20. "Carlyle," *Prose*, p. 176.

21. *Walt Whitman's Workshop*, edited by Clifton Joseph Furness, p. 49—hereafter cited as *Workshop*.

22. *Prose*, II, 380.

23. "Meditation VI," translated by Veitch, p. 91.

24. Descartes' own words are: ". . . j'aie un corps auquel je suis très étroitement conjoint; neanmoins, . . . il est certain que moi, *c'est-à-dire mon ame, par laquelle je suis ce que je suis*, est entierement et véritablement distincte de mon corps, et qu'elle peut être ou exister sans lui." *Oeuvre Philosophique de Descartes*, edited by Adolphe Garnier, p. 164.

25. Ralph Waldo Emerson, *Journals*, edited by W. E. Forbes and E. W. Emerson, V, 206.

26. *The Uncollected Prose and Poetry of Walt Whitman*, edited by Emory Holloway, II, 65—hereafter cited as *UPP*.

27. "The Body," *Reader's Edition*, p. 690.

28. Section 5, "Song of Myself," *Reader's Edition*, p. 33.

29. *UPP*, II, 64.

30. *Ibid.*, p. 66.

31. *Faint Clews & Indirections*, edited by Clarence Gohdes and Rollo G. Silver, p. 53.

32. Henry David Thoreau, *The Writings of Henry David Thoreau*, I, 364, and VII, 153, both quoted in Fred W. Lorch, "Thoreau and the Organic Principle in Poetry," *PMLA* (March, 1938), 290.

33. *An American Primer*, edited by Horace Traubel, p. 14.

34. *Ibid.*, p. 3.

35. Wallace Fowlie, *Mallarmé*, p. 264: ". . . more than on any other article of belief, the symbolists united with Mallarmé in his statements about poetic language. The theory of the suggestiveness of words comes from a belief that a primitive language, half-forgotten, half-living, exists in each man. It is language possessing extraordinary affinities with music and dreams." Quoted in William K. Wimsatt, Jr., and Cleanth Brooks, *Literary Criticism*, p. 596.

36. *UPP*, I, 258–59.

37. *Whitman*, p. 94.

38. "Our Eminent Visitors" in "November Boughs," *Prose*, II, 544.

39. Abrams, *Mirror and Lamp*, pp. 8–14.

40. "A Backward Glance O'er Travel'd Roads," *Reader's Edition*, p. 574.

41. Horace Traubel, *With Walt Whitman in Camden*, I, 58—hereafter cited as *WWWC*.

42. *UPP*, II, 75.

43. "Notes to Late English Books" in "November Boughs," *Prose*, II, p. 601.

CHAPTER II

1. "One's-Self I Sing," *Reader's Edition*, p. 1.

2. *The Critical Principle of the Reconciliation of Opposites as Employed by Coleridge*, pp. 11–12. Her quotation is from S. T. Coleridge, *Anima Poetae*, edited by E. H. Coleridge (London, 1895), p. 147.

3. S. T. Coleridge, *Biographia Literaria*, edited by John Shawcross, II, 12.

4. *Notes & Fragments*, edited by R. M. Bucke, p. 140—hereafter cited as *N & F*.

5. *UPP*, II, 66.

6. *Workshop*, p. 48.

7. *N & F*, p. 134.

8. "Carlyle" in "Specimen Days," *Prose*, I, 258.

9. "Democratic Vistas," *Prose*, II, 393–94.

10. *UPP*, II, 83.

11. "Hours for the Soul" in "Specimen Days," *Prose*, I, 174.

12. *N & F*, p. 93.

13. "Democratic Vistas," *Prose*, II, 394.

14. George Santayana, "The Poetry of Barbarism," *Interpretations of Poetry and Religion* (New York, 1900), printed in Louis Untermeyer, *The Poetry and Prose of Walt Whitman*, pp. 1043–48.

15. *UPP*, II, 96.

16. *Ibid.*

17. "Spiritual Characters Among the Soldiers" in "Specimen Days," *Prose*, I, 67–68.

18. "Preface, 1876," *Prose*, II, 467, footnote.

19. "Me Imperturbe," *Reader's Edition*, p. 11.

20. *WWWC*, I, 130.

21. *UPP*, II, 90.

22. "Freedom" in "Notes Left Over," *Prose*, II, 538.

23. "Democratic Vistas," *Prose*, II, 381.

24. *Ibid.*, pp. 391–92.

25. "Nationality—[And Yet.]" in "Notes Left Over," *Prose*, II, 514. The brackets are Whitman's.

26. *Prose*, II, 437.

27. *Leaves of Grass* (Brooklyn, New York, 1856), p. 362. See also *WWWC*, I, 385.

28. Gay Wilson Allen, *The Solitary Singer*, p. 345.

29. "Debris," *Leaves of Grass, Facsimile Edition of the 1860 Text*, p. 421; also in *Reader's Edition*, p. 605. See also Horace Traubel, "Round Table with Walt Whitman," *In Re Walt Whitman*, edited by Horace Traubel, p. 302, in which Traubel reports Whitman as saying, "one significant point of all first-class men is *caution*. Let us accept; let us whack away; let us absorb; *but don't let us be carried away*"—hereafter cited as *In Re.*

30. "Poetry To-day in America," *Prose*, II, 478.

31. "Last Saved Items" in "Good-bye My Fancy," *Prose*, II, 708.

32. "Darwinism" in "Notes Left Over," *Prose*, II, 523.

33. "Slang in America" in "November Boughs," *Prose*, II, 572.

34. See Allen, *Singer*, pp. 90–91.

35. *The Gathering of the Forces*, edited by Cleveland Rogers and John Black, I, 193.

36. Typewritten letter from Eldridge to J. H. Johnston, Washington, D.C., May 29, 1902 (original, signed, in Berg Collection, New York Public Library), quoted in Allen, *Singer*, p. 370; and Carpenter, *Days*, p. 38.

37. *WWWC*, I, 200.

38. *Ibid.*

39. *N & F*, p. 119.

40. *Ibid.*, p. 135.

41. *WWWC*, III, 70.

42. "Shakspere for America" in "Good-bye My Fancy," *Prose*, II, 675.

43. *WWWC*, I, 156–57.

44. "Preface, 1855," *Prose*, II, 454.

45. "Philosopher," p. 146.

46. *WWWC*, I, 105.

47. *Ibid.*

48. *Workshop*, p. 49.

49. For instance, in "I Sing the Body Electric," *Reader's Edition*, p. 97, the soul is specifically "the Female I see."

50. *Reader's Edition*, p. 255.

51. "Nationality" in "Notes Left Over," *Prose*, II, 514.

52. Section 3, "Song of Myself," *Reader's Edition*, p. 31.

53. *N & F*, p. 119.

54. *Gathering of Forces*, I, 51. One aspect of this image is discussed in Gay Wilson Allen, "The 'Long Journey' Motif," *Walt Whitman as Man, Poet, and Legend*, pp. 62–83 (reprinted, with revisions, from *The Journal of English and Germanic Philology*, XXXVIII [January, 1939], 76–95).

55. "'Going Somewhere,'" *Reader's Edition*, p. 525.
56. *The Correspondence*, edited by Edwin Haviland Miller, I, 324.
57. "A Song of the Rolling Earth," *Reader's Edition*, p. 220.
58. "Bumble-bees" in "Specimen Days," *Prose*, I, 124.
59. "Walt Whitman and his Poems," *In Re*, p. 15.
60. See also "As I Ponder'd in Silence," *Reader's Edition*, p. 2, which Whitman gives the honored place of the second "Inscription."
61. *UPP*, II, 68.
62. *The Complete Works of Ralph Waldo Emerson*, introduction and notes by Edward Waldo Emerson, II, 274.
63. *UPP*, I, 196.
64. "Chanting the Square Deific," *Reader's Edition*, pp. 443–45. See also introductory poem to "Songs of Insurrection," *Leaves of Grass* (1872), p. 363.
65. *N & F*, p. 19.
66. Carpenter, *Days*, pp. 49, 47.
67. "Leaves-Dropping," *Leaves of Grass* (1856), p. 357.
68. *Faint Clews*, pp. 40–41.
69. "Sunday Restrictions," October 20, 1854, *UPP*, I, 261. See also *UPP*, II, 76; *I Sit and Look Out*, p. 43.
70. "Stronger Lessons," *Reader's Edition*, p. 530.
71. *Correspondence*, III, pp. 4, 265–66. See also p. 154, where Whitman writes Stafford an account of a wrestling match.
72. *N & F*, p. 101.
73. "Preface, 1855," *Prose*, II, 457.
74. "City of Ships," *Reader's Edition*, p. 294.
75. *WWWC*, III, 118.
76. *N & F*, p. 129.
77. *I Sit and Look Out*, p. 160.
78. "America's Bulk Average" in "Good-bye My Fancy," *Prose*, p. 520.
79. "Democratic Vistas," *Prose*, II, 381.
80. *Works*, II, 271.
81. *Studies in Classic American Literature*, p. 177.
82. *Ibid.*, p. 179.
83. *The Great Chain of Being*, p. 24.
84. *Ibid.*, pp. 49–50.
85. "Democratic Vistas," *Prose*, II, 380.
86. *Workshop*, pp. 48–49.
87. Section 9, "To Think of Time," *Reader's Edition*, p. 440.
88. "Self-Reliance," *Works*, II, 70.
89. "Darest Thou Now O Soul," *Reader's Edition*, p. 441.
90. *N & F*, p. 134.
91. "To the Man-of-War Bird," *Reader's Edition*, p. 257.
92. "Ebb'd," *Reader's Edition*, p. 255.
93. "I Sing the Body Electric," *Reader's Edition*, p. 98.

94. Section 49, "Song of Myself," *Reader's Edition*, p. 87.
95. *WWWC*, II, 371.
96. Section 3, "Song of Myself," *Reader's Edition*, p. 31.
97. "Of the Terrible Doubt of Appearances," *Reader's Edition*, p. 120.
98. *UPP*, II, 66–67.
99. *Prose*, II, 456.
100. *UPP*, II, 83.
101. Section 33, "Song of Myself," *Reader's Edition*, p. 61.
102. "Whitman and his Poems," *In Re*, pp. 17–18.
103. "Democratic Vistas," *Prose*, II, 381.
104. Section 10, "Song of the Open Road," *Reader's Edition*, p. 155.
105. *N & F*, p. 35.
106. "Triadic Imagery," 99.
107. Allen, *Singer*, pp. 154–55.
108. Daiches, "Philosopher," p. 40.
109. *Studies in Human Time*, translated by Elliott Coleman, p. 342.
110. *Prose*, II, 409–10.
111. Poulet, p. 342.
112. "A Backward Glance O'er Travel'd Roads," *Reader's Edition*, p. 564.
113. "For Him I Sing," *Reader's Edition*, p. 8.
114. *N & F*, p. 108.
115. "With Antecedents," *Reader's Edition*, p. 241.
116. *N & F*, pp. 76–77.
117. "Genealogy" in "Specimen Days," *Prose*, I, 4–5.
118. See "Brooklyniana," *UPP*, II, 222–321.
119. Allen, *Singer*, pp. 121–22.
120. Section 5, "Song of Myself," *Reader's Edition*, p. 33.

CHAPTER III

1. "Preface, 1855," *Prose*, II, 444.
2. *Ibid.*, pp. 441–42.
3. *Correspondence*, III, 307.
4. John Burroughs, *Walt Whitman as Poet and Person*. The whole passage, in fact, not just the piece in quotation marks, may be Whitman's: see Frederick P. Hier, Jr., "The End of a Literary Mystery," *American Mercury*, I (April, 1924), 471–78; and, in response, Clara Barrus, "Whitman and Burroughs as Comrades," *Yale Review*, XV (October, 1925), 59–81, and *Workshop*, pp. 214–18.
5. Quoted in Allen, *Singer*, pp. 132–33.
6. "When The Full-Grown Poet Came," *Reader's Edition*, p. 550.
7. *UPP*, II, 65.

8. Quoted in Allen, *Singer*, p. 131.
9. *Workshop*, p. 189.
10. "Preface, 1855," *Prose*, II, 443.
11. *N & F*, p. 56.
12. *WWWC*, I, 131.
13. *N & F*, p. 89.
14. *WWWC*, III, 35–36; and I, 164.
15. "Abraham Lincoln," *Prose*, II, 603.
16. *N & F*, p. 70.
17. "Preface, 1876," *Prose*, II, 473.
18. *N & F*. p. 97.
19. See "The Bible as Poetry" in "November Boughs," *Prose*, II, 545–49.
20. *N & F*, p. 96.
21. *WWWC*, III, 35–36.
22. "Preface, 1855," *Prose*, II, 442.
23. *UPP*, II, 53–54.
24. *Ibid.*, p. 53.
25. *N & F*, p. 106.
26. *UPP*, II, 53.
27. "Democratic Vistas," *Prose*, II, 379–80.
28. *Readings in English Prose of the Nineteenth Century*, edited by Raymond M. Alden, pp. 239–42.
29. Quoted in Abrams, *Mirror and Lamp*, p. 26.
30. "Preface," "Prometheus Unbound," *Selected Poems, Essays, and Letters*, edited by Ellsworth Barnard, p. 95.
31. "A Defence of Poetry," *Selected Poems, Essays, and Letters*, p. 568.
32. *Works*, II, 289.
33. *Works*, III, 3–4.
34. Herman Melville, *Moby-Dick*, pp. 152–53.
35. Quoted in Abrams, p. 26.
36. "Jean Paul Friedrich Richter" (1827), *Works*, edited by H. D. Traill, XXVI, 20.
37. Abrams, pp. 175–76.
38. *Ibid.*, p. 176.
39. *Ibid.*, p. 224.
40. "Preface, 1855," *Prose*, II, 439–40.
41. *Workshop*, p. 40.
42. "Preface, 1876," *Prose*, II, 473.
43. *Literary Values, and Other Papers*, p. 231.
44. *Prose*, II, 573.
45. "Specimen Days," *Prose*, I, 292.
46. *Prose*, II, 424–25.
47. *Workshop*, p. 132.
48. "The Great Unrest of Which We Are Part" in "Specimen Days," *Prose*, I, 289.

49. "Carlyle," *Prose*, I, 260.
50. *N & F*, p. 61.
51. *UPP*, I, 140.
52. *Correspondence*, I, 45.
53. *N & F*, p. 78.
54. *Ibid.*, p. 56.
55. *WWWC*, I, 163.
56. *Ibid.*, p. 64.
57. Allen, *Singer*, pp. 131–32.
58. "Spontaneous Me," *Reader's Edition*, p. 103.
59. *WWWC*, I, 131.

CHAPTER IV

1. See Allen, *Singer*, pp. 498–500, 344–48.
2. *N & F*, p. 124. See also p. 169.
3. "Preface, 1876," *Prose*, II, 468, footnote.
4. Allen, *Singer*, pp. 237–38.
5. *WWWC*, I, 51.
6. "Preface, 1876," *Prose*, II, 471, footnote.
7. *Whitman's Manuscripts, Leaves of Grass* (1860), edited by Fredson Bowers, pp. 64–65.
8. Allen, pp. 421–25.
9. Quoted in Allen, p. 535.
10. Allen, p. 423.
11. "Here the Frailest Leaves of Me," *Reader's Edition*, p. 131.
12. "A Woman Waits for Me," *Reader's Edition*, p. 102.
13. "City of Orgies," *Reader's Edition*, p. 126.
14. "A Glimpse," *Reader's Edition*, p. 132.
15. "This Moment Yearning and Thoughtful," *Reader's Edition*, p. 128.
16. "City of Orgies," *Reader's Edition*, p. 126.
17. "To a Stranger," *Reader's Edition*, p. 127.
18. "We Two Boys Together Clinging," *Reader's Edition*, p. 130.
19. "Of the Terrible Doubt of Appearances," *Reader's Edition*, p. 120.
20. "Ages and Ages Returning at Intervals," *Reader's Edition*, p. 107.
21. Allen, *Singer*, p. 189.
22. That "bunch" means "poem" is also suggested by Allen and Davis, *Critical Aids*, p. 173, and Miller, *Guide*, p. 46.
23. "Preface, 1855," *Prose*, II, 440.
24. *Correspondence*, I, 347. Miller explains in a note that the "material in brackets has been supplied from the draft version. . . . Rossetti quoted this definition in a note; see *Poems by Walt Whitman*, 390 *n.*"
25. "To the Garden the World," *Reader's Edition*, p. 90.

26. "These I Singing in Spring," *Reader's Edition*, pp. 118–19.

27. "That Shadow My Likeness," *Reader's Edition*, p. 136.

28. "Recorders Ages Hence," *Reader's Edition*, p. 122.

29. "Trickle Drops," *Reader's Edition*, p. 125.

30. "I Saw in Louisiana a Live-Oak Growing," *Reader's Edition*, p. 127.

31. "These I Singing in Spring," *Reader's Edition*, p. 119. See also "To a Western Boy," *Reader's Edition*, p. 134.

32. "Among the Multitude," *Reader's Edition*, p. 135.

33. "Are You the New Person Drawn Toward Me?" *Reader's Edition*, p. 123. See also "Whoever You Are Holding Me Now in Hand," *Reader's Edition*, pp. 115–16.

34. See Esther Shephard, "An Inquiry into Whitman's Method of Turning Poetry into Prose," *Modern Language Quarterly*, XIV (March, 1953), 43–59.

35. See, for instance, *Workshop*, p. 132; "Preface, 1876," *Prose*, III, 470, footnote; "From Pent-up Aching Rivers," *Reader's Edition*, p. 91; "How Solemn as One by One," *Reader's Edition*, pp. 321–22; and, of course, "Whoever You Are Holding Me Now in Hand," *Reader's Edition*, pp. 115–16.

36. *In Re*, pp. 17–18.

37. The one exception is "As Adam Early in Morning," *Reader's Edition*, p. 111, which is didactic.

38. *Reader's Edition*, pp. 642–43, footnote. For commentary, see Allen and Davis, *Critical Aids*, pp. 5–8.

39. "Preface," *Some Imagist Poets*, pp. vi–vii. The six poets were Richard Aldington, H. D., F. S. Flint, Amy Lowell, John Gould Fletcher, and D. H. Lawrence.

40. *N & F*, p. 70.

41. *The Poetic Image* (London, 1947), p. 32.

42. "The Book of the Month," *The Poetry Review*, I (March, 1912), 133.

43. "Imagism," *Poetry*, I (March, 1913), 199.

44. Unpublished letter to Amy Lowell, November 10, 1917, quoted in Coffman, p. 168.

45. "Lecture on Modern Poetry," quoted in Coffman, p. 56. Pound stands somewhere between the two positions, though he leaned toward Hulme's. In a formal statement ("The Book of the Month," *The Poetry Review*, I [March, 1912], 133) he dismisses the pictorial theory as impressionism: "Impressionism belongs to paint, it is of the eye. . . . Poetry is in some odd way concerned with the specific gravity of things, with their nature . . . their nature and show, if you like; with the relation between them, but not with the show alone." But in a letter to Williams, suggesting principles for good poetry, he sounds like Aldington:

"1. To paint the thing as I see it.

"2. Beauty.

"3. Freedom from didacticism.

"4. It is only good manners if you repeat a few other men to at least do it better or more briefly,—utter originality is of course out of the question."

46. See Randall Jarrell, "Some Lines from Whitman" in *Poetry and the Age*, pp. 102–20, for a fine demonstration of Whitman's genius for metaphor.

47. "A March in the Ranks Hard-Prest, and the Road Unknown," *Reader's Edition*, pp. 305–6.

CHAPTER V

1. A *Child's Reminiscence*, edited by Thomas O. Mobbott and Rollo G. Silver (Seattle, 1930).

2. "Sea-Shore Fancies" in "Specimen Days," *Prose*, I, 139.

CHAPTER VI

1. Quoted in Matthiessen, *Renaissance*, p. 234.

2. *Ibid.*, p. 233.

3. *N & F*, p. 60.

4. *Faint Clews & Indirections*, p. 53.

5. *UPP*, II, 274.

6. "Sea-Shore Fancies" in "Specimen Days," *Prose*, I, 138–39.

7. *UPP*, II, 66.

8. Melville, *Moby-Dick*, pp. 152–53.

CHAPTER VII

1. "A Backward Glance O'er Traveled Roads," *Reader's Edition*, p. 570.

2. Furness, *Workshop*, pp. 57–58.

3. Furness, *Workshop*, p. 132.

4. *N & F*, pp. 69–70.

5. *Prose*, II, 503.

6. See, for example, Allen and Davis, *Critical Aids*, pp. 232–33; Chase, *Whitman*, p. 143; Feidelson, *Symbolism*, pp. 23–24; Mathiessen, *Renaissance*, p. 622; and Miller, *Guide*, p. 116.

7. "Death of Abraham Lincoln," *Prose*, II, 503.

8. "The Stupor Passes—Something Else Begins" in "Specimen Days," *Prose*, I, 31.

9. Quoted in Allen, *Singer*, p. 435.

BIBLIOGRAPHY

This bibliography is not a check list of Whitman studies, nor even a list of works consulted, but simply a record of the books and articles that have been in one way or another useful in the making of this book.

Abrams, Meyer H. *The Mirror and the Lamp*. New York: Oxford University Press, 1953.

Adams, Richard P. "Romanticism and the American Renaissance," *American Literature*, XXIII (January, 1952), 419–32.

———. "Whitman: A Brief Revaluation," *Tulane Studies in English*, V (1955), 111–49.

———. "Whitman's 'Lilacs' and the Traditional Pastoral Elegy," *Publications of the Modern Language Association*, LXXII (June, 1957), 479–87.

Alden, Raymond M. *Readings in English Prose of the Nineteenth Century*. Boston: Houghton Mifflin, 1917.

Aldington, Richard, H. D., F. S. Flint, Amy Lowell, John Gould Fletcher, and D. H. Lawrence. *Some Imagist Poets*. Boston: Houghton Mifflin, 1915.

Allen, Gay Wilson. *American Prosody*. New York: American Book Co., 1935.

———. *The Solitary Singer: A Critical Biography of Walt Whitman*. New York: Macmillan, 1955.

———. *Twenty-five Years of Walt Whitman Bibliography, 1918–1942*. Boston: F. W. Faxon Co., 1943.

——— (ed.). *Walt Whitman Abroad*. Syracuse: Syracuse University Press, 1955.

———. *Walt Whitman as Man, Poet, and Legend, with a check list of Whitman publications 1945–1960 by Evie Allison Allen*. Carbondale, Ill.: Southern Illinois University Press, 1961.

———. *Walt Whitman Handbook*. Chicago: Packard, 1946.

Arvin, Newton. *Whitman*. New York: Macmillan, 1938.

Asselineau, Roger. *The Evolution of Walt Whitman*. Vol. I. Translated by Richard Adams and the author. Cambridge, Mass.: Harvard University Press, 1960; II, 1962.

263

Barrus, Clara. "Whitman and Burroughs as Comrades," *Yale Review*, XV (October, 1925), 59–81.

———. *Whitman and Burroughs: Comrades*. Boston: Houghton Mifflin, 1931.

Bazalgette, Léon. *Walt Whitman, the Man and His Work*. Translated by Ellen Fitzgerald. Garden City: Doubleday, Page, and Co., 1920.

Beach, J. W. *The Concept of Nature in Nineteenth-Century English Poetry*. New York: Pageant Book Co., 1956.

Beaver, Joseph. *Walt Whitman—Poet of Science*. New York: King's Crown Press, 1951.

Bergman, Herbert. "Whitman in June 1885: Three Uncollected Interviews," *American Notes and Queries*, VIII (July, 1946), 51–56.

Blodgett, Harold. *Walt Whitman in England*. Ithaca: Cornell University Press, 1934.

Boatright, Mody C. "Whitman and Hegel," *Studies in English*, Vol. IX, *The University of Texas Bulletin* (July 8, 1929), 134–50.

Booth, Wayne C. *The Rhetoric of Fiction*. Chicago: University of Chicago Press, 1961.

Bradley, Sculley. "The Fundamental Metrical Principles of Whitman's Poetry," *American Literature*, X (January, 1939), 437–59.

———. "The Problem of a Variorum Edition of Whitman's *Leaves of Grass*," *English Institute Annual*. New York: Columbia University Press, 1942.

——— (ed.). *With Walt Whitman in Camden, January 21 to April 7, 1889* (from notes by Horace Traubel). Philadelphia: University of Pennsylvania Press, 1953.

Briggs, Arthur E. *Walt Whitman, Thinker and Artist*. New York: Philosophical Library, 1952.

Brooks, Van Wyck. *The Times of Melville and Whitman*. New York: E. P. Dutton, 1947.

Brown, Calvin S. *Music and Literature*. Athens: University of Georgia Press, 1948.

Bucke, R. M. *Walt Whitman*. Philadelphia, 1883.

Bullett, Gerald. *Walt Whitman, A Study and a Selection*. Philadelphia: Lippincott Co., 1925.

Burke, Kenneth. *The Philosophy of Literary Form*. Rev. ed. New York: Vintage Books, 1957.

———. "William James, Whitman, and Emerson," *Attitudes Toward History*. Rev. ed. Boston: Beacon Press, 1961.

Burroughs, John. *Notes on Walt Whitman as Poet and Person*. New

York, 1867. 2d ed., 1871, with supplementary section of eighteen pages.

———. "Suggestiveness," *Literary Values and Other Papers*. Boston: Houghton Mifflin, 1902.

———. *Walt Whitman, a Study*. Boston and New York, 1896.

Campbell, Killis. "The Evolution of Whitman as Artist," *American Literature*, VI (November, 1934), 254–63.

Canby, Henry S. *Walt Whitman, an American*. Boston: Houghton Mifflin, 1943.

Carlyle, Thomas. *Works*. Edited by H. D. Traill. Vol. XXVI. London: Chapman and Hall, 1905.

Carpenter, Edward. *Days with Walt Whitman*. London: George Allen, 1906.

Carpenter, F. I. "Walt Whitman's 'Eidolon,'" *College English*, III (March, 1942), 534–45.

Carpenter, George Rice. *Walt Whitman*. New York: Macmillan, 1909.

Catel, Jean. *Rhythme et Langage dans la Ire édition des "Leaves of Grass."* Paris: Les Éditions Rieder, 1930.

———. *Walt Whitman: La Naissance du Poete*. Paris, Les Éditions Rieder, 1929.

Chase, Richard. " 'Out of the Cradle' as a Romance," *The Presence of Whitman*. Edited by R. W. B. Lewis. New York: Columbia University Press, 1962.

———. *Walt Whitman Reconsidered*. New York: Sloane, 1955.

Coffman, Stanley K., Jr. " 'Crossing Brooklyn Ferry,' a Note on the Catalog Technique in Whitman's Poetry," *Modern Philology*, II (May, 1954), 225–32.

———. "Form and Meaning in Whitman's 'Passage to India,'" *Publications of the Modern Language Association*, LXX (June, 1955), 337–49.

———. *Imagism, a Chapter for the History of Modern Poetry*. Norman, Okla.: University of Oklahoma Press, 1951.

Coleridge, S. T. *Biographia Literaria*. Edited by John Shawcross. 2 vols. London: Oxford University Press, 1954.

Cowley, Malcolm. "Walt Whitman's Buried Masterpiece," *Saturday Review*, XLII (October 31, 1959), 11–13, 32–34.

Daiches, David. "The Philosopher," *Walt Whitman: Man, Poet, Philosopher*. Washington, D.C.: Library of Congress, 1955.

———. "Walt Whitman as Innovator," *The Young Rebel in American Literature*. Edited by Carl Bode. London: Heineman, 1959.

Day-Lewis, C. *The Poetic Image*. London: Oxford University Press, 1947.

Descartes, René. *The Methods, Meditations, and Selections from the Principles of Descartes*. Edited and translated by John Veitch. Edinburgh and London, 1887.

———. *Oeuvre Philosophique de Descartes*. Edited by Adolphe Garnier. Paris, 1835.

De Selincourt, Basil. *Walt Whitman, a Critical Study*. London: M. Secker, 1914.

Dutton, Geoffrey. *Whitman*. New York: Grove Press, 1961.

Eby, Edwin H. *A Concordance of Walt Whitman's "Leaves of Grass" and Selected Prose Writings*. Seattle: University of Washington Press, 1949–55.

Eliot, T. S. *The Three Voices of Poetry*. Cambridge: Cambridge University Press, 1954.

Emerson, Ralph Waldo. *The Complete Works of Ralph Waldo Emerson*. Edited and with an introduction by Edward Waldo Emerson. Vols. I–III. Boston: Houghton Mifflin, 1903.

———. *Journals*. Vol. V. Edited by W. E. Forbes and E. W. Emerson. Boston: Houghton Mifflin, 1911.

Falk, Robert P. "Walt Whitman and German Thought," *Journal of English and German Philology*, XL (July, 1941), 315–30.

Faner, Robert D. *Walt Whitman & Opera*. Philadelphia: University of Pennsylvania Press, 1951.

Feidelson, Charles, Jr. "Centenary of Leaves of Grass," *Yale Review*, XLV (September, 1955), 135–40.

———. *Symbolism and American Literature*. Chicago: University of Chicago Press, 1953.

Fiedler, Leslie A. "Introduction," *Whitman*. New York: Dell Publishing Co., 1959.

Foerster, Donald M. "The Critical Attack upon the Epic in the English Romantic Movement," *Publications of the Modern Language Association*, LXIX (June, 1954), 432–47.

Foerster, Norman. *American Criticism*. Boston: Houghton Mifflin, 1928.

———. *Nature in American Literature*. New York: Macmillan, 1923.

Frenz, Horst (ed.). *Whitman and Rolleston: A Correspondence*. Bloomington: University of Indiana Press, 1951.

Freyre, Gilberto. "Camerado Whitman" (translated by Benjamin M. Woodbridge, Jr.), *Walt Whitman Abroad*. Edited by Gay Wilson Allen. Syracuse: Syracuse University Press, 1955.

266

Frye, Northrup. *Anatomy of Criticism.* Princeton: Princeton University Press, 1957.

Furness, Clifton J. "Walt Whitman's Politics," *American Mercury,* XVI (April, 1929), 465–66.

Fussell, Paul, Jr. "Whitman's Curious Warble: Reminiscence and Reconciliation," *The Presence of Whitman.* Edited by R. W. B. Lewis. New York: Columbia University Press, 1962.

Gargano, James W. "Technique in 'Crossing Brooklyn Ferry': The Everlasting Moment," *Journal of English and Germanic Philology,* LXII (April, 1963), 262–69.

Gilbert, Katherine E., and Helmut Kuhn. A *History of Esthetics.* Bloomington: University of Indiana Press, 1953.

Glicksberg, Charles I. *Walt Whitman and the Civil War.* Philadelphia: University of Pennsylvania Press, 1933.

Griffith, Clark. "Sex and Death: The Significance of Whitman's Calamus Themes," *Philological Quarterly,* XXXIX (January, 1960), 18–38.

Hier, Frederick P., Jr. "The End of a Literary Mystery," *American Mercury,* I (April, 1924), 471–78.

Hindus, Milton (ed.). *Leaves of Grass One Hundred Years After.* Stanford, Calif.: Stanford University Press, 1955.

Howard, Leon. "For a Critique of Whitman's Transcendentalism," *Modern Language Notes,* XLVII (February, 1932), 79–85.

Hughes, Glenn. *Imagism and the Imagists.* Stanford, Calif.: Stanford University Press, 1931.

Jarrell, Randall. "Some Lines from Whitman," *Poetry and the Age.* New York, Vintage Press, 1955.

Johnson, Maurice O. "Whitman as a Critic of Literature," *University of Nebraska Studies in Language, Literature, and Criticism,* No. 16. Lincoln: University of Nebraska Press, 1938.

Jones, P. Mansell. *Modern French Poetry.* Cambridge: Cambridge University Press, 1951.

———. "Whitman and the Symbolists," *The Background of Modern French Poetry.* Cambridge: Cambridge University Press, 1951.

Kahn, Sholom. "The American Backgrounds of Whitman's Sense of Evil," *Scripta Hierosolymitana,* II (1955), 82–118.

———. "Whitman's Sense of Evil: Criticisms," *Walt Whitman Abroad.* Edited by Gay Wilson Allen. Syracuse; Syracuse University Press, 1955.

Kennedy, William Sloane. *The Fight of a Book for the World.* West Yarmouth, Mass.: Stonecroft Press, 1926.

267

Kennedy, William Sloane. *Reminiscences of Walt Whitman*. London, 1896.

Kinnaird, John. "The Paradox of an American Identity," *Partisan Review* V (1958), 380–405.

Lauter, Paul. "Walt Whitman: Lover and Comrade," *American Imago*, XVI (1959), 407–35.

Lawrence, D. H. *Studies in Classic American Literature*. Garden City: Doubleday, 1951.

Leary, Lewis (ed.). *Articles on American Literature: 1900–1950*. Durham, N.C.: Duke University Press, 1954.

Lehman, A. C. *The Symbolist Aesthetic in France, 1885–1895*. New York: Macmillan, 1950.

Lewis, R. W. B. *The American Adam*. Chicago: University of Chicago Press, 1955.

———— (ed.). *The Presence of Whitman*. New York: Columbia University Press, 1962.

————. "Walt Whitman," *Major Writers of America*. Vol. II. Edited by Perry Miller. New York: Harcourt, Brace, and World, 1962.

Lorch, Fred W. "Thoreau and the Organic Principle in Poetry," *Publications of the Modern Language Association*, (March, 1938), 286–302.

Lovejoy, A. O. *The Great Chain of Being*. Cambridge, Mass.: Harvard University Press, 1936.

Lovell, John, Jr. "Appreciating Whitman: 'Passage to India,'" *Modern Language Quarterly*, XXI (June, 1960), 131–41.

Lowenfels, Walter (ed.). *Walt Whitman's Civil War*. New York: Knopf, 1961.

Marks, Alfred H. "Whitman's Triadic Imagery," *American Literature*, XXIII (March, 1951), 99–126.

Matthiessen, F. O. *American Renaissance*. London: Oxford University Press, 1941.

Melville, Herman. *Moby-Dick*. Boston, 1892.

Meyers, Henry Alonso. "Whitman's Consistency," *American Literature*, VIII (November, 1936), 243–57.

Miller, James E., Jr. *A Critical Guide to Leaves of Grass*. Chicago: University of Chicago Press, 1957.

————. *Walt Whitman*. New York: Twayne Publishers, 1962.

————. "Whitman's 'Calamus': The Leaf and the Root," *Publications of the Modern Language Association*, LIX (March, 1957), 244–71.

————, Karl Shapiro, and Berenice Slote. *Start with the Sun: A Study in Cosmic Poetry*. Lincoln: University of Nebraska Press, 1960.

Murry, J. Middleton. "Whitman: Poet-prophet of Democracy," *Unprofessional Essays*. London: Oxford University Press, 1956.

Musgrove, S. T. S. *Eliot and Walt Whitman*. Wellington: New Zealand University Press, 1952.

Parrington, Vernon. "The Afterglow of the Enlightenment," *Main Currents in American Thought*. Vol. III. New York, 1930.

Parsons, Olive W. "Whitman the Non-Hegelian," *Publications of the Modern Language Association*, LVIII (December, 1943), 1073–93.

Pater, Walter. *Appreciations*. London: Macmillan, 1913.

Pearce, Roy Harvey. *The Continuity of American Poetry*. Princeton, N.J.: Princeton University Press, 1961.

———. "On the Continuity of American Poetry," *Hudson Review*, X (1957), 518–39.

———. "Towards an American Epic," *Hudson Review*, XII (Autumn, 1959), 362–77.

——— (ed.). *Whitman, a Collection of Critical Essays*. Englewood, N.J.: Prentice Hall, 1962.

———. "Whitman Justified," *The Presence of Whitman*. Edited by R. W. B. Lewis. New York: Columbia University Press, 1962.

Peckham, Morse. "Toward a Definition of Romanticism," *Publications of the Modern Language Association*, LXVI (March, 1951), 5–23.

Perry, Bliss. *Walt Whitman*. Boston: Houghton Mifflin, 1906.

"The Poet of Democracy," translated by Stephen Stepanchev, *Walt Whitman Abroad*. Edited by Gay Wilson Allen. Syracuse: Syracuse University Press, 1955.

Poulet, Georges. *Studies in Human Time*. Translated by Elliott Coleman. Baltimore: Johns Hopkins Press, 1956.

Pound, Ezra. "The Book of the Month," *The Poetry Review*, I (March, 1912), 133.

———. "Imagism," *Poetry*, I (March, 1913), 199.

———. *Personae, the Collected Poems of Ezra Pound*. Norfolk, Conn.: New Directions, 1938.

———. "Walt Whitman," *American Literature*, XXVII (1955), 59–61.

Reed, H. B. "The Heraclitan Obsession of Whitman," *Personalist*, XV (Spring, 1934), 125–38.

Reiss, Edmund. "Whitman's Debt to Animal Magnetism," *Publications of the Modern Language Association*, LXXVIII (March, 1963), 80–88.

Rountree, Thomas I. "Whitman's Indirect Expression and Its Application to 'Song of Myself,'" *Publications of the Modern Language Association*, LXXIII (December, 1958), 549–55.

Schumann, Detlev W. "Enumerative Style and Its Significance in Whitman, Rilke, Werfel," *Modern Language Quarterly*, III (1942), 171–204.

Schyberg, Frederik. *Walt Whitman*. Translated by Evie Allison Allen. New York: Columbia University Press, 1951.

Shelley, Percy Bysshe. *Selected Poems, Essays, and Letters*. Edited by Ellsworth Barnard. New York: Odyssey Press, 1944.

Shepard, Esther. "An Inquiry into Whitman's Method of Turning Prose into Poetry," *Modern Language Quarterly*, XIV (March, 1953), 43–59.

———. *Walt Whitman's Pose*. New York: Harcourt Brace and Co., 1938.

Smith, Thomas K. *Whitman's Leaves of Grass. Style and Subject Matter with Special Reference to Democratic Vistas*. Königsberg: Druk von Karg und Manneck, 1914.

Snyder, Alice D. *The Critical Principle of the Reconciliation of Opposites as Employed by Coleridge*. Ann Arbor, Mich.: Ann Arbor Press, 1918.

Spiller, Robert E. "Romantic Crisis: Melville, Whitman," *Cycle of American Literature*. New York: Macmillan, 1955.

Spitzer, Leo. "Explication de Texte Applied to Walt Whitman's Poem 'Out of the Cradle Endlessly Rocking,'" *Journal of English Literary History*, XVI (September, 1949), 229–49.

Story, Irving C. "The Growth of Leaves of Grass: A Proposal for a Variorum Edition," *Pacific University Bulletin*, XXXVII (February, 1941), 1–11.

Stovall, Floyd. "Main Drifts in Whitman's Poetry," *American Literature*, IV (March, 1932), 3–21.

———. "Notes on Whitman's Reading," *American Literature*, XXVI (November, 1954), 337–62.

———. "Walt Whitman and the American Tradition," *Virginia Quarterly Review*, XXXI (1955), 540–57.

———. "Walt Whitman and the Dramatic Stage," *Studies in Philology*, L (July, 1953), 515–39.

Strauch, Carl F. "The Structure of Walt Whitman's Song of Myself," *English Journal*, XXVII (September, 1938), 597–607.

Sutton, Walter. "The Analysis of Free Verse Form, Illustrated by a Reading of Whitman," *Journal of Aesthetics and Art Criticism*, XVIII (December, 1959), 241–54.

Swayne, Mattie. "Whitman's Catalogue Rhetoric," *University of Texas Studies in English*, XXI (1941), 162–78.

270

Swinburne, Algernon C. *William Blake*. London, 1868.

Symonds, John Addington. *Walt Whitman, a Study*. London, 1893.

Thorp, Willard. "Whitman," *Eight American Authors: A Review of Research and Criticism*. Edited by Floyd Stovall. New York: Modern Language Association of America, 1956.

Traubel, Horace (ed.). *In Re Walt Whitman*. Philadelphia, 1893.

―――. *With Walt Whitman in Camden*. Vol. I; Boston: Small, Maynard, and Co., 1906. Vol. II; New York: D. Appleton and Co., 1908. Vol. III; New York: M. Kennerly, 1914.

Untermeyer, Louis. *The Poetry and Prose of Walt Whitman*. New York: Simon and Schuster, 1949.

Van Doren, Mark. "Walt Whitman, Stranger," *The Private Reader*. New York: Henry Holt and Co., 1942.

Walt Whitman Review. Detroit, 1955–65. Title changed from *Walt Whitman Newsletter*, 1959.

Wellek, René. "Emerson and German Philosophy," *New England Quarterly*, XVI (March, 1943), 43–62.

Werner, W. L. "Whitman's 'The Mystic Trumpeteer' as Autobiography," *American Literature*, VII (January, 1936), 455–58.

Whicher, Stephen. "Whitman's Awakening to Death," *The Presence of Whitman*. Edited by R. W. B. Lewis. New York: Columbia University Press, 1962.

Whitman, Walt. *An American Primer*. Edited by Horace Traubel. Boston: Small, Maynard Co., 1904.

―――. *Calamus* (letters to Peter Doyle, 1860–80). Edited and with an introduction by R. M. Bucke. Boston, 1897.

―――. *A Child's Reminiscence*. Edited by Thomas O. Mobbott and Rollo G. Silver. Seattle: University of Washington Book Store, 1930.

―――. *The Collected Writings of Walt Whitman*. Edited by Gay Wilson Allen and Sculley Bradley. 15 vols. New York: New York University Press, 1961―.

―――. *Complete Poetry and Selected Prose and Letters*. Edited by Emory Holloway. New York: Random House, 1938.

―――. *Complete Prose Works*. Philadelphia, 1892.

―――. *The Correspondence*. Edited by Edwin Haviland Miller. 4 vols. New York: New York University Press, 1961―.

―――. *1855–56 Whitman Notebook: Toward the Second Edition of Leaves of Grass*, Introduction by Harold W. Blodgett, notes by William White, and foreward by Charles E. Feinberg. Carbondale, Ill.: Southern Illinois Press, 1959.

271

Whitman, Walt. *Faint Clews and Indirections.* Edited by Clarence Gohdes and Rollo G. Silver. Durham, N.C.: Duke University Press, 1949.

———. *The Gathering of the Forces.* Edited by Cleveland Rogers and John Black. 2 vols. New York: G. P. Putnam's Sons, 1920.

———. *The Half-Breed and Other Stories.* Edited by Thomas O. Mobbott. New York: Columbia University Press, 1927.

———. *I Sit and Look Out.* Edited by Emory Holloway and Vernolian Schwarz. New York: Columbia University Press, 1932.

———. *Leaves of Grass.* Facsimile of 1855 edition with introduction by Clifton Joseph Furness. New York: Columbia University Press, 1939.

———. *Leaves of Grass.* First (1855) edition, edited with an introduction by Malcolm Cowley. New York: Viking, 1959.

———. *Leaves of Grass.* Brooklyn, 1856.

———. *Leaves of Grass.* Facsimile Edition of the 1860 text with introduction by Roy Harvey Pearce. Ithaca, N.Y.: Great Seal Books, 1961.

———. *Leaves of Grass.* Washington, 1872.

———. *Leaves of Grass, Comprehensive Reader's Edition.* Edited by Harold Blodgett and Sculley Bradley. New York, New York University, 1964.

———. *Leaves of Grass, Inclusive Edition.* Edited by Emory Holloway. Garden City: Doubleday, Page, and Co., 1924.

———. *The Letters of Anne Gilchrist and Walt Whitman.* Edited by T. B. Harned. Garden City: Doubleday, Page and Co., 1919.

———. *New York Dissected.* Edited by Ralph Adimari and Emory Holloway. New York: R. R. Wilson, Inc., 1936.

———. *Notes & Fragments.* Edited by R. M. Bucke. London and Ontario, 1899.

———. *Pictures.* Edited and with an introduction by Emory Holloway. New York: June House, 1927; London: Faber and Gwyer, 1928.

———. *Prose Works, 1892.* Edited by Floyd Stovall. 2 vols. New York: New York University Press, 1963–64.

———. "Seven Letters of Walt Whitman," edited by Rollo G. Silver, *American Literature,* VII (March, 1935), 46–81.

———. *The Uncollected Prose and Poetry of Walt Whitman.* Edited by Emory Holloway. 2 vols. Garden City: Doubleday, Page and Co., 1921.

———. *Walt Whitman of the New York Aurora.* Edited by Jay Rubin and Charles H. Brown. State College: Pennsylvania State University Press, 1950.

———. *Walt Whitman's Backward Glances.* Edited and with an introduction by Sculley Bradley and John A. Stevenson. Philadelphia: University of Pennsylvania Press, 1947.

———. *Walt Whitman's Diary in Canada*. Edited by William S. Kennedy. Boston: Small, Maynard and Co., 1904.

———. *Walt Whitman's Drum-Taps* (1865) *and Sequel to Drum-Taps* (1865–66). Edited and with an introduction by F. DeWolfe Miller. Gainesville, Fla.: Scholars Facsimiles and Reprints, 1959.

———. *Walt Whitman's Poems: A Selection, with Critical Aids*. Edited by Gay Wilson Allen and Charles T. Davis. New York: New York University Press, 1955.

———. *Walt Whitman's Workshop*. Edited and with an introduction and notes by Clifton Joseph Furness. Cambridge, Mass.: Harvard University Press, 1928.

———. *Whitman's Manuscripts, Leaves of Grass* (1860). Edited by Fredson Bowers. Chicago: University of Chicago Press, 1955.

Willard, Charles B. *Whitman's American Fame*. Providence, R.I.: Brown University Press, 1950.

Williams, William Carlos. *The Collected Earlier Poems of William Carlos Williams*. Norfolk, Conn.: New Directions, 1938.

Wimsatt, William K. "The Structure of Romantic Nature Imagery," *The Verbal Icon*. Lexington: University of Kentucky Press, 1954.

——— and Cleanth Brooks. *Literary Criticism*. New York: Knopf, 1957.

Wright, James A. "Whitman's Delicacy," *The Presence of Whitman*. Edited by R. W. B. Lewis. New York: Columbia University Press, 1962.

INDEX

275